BODILY NATURES

SCIENCE, ENVIRONMENT, AND THE MATERIAL SELF

STACY ALAIMO

Indiana University Press

Bloomington & Indianapolis

This book is a publication of

Indiana University Press
601 North Morton Street
Bloomington, Indiana 47404-3797 USA

www.iupress.indiana.edu

Telephone orders: 800-842-6796
Fax orders: 812-855-7931
Orders by e-mail: iuporder@indiana.edu

♾ The paper used in this publication meets the
minimum requirements of the American National
Standard for Information Sciences—Permanence
of Paper for Printed Library Materials,
ANSI Z39.48-1992.

Manufactured in the United States of America

Library of Congress Cataloging-in-Publication Data

Alaimo, Stacy, [date]
  Bodily natures : science, environment, and the material
self / Stacy Alaimo.
      p. cm.
  Includes bibliographical references and index.
  ISBN 978-0-253-35532-4 (cl : alk. paper) —
ISBN 978-0-253-22240-4 (pb : alk. paper) 1. Human
ecology—Philosophy. 2. Human beings—Effect of
environment on. 3. Human body (Philosophy) I. Title.
  GF41.A385 2010
  304.2—dc22
                              2010012635

1 2 3 4 5   15 14 13 12 11 10

For environmental activists everywhere

CONTENTS

Acknowledgments | ix

1 | 1
Bodily Natures

2 | 27
Eros and X-rays
Bodies, Class, and "Environmental Justice"

3 | 61
Invisible Matters
The Sciences of Environmental Justice

4 | 85
Material Memoirs
Science, Autobiography, and the Substantial Self

5 | 113
Deviant Agents
*The Science, Culture, and Politics of
Multiple Chemical Sensitivity*

6 | 141
Genetics, Material Agency, and the
Evolution of Posthuman Environmental
Ethics in Science Fiction

Notes | 159
Works Cited | 173
Index | 189

ACKNOWLEDGMENTS

This book began before the edited collection *Material Feminisms,* but took longer to complete. In the process, *Bodily Natures* was enriched by the scholarship in *Material Feminisms* as well as by many fruitful theoretical discussions with my co-editor, Susan J. Hekman. Susan's extensive knowledge of feminist theory and philosophy and her friendship have been invaluable. I am also grateful to my colleagues at the University of Texas at Arlington, especially Wendy Faris, Penny Ingram, Cedrick May, Neill Matheson, Chris Morris, Tim Morris, Ken Roemer, Johanna Smith, and Jackie Stodnick, for their interest in this project. Susan Hekman and Johanna Smith provided many perceptive critiques of the introductory chapter, and Ken Roemer shared his wealth of knowledge about Native American literature. Participants in our short-lived UTA/SMU summer reading group discussed a rough draft of the chapter on multiple chemical sensitivity; thanks to Suzanne Bost, Dennis Foster, Jeanne Hamming, Bruce Levy, Beth Newman, Nina Schwartz, Erin Smith, and Rajani Sudan for their ideas. I should note that the University of Texas at Arlington provided a one-semester leave for this book, and the College of Liberal Arts supported my research with funds for travel and materials. Wendy Faris, the chair of the English Department, has been remarkably encouraging throughout this long process.

I have been extremely fortunate to enjoy the friendship, intellectual provocations, and camaraderie of many scholars across the United States and Canada whose work I admire, especially Karla Armbruster, Dianne Chisholm, Giovanna Di Chiro, Ursula Heise, Robert Markley, Cate Mortimer-Sandilands, Dan Phillipon, and Rachel Stein. Lively conversations with both Giovanna and Ursula have been especially valuable for revealing connections among theory, politics, and daily life. In pursuit of alliances between science studies and the environmental humanities, I have coordinated several panels at conferences of the Association for the Study of Literature and Environment and of the Society for Literature, Science, and the Arts, as well as a science studies workshop at ASLE. I would like to thank everyone who participated in these sessions; I learned a great deal. I am also grateful for the many lively and thought-provoking conversations I have had at the ASLE conferences over the years; I regret that I cannot list here all of the people who have helped to create a rich intellectual community devoted to the environmental humanities. Finally, I would like to express how grateful I am to both Donna Haraway and Cary Nelson for their inspiring work.

I have very much appreciated the invitations to speak and contribute essays that I have received over the last several years. My sincere thanks to the following people for invitations to these memorable events: Gregory Caicco ("Ethics in Place: Architecture, Memory, and Environmental Ethics"), Cate Mortimer-Sandilands and Megan Salhus ("Nature Matters"), Cate Mortimer-Sandilands and Bruce Erickson ("Queer Ecologies"), Todd Richardson (UT Permian Basin Distinguished Lecture Series), and Hilda Rømer Christensen, Helene Hjorth Oldrup, and Michala Hvidt Breengaard (Gendering Climate and Sustainability Conference). I also thank Nina Lykke for her challenging response to my talk; Dan Phillipon, Bruce Braun, the press, and the Institute for Advanced Study at the University of Minnesota (the Quadrant Project); and Sylvia Mayer, Christof Mauch, and Meike Zwingenberger ("Green Cultures").

Working with graduate students has been the best part of my job. My thanks especially to Bridgitte Barclay, Kim Bowers, Trae Clough, Dyane Fowler, Justin Lerberg, Matthew Lerberg, Christy Tidwell, David Wallace and Mary Warejcka for their interest and engagement in feminist theory, environmental humanities, and science studies. (Additional thanks to Matthew and Justin for the climbing.) I also thank the graduate students who bravely participated in the "Telling Matter" science studies seminar in which I worked through some initial ideas: Brian Chen, Toni Manning, Barbara C. Noyes, Rodney Rather, Michele Sanders, and Christy Tidwell. Thanks as well to the undergraduate students whose passion for intellectual inquiry, environmentalism, and social justice makes teaching worthwhile (you know who you are).

I am very grateful to Rhonda Zwillinger for granting permission to reprint four of her captivating photos from *The Dispossessed: Living with Multiple Chemical Sensitivities* and for speaking with me about her life and work. Thanks to the Environmental Justice Foundation, which kindly allowed me to include two photos from its website. I am also grateful to the digital artist Fawaz AlOlaiwat for permission to use his fabulous artwork *Toxic Girl* on the cover. See http://www.fawazalolaiwat.com for more on his work. Simon J. Ortiz generously allowed me to quote from his poetry.

Early versions of some sections of this book were published elsewhere. Parts of chapter 1 appeared in the introduction to *Material Feminisms* and in my essay in that volume, "Trans-Corporeal Feminism and the Ethical Space of Nature." A short version of chapter 5 of this book was published in *TOPIA: Canadian Journal of Cultural Studies* as "MCS Matters: Material Agency in the Science and Practices of Environmental Illness," and a very early version of half of chapter 2 was published in *ISLE: Interdisciplinary Studies in Literature and Environment* as "'Comrades of Surge': Meridel Le Sueur, Cultural Studies, and the Corporeal Turn."

I am indebted to the two anonymous readers of this book for their rigorous reading and their many helpful comments. Thanks to my editor, Dee Mortensen, who is such a pleasure to work with, and to Dan Pyle for his fast and resourceful work on the illustrations. It has been a relief to have the project in such good hands.

I would like to thank Evan Engwall for his many insights and for his flexible co-parenting, without which I would be unable to write or travel. I'd also like to acknowledge my animal companions, Carmel, Pip, and Crackers, for making me walk and play. Emma Alaimo and Kai Engwall have been pretty good sports about letting me work and letting me leave town to give talks. They also make the life that is not work much more fun. Many thanks, of course, to Jeanne Hamming for her intelligence, energy, enthusiasm, and support.

BODILY NATURES

ONE

Bodily Natures

[Matter] is not little bits of nature, or a blank slate, surface, or site passively awaiting signification, nor is it an uncontested ground for scientific, feminist, or Marxist theories. Matter is not immutable or passive. Nor is it a fixed support, location, referent, or source of sustainability for discourse.

—Karen Barad, *Meeting the Universe Halfway*

And the word *environment*. Such a bloodless word. A flat-footed word with a shrunken heart. A word increasingly disengaged from its association with the natural world. Urban planners, industrialists, economists, developers use it. It's a lost word, really. A cold word, mechanistic, suited strangely to the coldness generally felt toward nature.

—Joy Williams, *Ill Nature*

Karen Barad and Joy Williams alert us to the rather shabby theoretical and rhetorical treatment of "matter" and "environment" in the late twentieth and early twenty-first centuries. *Matter,* the vast stuff of the world and of ourselves, has been subdivided into manageable "bits" or flattened into a "blank slate" for human inscription. The *environment* has been drained of its blood, its lively creatures, its interactions and relations—in short, all that is recognizable as "nature"—in order that it become a mere empty space, an "uncontested ground," for human "development."

If nature is to matter,[1] we need more potent, more complex understandings of materiality. Side by side, Barad's critique of the linguistic turn and Williams's appraisal of the word *environment* suggest a troubling parallel between the immateriality of contemporary social theory and a widespread, popular disregard for nonhuman nature. This book will address the dematerializing networks that cross through academic theory, popular culture, contemporary discourse, and everyday practices by focusing on the possibilities for more robust and complex conceptions of the materiality of human bodies and the more-than-human world. Specifically, *Bodily Natures* explores the interconnections, interchanges, and transits between human bodies and nonhuman natures. By attending to the material interconnections between the human and the more-than-human world, it may be possible to conjure an ethics lurking in an idiomatic definition of *matter* (or *the matter*): "The condition of or state of things regarding a person or thing, esp. as a subject of concern or wonder" (*Oxford English Dictionary*). Concern and wonder converge when the context for ethics becomes not merely social but material—the emergent, ultimately unmappable landscapes of interacting biological, climatic, economic, and political forces.

Potent ethical and political possibilities emerge from the literal contact zone between human corporeality and more-than-human nature. Imagining human corporeality as trans-corporeality, in which the human is always intermeshed with the more-than-human world, underlines the extent to which the substance of the human is ultimately inseparable from "the environment." It makes it difficult to pose nature as mere background, as Val Plumwood would put it,[2] for the exploits of the human since "nature" is always as close as one's own skin—perhaps even closer. Indeed, thinking across bodies may catalyze the recognition that the environment, which is too often imagined as inert, empty space or as a resource for human use, is, in fact, a world of fleshy beings with their own needs, claims, and actions. By emphasizing the movement across bodies, trans-corporeality reveals the interchanges and interconnections between various bodily natures. But by underscoring that *trans* indicates movement across different sites, trans-corporeality also opens up a mobile space that acknowledges the often unpredictable and unwanted actions of human bodies, nonhuman creatures, ecological systems, chemical agents, and other actors. Emphasizing the material interconnections of human corporeality with the more-than-human world—and, at the same time, acknowledging that material agency necessitates more capacious epistemologies—allows us to forge ethical and political positions that can contend with numerous late twentieth- and early twenty-first-century realities in which "human" and "environment" can by no means be considered as separate.

Two particularly striking movements of the late twentieth century—environmental justice and environmental health—mark significant material interchanges between human bodies and the environment. Thus, much of this book focuses on the literature, science, and popular culture of these two movements, quite broadly conceived, including the erotic early twentieth-century "environmental justice" writings of Meridel Le Sueur, contemporary accounts of environmental racism, environmental memoirs in which the material world becomes the very substance of self, and the volatile scientific and political struggles to define or dismiss the syndrome of multiple chemical sensitivity. As they promote substantial interconnections between humans and the wider world, environmental health and environmental justice accounts often reconceptualize material agencies—the often unpredictable and always interconnected actions of environmental systems, toxic substances, and biological bodies. Strangely, popular renderings of genetics ascribe agency to genes, but tend to disconnect genes from the environment and evolution. Thus, the final chapter envisions a posthuman environmental ethics in which genetics, evolution, and environment are imbricated in and affect the emergence as well as the unraveling of the human.

This chapter introduces some of the theoretical models, questions, and arguments of the book, focusing on how feminist corporeal theory, disability studies, environmental humanities, and science studies productively engage with the materiality of human bodies and nonhuman natures. Ironically, despite the tremendous outpouring of feminist theory and cultural studies of "the body," much of this work tends to focus exclusively on how various bodies have been discursively produced, which casts the body as passive, plastic matter. As Elizabeth Wilson puts it, "The body at the center of these projects is curiously abiological—its social, cultural, experiential, or psychical construction having been posited against or beyond any putative biological claims" (*Neural Geographies* 15). Bracketing the biological body, and thereby severing its evolutionary, historical, and ongoing interconnections with the material world, may not be ethically, politically, or theoretically desirable. Trans-corporeality offers an alternative. Trans-corporeality, as a theoretical site, is where corporeal theories, environmental theories, and science studies meet and mingle in productive ways. Furthermore, the movement across[3] human corporeality and nonhuman nature necessitates rich, complex modes of analysis that travel through the entangled territories of material and discursive, natural and cultural, biological and textual.

Throughout the book, I will examine how various models of trans-corporeality are emerging not only in a broad expanse of scholarship and theory, but in popular culture, literary texts, and social practices. My intention is not to conjure up a new theory so much as to work across separate fields, forging connections and suggesting ethical and political perspectives. If trans-corporeality were some sort of rarefied, new theoretical invention, it would not travel very well across intellectual, scientific, political, and popular domains. Moreover, the fact that "bodily natures" are emerging across different domains suggests that the concept has the potential to perform potent cultural work. Although most of this book does not address cultural studies directly, cultural studies models— that take popular culture seriously, that trace peculiar but potent intersections, and that insist upon the political relevance of academic practice—deeply inform my approach. I find the many bodily natures discussed throughout this book—of science studies, environmental health, environmental justice, popular epidemiology, disability studies, corporeal feminism, film, photography, material memoir, science fiction, and evolution—to be both theoretically provocative and politically potent, as they recast our most basic understandings of self and world as separate entities.

Pheng Cheah, critiquing the disdain for nature and "the given" in contemporary cultural theory, argues that this "obsessive pushing away of nature may well constitute an acknowledgement-in-disavowal that humans may be natural creatures after all" (108). I think it is crucial to address this "obsessive pushing away of nature," which has not only dominated social theory and humanities scholarship, but also infuses everyday beliefs and practices, rendering environmentalism a distant, dismissible enterprise. Rather than arguing, however, that humans are natural creatures, that nonhuman animals are cultural creatures, and that the nature/culture divide is not sustainable (all of which I believe), I will locate my inquiry within the many interfaces between human bodies and the larger environment. Those particular sites of interconnection demand attention to the materiality of the human and to the immediacy and potency of all that the ostensibly bounded, human subject would like to disavow. Trans-corporeality, emerging in social theories, science, science studies, literature, film, activist websites, green consumerism, popular epidemiology, and popular culture, counters and critiques the obdurate, though postmodern, humanisms that seek transcendence or protection from the material world. Thus, *Bodily Natures* grapples with the ways in which environmental ethics, social theories, popular understandings of science, and conceptions of the human self are profoundly altered by the recognition that "the environment" is not located somewhere out there, but is always the very substance of ourselves.

Feminist Theory's Flight from Nature and Biology

Nature has long been waged as a philosophical concept, a potent ideological node, and a cultural repository of norms and moralism against women, people of color, indigenous peoples, queers, and the lower classes. In *Undomesticated Ground: Recasting Nature as Feminist Space,* I argued that because *woman* has long been defined in Western thought as a creature mired in "nature" and thus outside the domain of human transcendence, rationality, subjectivity, and agency, most feminist theory has worked to disentangle *woman* from *nature.* Working within rather than against predominant dualisms, many important feminist arguments and concepts necessitate a rigid opposition between nature and culture. For example, feminist theory's most revolutionary concept—the concept of gender, as distinct from biological sex—is predicated upon a sharp opposition between nature and culture. Even as it would be difficult to overestimate the explanatory and polemical force of feminist theories of social construction, such theories are haunted by the pernicious notions of nature that propel them. Thrust aside, completely removed from culture, this nature—the repository of essentialism and stasis—nonetheless remains dangerously intact. Rather than fleeing from this debased nature, which is associated with corporeality, mindlessness, and passivity, it would be more productive for feminist theory to undertake the transformation of gendered dualisms—nature/culture, body/mind, object/subject, resource/agency, and others—that have been cultivated to denigrate and silence certain groups of human as well as nonhuman life (Alaimo, *Undomesticated Ground* 4–14).

Human corporeality, especially female corporeality, has been so strongly associated with nature in Western thought that it is not surprising that feminism has been haunted not only by the specter of nature as the repository of essentialism, but by, as Lynda Birke puts it, "the ghost of biology" (44). She charges that the "underlying assumption that some aspects of 'biology' are fixed becomes itself the grand narrative (albeit implicit) from which feminist and other social theorists are trying to escape" (ibid.). Nancy Tuana, noting a resurgence of popular belief in racial and sexual determinism, charges that "we feminists have been epistemically irresponsible in leaving in place a fixed, essential, material basis for human nature, a basis which renders biological determinism meaningful" ("Fleshing Gender" 57). Only by directly engaging with matter itself can feminism do as Tuana advocates: render biological determinism "nonsense." For instance, rather than bracketing the biological body, Birke insists upon the need to understand it as "changing and changeable, as *transformable*" (45). Cells "constantly renew themselves," bone "is always remodeling," and "bodily interiors" "constantly react to change inside or out, and act upon the world" (ibid.). Even with these few examples, it is clear that the notion of biology as destiny, which has long haunted feminism, depends on a particular—if not peculiar—notion of biology that can certainly be displaced by other models. Since biology, like nature, has long been drafted to serve as the armory for racist, sexist, and heterosexist norms, it is crucial that feminists recast the norms, values, and assumptions that permeate this field. For example, Hird in "Naturally Queer" offers an abundance of biological examples that make heterosexism seem utterly unnatural: "The *vast* majority of cells in the human body are intersex"; "most of the organisms in four out of the five kingdoms do not require sex for reproduction"; and, marvelously, the Schizophyllum "has more than 28,000 sexes." She concludes by arguing, "We may no longer be certain that it is nature that remains static and culture that evinces limitless malleability" (85–86, 88). If this biology sounds queer, all the better.[4] As a "situated knowledge" (see Haraway, "Situated Knowledges"), this queer biology contests not only the content and the ramifications of normative hetero-biology, but its claim to objectivity and neutrality.

Perhaps the only way to truly oust the twin ghosts of biology and nature is, paradoxically, to endow them with flesh, to allow them to materialize more fully, and to attend to their precise materializations. The theories, literature, activist websites, photography, and other texts and practices discussed in this book perform exactly this sort of cultural work as they grapple with both apparent and seemingly apparitional materializations.

The Material Turn in Feminist Theory, Environmental Humanities, and Science Studies

Wondering whether it makes her a "survivor or a traitor of the age of (post)structuralism," Teresa de Lauretis boldly suggests:

> [N]ow may be a time for the human sciences to reopen the questions of subjectivity, materiality, discursivity, knowledge, to reflect on the *post* of posthumanity. It is a time to break the piggy bank of saved conceptual schemata and reinstall uncertainty in all theoretical applications, starting with the primacy of the cultural and its many "turns": linguistic, discursive, performative, therapeutic, ethical, you name it. (368)

What has been most notably excluded by the "primacy of the cultural" and the turn toward the linguistic and the discursive is the "stuff" of matter. Theorists within the overlapping fields of feminist theory, environmental theory, and science studies, however, have put forth innovative understandings of the material world. Some feminist theorists, such as Moira Gatens, Claire Colebrook, and Elizabeth Bray, have embraced the work of Spinoza and Deleuze as countertraditions to the linguistic turn. Others have reread theorists at the heart of poststructuralism—for example, Jacques Derrida (Vicki Kirby and Elizabeth Wilson), Michel Foucault (Ladelle McWhorter and Karen Barad), and Judith Butler (Karen Barad). Together, these theorists, along with others, constitute the material turn in feminist theory, a wave of feminist theory that takes matter seriously.[5] Such radical rethinkings of materiality are difficult to sustain within a discursively oriented theoretical cosmos. For example, Donna Haraway's influential figure of the cyborg, which muddles nature/culture dualisms, has been celebrated in most feminist theory and cultural studies as a figure that blurs the bounds between humans and technology—but, in this latest flight from nature, the cyborg is rarely embraced as an amalgamation of human and nature. Significantly, feminist cultural studies have embraced the cyborg as a social and technological *construct* but have ignored, for the most part, the *matter* of the cyborg, a materiality which is as biological as it is technological, both fleshy and wired, since the cyborg encourages human "kinship with animals" as well as with machines ("A Cyborg Manifesto" 154). Disturbingly, the critical reception of the cyborg as technological but not biological insinuates a transcendent cyber-humanism that shakes off worldly entanglements.

The material turn is by no means exclusive to feminist theory. New conceptions of materiality that are neither biologically reductive nor strictly social construc-tionist are emerging in many disciplines: environmental philosophy, corporeal feminism, disability studies, transgender theory, science studies, animal stud-ies, new media studies, race theory, and other areas. The work of Gilles Deleuze and Felix Guattari, especially *A Thousand Plateaus,* and of Brian Massumi, who criticizes cultural theories of the body in which "matter, bodily or otherwise, never figures into the account *as such*" (4), presents palpable models of material-ity. The body, "as such," is also essential to disability studies. Tobin Siebers, for example, in his essay "Disability in Theory: From Social Constructionism to the New Realism of the Body," contends that the "disabled body seems difficult for the theory of social construction to absorb: disability is at once its best example and a significant counterexample" (740). Transgender theory, according to Ber-nice L. Hausman, must examine the body as "a material entity, beginning with an interrogation of those categories, like gender, that have contributed to the body's contradictory status by serving as an alibi for a notion of identity that exists as pure information" (212). Scholars are even beginning to consider the dangerous proposition—given the virulent history of racial essentialism—that analyses of race need to attend to materiality. Michael Hames-Garcia in "How Real Is Race?" argues:

> [T]here are important reasons not to eliminate all considerations of biology and the body from our discussions of race, provided we understand biology as mutu-ally constituted with culture and as significantly less determinate than it is often taken to be. In particular . . . an important dimension of what race is and how it functions results from the interaction of social ideologies of race with visible human difference. (324)

While it is still crucial to analyze and critique how "nature" and the "envi-ronment" circulate as potent discursive formulations, many of us would like to find ways to complement and complicate that sort of analysis with investigations that account for the ways in which nature, the environment, and the material world itself signify, act upon, or otherwise affect human bodies, knowledges, and practices.[6] Notwithstanding the fact that theories of social construction have performed invaluable cultural work by critiquing the naturalized and oppressive categories of race, class, gender, sexuality, and ability, from an environmentalist perspective, such theories may bracket or minimize the significance, substance, and power of the material world. David W. Kidner, in an essay in *Environmental Ethics,* argues that social constructionism "colludes with commercialism in the long-term industrialist project of replacing the natural by the artifactual, defining a form of human existence which claims independence from natural processes and rhythms. Social constructionism therefore provides a model of nature which fits seamlessly into the industrialist view of the world" (352). Not surprisingly, many environmentally-oriented scholars seek to engage with the material world as something more than a humanly made concept or a plastic resource for human use. Charles E. Scott, in *The Lives of Things,* critiques the word *nature* in part because the meanings of the word "often draw us to an abstracting process rather than to the lives of things in their nondiscursive, dynamic interactions" (23). Scott uses the term *physicality* instead in order to evoke how "the lives of things show a considerable excess to meaning and sense" (73). Environmental phenomenology, such as that of Edward Casey and David Abram, locates human experience and perception within specific places. Casey asserts that "places serve as the *condition* of all living things" (15; emphasis in original). Similarly, Lawrence Buell contends that insofar as "human beings are biocultural creatures constructing themselves in interaction with surroundings they cannot not inhabit, all their artifacts may be expected to bear traces of that" (*Writing* 2). Thus, ecocriticism must develop modes of analysis that do not continue to emphasize the "disjunction between text and world" (Buell, *Environmental Imagination* 84), but instead reveal the environmental traces within all texts. Environmental historians, such as Richard Grove, Carolyn Merchant, William Cronon, Richard White, Ted Steinberg, and others, trace how the natural world impacts human history. Steinberg contends that "viewing nature as an active, shaping force in the past can help us change our understanding of some conventional topics in American history" ("Down to Earth" n.p.). He urges us to consider, for example, "how the ecological consequences of eating and flushing become so invisible, so enmeshed in the wish to forget" (ibid.). Forgetting that bodily waste must go somewhere allows us to imagine ourselves as rarefied rational beings distinct from nature's muck and muddle.

Such comforting distinctions are often challenged by science studies scholars who work at the crossroads of cultural formations and material worlds. Science studies, because it is informed by social and political theories and yet also contends with material substances, actions, and agencies, puts forth provocative, even jolting, methodologies and reconceptualizations. Bruno Latour, in *We Have*

Never Been Modern, contends that our "intellectual life is out of kilter" due to the severing of scientific, sociological, and textual knowledge practices: "We may glorify the sciences, play power games or make fun of the belief in a reality, but we must not mix these three caustic fields" (5, 6). And yet the multitude of nature/culture "hybrids" that surround us cannot be understood in such segregated terms:

> The ozone hole is too social and too narrated to be truly natural; the strategy of industrial firms and heads of state is too full of chemical reactions to be reduced to power and interest; the discourse of the ecosphere is too real and too social to boil down to meaning effects. Is it our fault if the networks are *simultaneously real, like nature, narrated, like discourse, and collective, like society*? (6; emphasis in original)

Networks, then, require analyses that can grapple with their reality, narrativity, and collectivity—which is surely no small feat, given that scholars are trained, for the most part, to engage in only one of these three modes of investigation.

Drawing upon Latour, Susan Squier, in *Liminal Lives: Imagining the Human at the Frontiers of Biomedicine,* urges us to "examine the notion of social construction as critically as we do the notion of the natural, realizing that there is a material base to even the most seemingly socially constructed experiences or entities. It further counsels us to remember that the material world exercises a shaping effect on 'the literary,' as well as 'the scientific'" (46). Departing from the standard practices of literary studies, Squier insists not only that "language helps structure our sense of possibilities," but that "material conditions shape and reshape what we can put into words" (57). Scholarly analysis may reveal those material conditions; at the same time, the producers of various works of literature, art, and activism may themselves grapple with ways to render murky material forces palpable or recognizably "real." As the next chapter will demonstrate, Muriel Rukeyser, in her early twentieth-century poem *The Book of the Dead,* documented the medical, environmental, and social devastation wrought by silicosis in one particularly infamous industrial disaster. Rukeyser, determined to disclose the substantial nature of this disaster, turns to scientific and medical technologies capable of tracing the often invisible, but nonetheless material, flows of substances and forces between people, places, and economic/political systems.

Even as my desire to find more robust modes of analysis that make space for materiality is, in large part, motivated by my own environmentalist stance, there are no guarantees that emerging models of materiality will cultivate environmentalisms. Some recent models of materiality do not, in fact, value nature, nonhuman creatures, or ecological systems. Many make the cut so familiar to humanism, severing the person from all that surrounds them. "The body," meaning the human body, of course, may be endowed with agency and substance, but the critical interest ends at the skin. Pamela Moss and Isabel van Dyck, for example, in "Inquiry into Environment and Body: Women, Work, and Chronic Illness," aim to "situate body both in its material and representational form" (746) and to analyze the environment in both material and discursive terms. Even as they open up significant questions regarding the "spatiality of body and environment" (749), "environment" appears as a "socially negotiated space inclusive of its material aspects" (746). They use the term *environment,* rather than *place,* not because it invokes the natural world but "because it incorporates more widely the multiple positions individuals occupy in the various sets of relations they engage in and cautions against individualistic conceptions of place as in humanistic definitions" (739). Even as people are embodied within this analysis, the term *environment* is used for its analytical convenience: the material world vanishes into a humanly made, abstract calculus of power and identity. Such a formulation not only renders nature invisible but forecloses possible alliances between disability activism and environmentalism, as well as a consideration of how various toxins may exacerbate or cause chronic illnesses. By contrast, in chapter 5, I argue that reading multiple chemical sensitivity as a mode of trans-corporeality forges productive alliances among environmentalism, disability activism, and an ethical and political conception of the "deviant agencies" cutting across bodies and places.

Elizabeth Grosz, whose influential book *Volatile Bodies* is a founding corporeal feminist text, argues for the significance of Darwin in her more recent books, *Time Travels: Feminism, Nature, Power* and *The Nick of Time.* Grosz calls for philosophers and social theorists to reconsider Darwinian theory and, more generally, to attend to biology and materiality. She asks, provocatively, "what would a new conception of culture, one which refuses to sever it from nature, look like?" (*Time Travels* 52). Many of her analyses underscore materiality. For example, she reveals that *The Nick of Time* was "written as a remembrance of what we have forgotten—not just the body, but that which makes it possible and which limits its actions: the precarious, accidental, contingent, expedient, striving, dynamic status of life in a messy, complicated, resistant, brute world of materiality" (2). Pertinent to my focus on trans-corporeality, she insists that "we need to understand the body, not as an organism or entity in itself, but as a system, or series of open-ended systems, functioning within other huge systems it cannot control through which it can access and acquire its abilities and capacities" (3). At first glance, Grosz's project would seem allied with other environmentally-oriented theories, as she advocates "reconceptualizing the relations between the natural and the social, between the biological and the cultural, outside the dichotomous structure in which these terms are currently enmeshed" (*Time Travels* 30). Grosz, however, clearly distinguishes herself from "eco-feminist and eco-philosophy," which she characterizes as "offshoots" "of the ecology movement" (34, 47). Resisting "an ecological understanding of the natural order," her reading of Darwin corrects outmoded notions of ecological equilibrium or stasis. But her philosophical vision does much more; it calls up a perspective that transcends any sort of environmentalism: "If an ecology that values not only the living—the present—but also the future could be possible, it would be very close to the (non)moral ontology of Darwinism, which mourns no particular extinction and which waits, with surprise, to see what takes the place of the extinct" (ibid., n. 4, 220–221). Grosz projects a Darwinian philosophy that is rich with both a recognition of materiality and a sense of wonder—yet dismisses environmental concerns. The subject here, oddly, is not a person but "Darwinism" itself, "which waits, with surprise, to see what takes the place of the extinct." In this strange moment, Darwinism becomes a disembodied, transcendent, omniscient observer, reinstalling a rather humanist, even deified subject. This disengaged philosophical platform is uninhabitable for anyone with ethical and political commitments to environmentalism and environmental justice. By contrast, trans-corporeality, as a descendant of Darwinism, insists that the human is always the very stuff of the messy, contingent, emergent mix of the material world.

Maps of Transit

In a book review entitled "The 'Environment' Is Us," Harold Fromm gives this arresting image of what I'm calling trans-corporeality: "The 'environment,' as we now apprehend it, runs right through us in endless waves, and if we were to watch ourselves via some ideal microscopic time-lapse video, we would see water, air, food, microbes, toxins entering our bodies as we shed, excrete, and exhale our processed materials back out" (2). Fromm argues that the "environment" "looks more and more to be the very substance of human existence in the world" (ibid.). Edward S. Casey, drawing upon Merleau-Ponty, makes a similar argument: "my body and natural things are not just coterminous but continuous with each other. . . . The fibers of culture and nature compose one continuous fabric" (255, 256). The recognition that bodies and places are continuous incites transit across traditional disciplinary boundaries. Christopher Sellers argues "for an environmental history of the body and for a more embodied environmental history," contending that environmental historians can "encourage and extend mediation between naturalist and culturalist perspectives" ("Thoreau's Body" 504, 501). Linda Nash places "the human body at the center of an environmental history" in her book *Inescapable Ecologies: A History of Environment, Disease, and Knowledge.* She asks, "Where does the body end and 'nonhuman nature' begin?" asserting that "environments have shaped human flesh in minute and profound ways," thus it is a mistake to write the history of human health without considering the environment (8, 9). Disability studies, in particular, may reject medical models of the enclosed body in order to trace material/social interchanges between body and place. Rosemarie Garland-Thomson explains, "Disability studies reminds us that all bodies are shaped by their environments from the moment of conception. We transform constantly in response to our surroundings and register history on our bodies. The changes that occur when body encounters world are what we call disability" (524). If, as Garland-Thomson argues, "all bodies are shaped by their environments from the moment of conception," then there is never a time in which the human can be anything but trans-corporeal. Moreover, disability studies may be enriched by attending not only to the ways in which built environments constitute or exacerbate "disability," but to how materiality, at a less perceptible level—that of pharmaceuticals, xenobiotic chemicals, air pollution, etc.—affects human health and ability.

What are some of the routes through person and place? What ethical or political positions emerge from the movement across human and more-than-human flesh? Perhaps the most palpable trans-corporeal substance is food, since eating transforms plants and animals into human flesh. While eating may seem a straightforward activity, peculiar material agencies may reveal themselves during the route from dirt to mouth. Ladelle McWhorter, in *Bodies and Pleasures: Foucault and the Politics of Sexual Normalization,* boldly undertakes a genealogy of her own body. Although her book focuses on sexual orientation, it also includes accounts of "becoming white" as well as a rather surprising philosophical account of "becoming dirt." She tells how her quest to grow a real, flavorful tomato ends not only with a "high regard for dirt," but with a sense of kinship to this degraded substance. Munching on a bag of Doritos, she is about to toss the crumbs in her composting trench but stops:

> "Nope," I thought, "can't feed that crap to my dirt." I threw the crumbs in the trash and reached for that one last chip. It was halfway to my mouth before I was struck by what I'd just said. I looked out the kitchen window at my garden, my trenches, my dirt, and then my gaze turned downward toward my Dorito-stained hand. Dirt and flesh. Suddenly it occurred to me that, for all their differences, these two things I was looking at were cousins—not close cousins, but cousins, several deviations once removed. I haven't purchased a bag of Doritos since. (167)

As that last Dorito hangs—in midair—the epiphanic narrative surrounds it with a humorous recognition that this precarious sense of kinship between dirt and flesh may not only elevate dirt to the status of family member but, in this case, elevate the very substance of the self into something worthy of proper care and feeding. A queer, green, ethical family, indeed. We can trace the literal route though which dirt becomes flesh via the tomato, but McWhorter doesn't belabor that point, perhaps because dwelling on food, rather than on dirt, the very matrix of life, serves up nature as an ingestible morsel. True, we are transformed by the food we consume (as the film *Supersize Me* attests), but for the most part the model of incorporation emphasizes the outline of the human: food disappears into the human body, which remains solidly bounded.

In their revealing article "Incorporating Nature," Margaret FitzSimmons and David Goodman argue for a model of incorporation "as metaphor and as process—as a useful way of bringing nature into the body of social theory and, more literally, into the body of living organisms, including ourselves" (194). FitzSimmons and Goodman's complex model, which accounts for the agency of nature, as well as social, economic, and political forces, promotes the notion of incorporation "to capture the relational materiality of ecologies and bodies that characterizes agro-food networks" (216). While this formulation provides an illuminating way of thinking through the productions of nature/culture, ultimately the production of food is a rather one-sided affair, as the model of incorporation is only one bite away from capitalist consumption. Although McWhorter begins with a simple desire for a tomato, her scenario moves in the opposite direction, extending her own flesh to the dirt, rather than merely incorporating the fruits of the dirt into herself. McWhorter's Foucauldian analysis of corporeality, which for most of the book concerns not ecological issues but the regulatory regimes of sexual identity, reaches into the ground, becoming a thorough redefinition of the stuff of matter.

Drawing upon Spinoza rather than Foucault, Moira Gatens similarly describes human bodies that open out into the more-than-human world. The identity of the human body "can never be viewed as a final or finished product as in the case of the Cartesian automaton, since it is a body that is in constant interchange with its environment. The human body is radically open to its surroundings and can be composed, recomposed and decomposed by other bodies" (110). Whereas in a model of incorporation, the human self remains the selfsame, in Gatens's reading of Spinoza, the human body is never static because its interactions with other bodies always alter it. Gatens explains that these "'encounters' with other bodies are good or bad depending on whether they aid or harm our characteristic constitution" (ibid.). Oddly, Spinoza's understanding of the body seems particularly akin to some twenty-first-century models of corporeality, such as that of the environmental health movement, which warns that particular "interchange[s] with [the] environment" may result in disease, illness, or death. Indeed, the many protests against genetically modified foods warn that these engineered substances may not be benignly incorporated into the human body. Genetically modified foods may have unintended effects, on humans or other creatures, that science may not discover for decades.

While the gastronomical relations between earth and stomach exhibit a digestible example of trans-corporeal transit, Vicki Kirby presents a counterintuitive account of how human corporeality opens onto the more-than-human world. Kirby, in *Telling Flesh: The Substance of the Corporeal,* interprets Jacques Derrida's famous dictum "there is no outside of text": "It is as if the very tissue of substance, the ground of Being, is this mutable intertext—a 'writing' that both circumscribes and exceeds the conventional divisions of nature and culture" (Kirby 61). Kirby considers the possibility "that nature scribbles or that flesh reads": "For if nature is literate, then the question 'What is language?'—or more scandalously, 'Who reads?'—fractures the Cartesian subject to its very foundation" (127). She extends the poststructuralist model of textuality to such a degree that its most basic terms are radically rewritten:

> What I am trying to conjure here is some "sense" that word and flesh are utterly implicated, not because "flesh" is actually a word that mediates the fact of what is being referred to, but because the entity of a word, the identity of a sign, the system of language, and the domain of culture—none of these are autonomously enclosed upon themselves. Rather they are all emergent *within* a force field of differentiations that has no exteriority in any final sense. (ibid.)

Kirby's critique transforms poststructuralism into a truly posthumanist horizon, as it refuses to delineate the human, the cultural, or the linguistic against a background of mute matter. Nature, culture, bodies, texts all unravel into a limitless "force field of differentiation." For McWhorter, Gatens, and Kirby, that which had been exclusive to the human opens out into a wider realm in which the substance of human corporeality and, in Kirby's case, even human linguistic systems are not ultimately separable from that which it is difficult not to call "nature." These theorists can be read as a sort of postscript to feminism's many invocations of nature as an undomesticated, literally nondomestic, space. For the walls of domestic enclosure that would separate human from nature and define the human as such are nowhere to be found, as human corporeality and textuality effortlessly extend into the more-than-human world. Word, flesh, and dirt are no longer discrete.

Nancy Tuana's remarkable essay "Viscous Porosity: Witnessing Hurricane Katrina" captures similar indiscretions—as it swirls together wind, rain, floods, flesh, racism, politics, psychology, hydrology, poverty, and PVCs, arguing that Hurricane Katrina must be understood as "a complex interaction" of both "social practices and natural phenomena" (193). This interactionist ontology is encapsulated by her conception of "viscous porosity." She asserts that there is "a viscous porosity of flesh—my flesh and the flesh of the world. This porosity is a hinge through which we are of and in the world. I refer to it as viscous for there are membranes that effect [*sic*] the interactions. These membranes are of various types—skin and flesh, prejudgments and symbolic imaginaries, habits and embodiments" (199–200).

Significantly, Tuana's notion of viscosity allows her to highlight "distinctions" as ethical and political matters. Even as she argues that Katrina demonstrated that "there is no sharp ontological divide" between the natural and social factors that caused the hurricane, "but rather a complex interaction of phenomena," she insists upon accountability:

> This does not mean that we cannot attempt to determine the extent to which human factors increased the intensity of a hurricane or some other weather related phenomena. Indeed issues of distributive justice may require that such a distinction be made in order to determine how to apportion responsibility across nations for harm from human-induced climate change as may be done if we adopt a "polluter-pays" principle of responsibility. Again, distinctions can be made, which is why I employ the phrase "viscous porosity," rather than fluidity. (193)

Viscous porosity, then, with its emphasis on mediating membranes, which may be biological, social, and political, is a powerful model for understanding material interactions in scientific/ethical/political terms and epitomizes the trans-corporeality that I advocate throughout *Bodily Natures*.

Trans-Corporeality and Environmentalism

Because trans-corporeality brings the human body into focus, it is possible to charge that it reinstalls anthropocentrism. Jhan Hochman, for instance, would probably condemn trans-corporeality as another sort of "creeping metonymy," in which "culture invades nature by calling itself *natural* or *part of nature*" (171). Hochman asserts that "what nature needs is not a bond with culture but a separation or divorce, some autonomy, at last some protection through 'shelters' (preserves), offering sanctuary from culture's constant battering and stalking" (188). The personification of nature as a battered wife is creepy, but worse, it doesn't begin to convey the complicated dynamics between cultures and environments. It is true that the survival of many species depends on protecting ecosystems and habitats from plunder and degradation, but sustainable human practices within particular environments can also help maintain environments. At this point in time, with global climate change proceeding even more rapidly than was projected, we hardly have the luxury of imagining any expanse of land or sea as beyond the reach of humanly-induced harm. Matters of environmental concern and wonder are always "here," as well as "there," simultaneously local and global, personal and political, practical and philosophical. Although trans-corporeality as the transit between body and environment is exceedingly local, tracing a toxic substance from production to consumption often reveals global networks of social injustice, lax regulations, and environmental degradation. I agree with Ursula Heise, who argues in *Sense of Place and Sense of Planet: The Environmental Imagination of the Global* that "what is crucial for ecological awareness and environmental ethics is arguably not so much a sense of place as a sense of planet—a sense of how political, economic, technological, social, cultural, and ecological networks shape daily routines" (55). Heise advocates "eco-cosmopolitanism," which is "an attempt to envision individuals and groups as part of planetary 'imagined communities' of both human and nonhuman kinds" (61). My project may be allied with Heise's in that recognizing trans-corporeality may incite inquiry into global networks. Thus, although the notion of trans-corporeality may seem anthropocentric, ultimately the ostensible center is extended throughout multiple, often global, networks. Moreover, inquiry as a sustained practice is as crucial for trans-corporeal environmentalism as it is for Heise's notion of eco-cosmopolitanism, which, she argues, values "the abstract and highly mediated kinds of knowledge and experience that lend equal or greater support to a grasp of biospheric connectedness" (62). This book makes a somewhat similar argument: an understanding of the material interchanges between bodies (both human and nonhuman) and the wider environment often requires the mediation of scientific information.

The need to cultivate a tangible sense of connection to the material world in order to encourage an environmentalist ethos is underscored by the pervasive sense of disconnection that casts "environmental issues" as containable, eccentric, dismissible topics. Even as environmental health, environmental justice, popular epidemiology, and green consumerism gain strength, they remain peripheral movements. The most pervasive assumption within the United States would seem to be that people are separate from nature, the environment, and other material substances and forces. Witness, for example, the blasé use of dangerous pesticides and herbicides at home (the attitude may be offhand, but the poison isn't). Observe, as well, the multitude of horror movies that shock us with the prospect of monstrous human-animal hybrids (the giant cockroach that looks like a man, the seductive woman who is really a cat-beast), only to conclude with the triumphant transcendence of "man."[7] Or consider the astounding right-wing denial of global warming, which casts it as a matter of personal "belief." It seems we have been granted the right to choose whether or not we "believe in" global warming, as if (quasi-religious) beliefs or personal opinions could insulate us from the emergent processes of material/political realities.[8] Indeed, huge McMansions, giant trucks, and gas-guzzling SUVs (all of which contribute to the vast amounts of carbon being emitted into the atmosphere) serve to insulate their inhabitants from the world.[9] Attention to the material transit across bodies and environments may render it more difficult to seek refuge within fantasies of transcendence or imperviousness.

If the predominant understanding of environmental ethics has been that of a circle that has expanded in such a way as to grant "moral consideration to animals, to plants, to [nonhuman] species, even to ecosystems and the Earth" (Light and Rolston 7), trans-corporeality denies the human subject the sovereign, central position. Instead, ethical considerations and practices must emerge from a more uncomfortable and perplexing place where the "human" is always already part of an active, often unpredictable, material world. Many of the subjects of *Bodily Natures* are akin to the "ecological subjects" so beautifully elaborated by Lorraine Code, subjects that are "well placed, collectively and singly, to own and take responsibility for their epistemic-moral-political activity" (5). Code advocates "ecological thinking," which "relocates inquiry 'down on the ground' where knowledge is made, negotiated, circulated," and which "proposes a way of engaging . . . with the implications of patterns, places, and the interconnections of lives and events in and across the human and nonhuman world, in scientific and secular projects of inquiry" (5, 4). She argues that, in ecological thinking, "knowers are repositioned as self-consciously part of nature, while anthropocentric projects of mastery are superseded by projects of displacing Enlightenment 'man' from the center of the universe" (32). This explains how an epistemological shift can become an ethical matter; trans-corporeal subjects must also relinquish mastery as they find themselves inextricably part of the flux and flow of the world that others would presume to master.

Code proposes a coherent conception of ecological thinking, which she sees as "infusing, shaping and circulating throughout the social-material-intellectual atmosphere(s)" (28).[10] Even as I endorse the epistemology she advocates, my purpose here is not to propose a particular epistemology, but instead to trace how trans-corporeality often ruptures ordinary knowledge practices. *Bodily Natures* analyzes particular moments of confusion and contestation that occur when individuals and collectives must contend not only with the materiality of their very selves but with the often invisibly hazardous landscapes of risk society, which require scientific mediation. Moreover, the cultural artifacts I investigate do not yield one consistent sort of epistemology, but instead reveal that a recognition of trans-corporeality entails a rather disconcerting sense of being immersed within incalculable, interconnected material agencies that erode even our most sophisticated modes of understanding.

Toxic Bodies, Science, and the Material Self

One of the most vivid examples of this immersion in often unpredictable material agencies is the now all too familiar idea that human bodies are toxic. The *Onion* lampooned this clichéd figure in a mock news story:

> The Environmental Protection Agency issued a bulletin Tuesday warning the bodies of American citizens, with their large concentrations of artificial, synthetic, and often toxic substances, have been reclassified as industrial waste. "The average human body is now only 35 percent organic," EPA chief Ralph Johnson

said. "Due to changes brought about by modern detergents, silicone implants, and processed cheese food product, it is no longer safe to allow human tissue to come into contact with our nation's topsoil." ("EPA Warns" n.p.)

Classifying human bodies as dangerous hazardous waste is a striking example of what many people already know but either cynically accept or try to deny—that all that scary stuff, supposedly out there, is already within. Consumer products manufactured to do what they are supposed to do—taste like cheese yet squirt out of a bottle—may do other, unwanted things as well, such as cause cancer or litter the planet. When McWhorter thinks she'd better protect her dirt from the very Doritos she happily consumes, and the imagined EPA pronounces it must protect the U.S. topsoil from the bodies of its citizens, these bizarre moments tear through conventional conceptual landscapes that allow us to take refuge within the outlines of an impermeable, even disembodied, human figure.

The existence of toxic bodies, both human and nonhuman—however clichéd, however repressed or denied—still mixes things up. Since the same chemical substance may poison the workers who produce it, the neighborhood in which it is produced, and the web of plants and animals who end up consuming it, the traffic in toxins reveals the interconnections among various movements, such as environmental health, occupational health, labor, environmental justice, popular epidemiology, environmentalism, ecological medicine, disability rights, green living, antiglobalization, consumer rights, and children's health and welfare. The traffic in toxins may render it nearly impossible for humans to imagine that our own well-being is disconnected from that of the rest of the planet or to imagine that it is possible to protect "nature" by merely creating separate, distinct areas in which it is "preserved." In other words, the ethical space of trans-corporeality is never an elsewhere but is always already here, in whatever compromised, ever-catalyzing form. A nearly unrecognizable sort of ethics emerges—one that demands that we inquire about all of the substances that surround us, those for which we may be somewhat responsible, those that may harm us, those that may harm others, and those that we suspect we do not know enough about. A trans-corporeal ethics calls us to somehow find ways of navigating through the simultaneously material, economic, and cultural systems that are so harmful to the living world and yet so difficult to contest or transform.

Tracing the traffic in toxins, for example, may allow us to notice that carcinogenic chemicals are produced by some of the same companies that sell chemotherapy drugs. This may be a useful thing to notice, but not an easy thing to remedy. It is certainly difficult, in a world of simulacra and slick public relations campaigns, to shift our focus from image to substance. Breast Cancer Action, the "bad girls of breast cancer," attempt just that. They expose corporations that "pinkwash" their products by claiming they "care about breast cancer by promoting a pink ribbon campaign, but manufacture products that are contributing to the epidemic" (Breast Cancer Action website). Cosmetics companies, food manufacturers, automobile manufacturers, and others decorate their complicity in the (breast) cancer epidemic with that ubiquitous pink ribbon. Significantly, that pink ribbon, which is a symbol without substance, is pasted on myriad consumer goods and services for fundraising and "awareness." Breast Cancer Action, however, focuses attention on the ingredients within the products, revealing their carcinogenicity and thus provoking recognition that these things that surround us are not benign—the pink ribbon suddenly becomes sinister!—but are substances that betray human permeability and vulnerability. This disturbing sense of trans-corporeality is a universe apart from the glib call of the Susan G. Komen Foundation for people to join "Passionately Pink for the Cure": "You'll help raise awareness among your friends, family or co-workers; and help end breast cancer forever!" (Susan G. Komen for the Cure website). The women in the photographs on the Komen website are inexplicably happy, perhaps because "awareness" is a comforting, mental, even ethereal, state; it is magical thinking to protect us from harm. Being aware of breast cancer will not, however, do anything to end it, especially since the actual content of this awareness is vague, at best, and blatantly ignores the role that toxicants in food, air, water, cosmetics, and other consumer products play in causing cancer.

True awareness eludes most, if not all, members of risk society. As Ulrich Beck asserts, the "risks" of modernization are difficult, if not impossible, for individuals to apprehend without access to scientific technology or institutions. Understanding the risks requires "the 'sensory organs' of science—*theories, experiments, measuring instruments—in order to become visible or interpretable as hazards at all*" (27; emphasis in original). The trans-corporeality of environmental health and environmental justice that I examine in this book emerges from exactly this sense of risk society, in which individuals require scientific knowledge not only to assess risks but to survey the landscape of the self.

Environmental activism and green consumerism have emerged from and contribute to the recognition that our material interconnection with the wider world puts us at risk. Greenpeace, for example, launched a campaign during 2004–2005 against mercury, which encouraged people to send in a sample of their own hair to be tested for mercury contamination. Such an action renders palpable one's own corporeal connection to global economic, industrial, and environmental systems as well as to global environmental campaigns, especially since Greenpeace, in turn, informed the participants of the levels of mercury in their bodies, explained the significance of that number in terms of possible health effects, and discussed how to minimize mercury exposure through both dietary and political means. Someone who participated in this campaign may well have considered how her own body was literally enmeshed within the wider world. When I received my results, I imagined various routes that mercury may have taken to my body (tuna sandwiches in childhood? Dallas air pollution?), but I was also struck by the bare number on the page (.35) and the process by which scientific testing transformed my hair into a chunk of data (not unlike Latour's "circulating reference").[11] It is more than a little unnerving, I think, not only to receive scientific data about the toxicity of one's own body but to consider how this particular bit of knowledge appears only after traveling through contingent networks that intermesh science and activism. Not only did I not have access to this number before I happened to open a random letter from Greenpeace, but I did not know that I would want such a number or even that such a number could exist. Traveling through the mail as well as through networks interlacing power and knowledge, this chunk of hair became a primer for trans-corporeal risk society.

What I argue throughout this book is that understanding the substance of one's self as interconnected with the wider environment marks a profound shift in subjectivity. As the material self cannot be disentangled from networks that are simultaneously economic, political, cultural, scientific, and substantial, what was once the ostensibly bounded human subject finds herself in a swirling landscape of uncertainty where practices and actions that were once not even remotely ethical or political matters suddenly become the very stuff of the crises at hand. This is especially evident in the case of global climate change: an individual, household, business, university, city, state, nation, or continent can calculate the carbon footprint left by the stunning range of human activities that emit carbon.[12] I think it is crucial to emphasize, however, that trans-corporeality, as it emerges in environmental health, environmental justice, web-based subcultures, green consumerism, literature, photography, activist websites, and films, is a recognition not just that everything is interconnected but that humans are the very stuff of the material, emergent world. Thus, the pursuit of self-knowledge, which has been a personal, philosophical, psychological, or discursive matter, now extends into a rather "scientific" investigation into the constitution of our coextensive environments. Science, however, offers no steady ground, as the information may be biased, incomplete, or opaque and the ostensible object of scientific inquiry—the material world—is extremely complex, overwrought with agencies, and ever emergent.

Take, for example, the state of knowledge about xenobiotic chemicals. Obviously, powerful entities, such as the chemical and pharmaceutical industries, greatly influence what knowledge is produced and how it is delivered to the public. As Robert N. Proctor argues in *Cancer Wars: How Politics Shapes What We Know and Don't Know about Cancer:* "ignorance and uncertainty can be manufactured, maintained, and disseminated" (8). But even after bracketing the intentional production of ignorance, uncertainty, and blatant misinformation, the fact remains that it may not even be possible to predict the staggeringly vast number of chemical interactions that may occur as a result of the "*billions* of pounds of toxic chemicals being routinely emitted" in the United States alone (Steingraber, *Living Downstream* 102). The problem is not only that, as Sandra Steingraber informs us, "[t]wo-thirds of the most widely used chemicals have still not gone through basic carcinogenicity tests," but that far less is known about how various chemical combinations inter- and intra-act in bodies and environments (281, 258). The interactions of chemicals may be understood within the wider onto-epistemology of Karen Barad, which stresses both material agency and the nearly inconceivable concept of intra-action. Barad's concept of intra-action, which she develops from quantum physics and particularly from the work of Niels Bohr, rejects an ontology whereby "things" precede their relations. Instead, "relata" (as opposed to discrete "things") "do not preexist relations; rather, relata-within-phenomena emerge through specific intra-actions" (Barad, *Meeting the Universe Halfway* 140). Understanding the material world as agential and considering that things, as such, do not precede their intra-actions are, I think, crucial for twenty-first-century environmentalisms in which the existence of anything—any creature, ecosystem, climatological pattern, ocean current— cannot be taken for granted as simply existing out there. Even though Barad's theory, based on quantum physics, is a timeless onto-epistemology, it strikes me as being particularly relevant for our contemporary state of environmental crisis in which elaborate, colossal human practices, extractions, transformations, productions, and emissions have provoked heretofore unthinkable intra-actions at all levels. If the material environment is a realm of often incalculable, interconnected agencies, then we must somehow make political, regulatory, and even personal decisions within an ever-changing landscape of continuous interplay, intra-action, emergence, and risk.

Ulrich Beck notes that an "implicit ethics" exists within risk society, as the question "how do we wish to live?" arises against a "normative horizon of lost security and broken trust" (28). Beck argues that the determination of risk is itself a form of ethics and that such determinations are an "unrecognized, still undeveloped symbiosis of the natural and the human sciences, of everyday and expert rationality, of interest and fact" (ibid.). Many of the texts discussed in *Bodily Natures* struggle with implicit and explicit ethical matters, as they document what it is to know, to live, and to act within risk culture. Steingraber, whose work is considered further in chapter 5, advocates that the "precautionary principle" guide us within these landscapes of risk. The precautionary principle states, "When an activity raises threats of harm to human health or the environment, precautionary measures should be taken even if some cause and effect relations are not fully established scientifically. In this context, the proponent of an activity, rather than the public, should bear the burden of proof" (*Living Downstream* 284).

The recognition that material agencies can be neither adequately predicted nor safely mastered encourages caution. The precautionary principle serves as a practical, commonsensical procedural map and as a manifestation of how trans-corporeality demands more responsible, less confident epistemologies. It drama-tizes how early twenty-first-century peoples require scientific knowledge in order to navigate through the many invisible dangers that surround us and, simultane-ously, how our scientific understanding of unpredictable material agencies will never be sufficient to protect us from unforeseen harms.[13] As a particularly vivid example of trans-corporeal space, toxic bodies insist that environmentalism, hu-man health, and social justice cannot be severed. They encourage us to imagine ourselves in constant interchange with the environment and, paradoxically per-haps, to imagine an epistemological space that allows for both the unpredictable becomings of other creatures and the limits of human knowledge. Toxic bodies may provoke material, trans-corporeal ethics that turn from the disembodied values and ideals of bounded individuals toward an attention to situated, evolv-ing practices that have far-reaching and often unforeseen consequences for mul-tiple peoples, species, and ecologies.

Chapter Summaries

Bodily Natures continues with two chapters that foreground environmental jus-tice models of the corporeal manifestations of race, class, and gender, asking what it means to posit such a thing as a "proletarian lung" or to insist that some-one's blood is not his own. As in other instances of trans-corporeality, biology and politics merge as people, places, and substances amalgamate. The environ-mental justice struggles in chapters 2 and 3 raise questions about the nature of evidence, the activists' need for science and technology, and the scientific refusal of dispassionate objectivity. Chapter 2, "Eros and X-rays: Bodies, Class, and 'Environmental Justice,'" explores the work of two early twentieth-century writers, Meridel Le Sueur and Muriel Rukeyser, who construct radically dif-ferent relations between working-class bodies and the environment. Le Sueur's startling portrayal of erotic, corporeal natures, imbued with working-class vital-ity and values, contrasts with Rukeyser's depiction of miners dying of silicosis, their illness rendered visible by X-rays. Le Sueur's and Rukeyser's work manifests conceptions of "environmental justice," avant la lettre, and, at the same time, prefigures discord between anthropocentric and ecocentric ethics. This chapter illustrates the movement from cultural studies models of discursive contesta-tion to more materially-oriented modes of analysis. I contend that, in order to understand the political aims of both Le Sueur and Rukeyser, it is necessary to invoke corporeal theories that push through the bounds of discursive paradigms in order to understand the imbrication of culture and matter.

Chapter 3, "Invisible Matters: The Sciences of Environmental Justice," analyzes the intersection of raced bodies, toxic environments, and the scientific mediation of knowledge within environmental justice activism and literature. Civil rights, affirmative action, and identity politics models of social justice—all of which assume that individuals are bounded, coherent entities—become profoundly altered by the recognition that human bodies, human health, and human rights are interconnected with the material, often toxic, flows of particular places. Several works of contemporary U.S. literature depict the struggle to know the invisible risks that travel across bodies and landscapes. Ana Castillo's novel *So Far from God* and Simon Ortiz's poetry, for example, dramatize the onto-epistemological ruptures that occur when people confront the troubling invisibility of the dangerous substances and forces of risk society. Percival Everett's novel *Watershed* charts how, within an environmental justice crisis, the notion of scientific objectivity becomes complicated by a political struggle that both does and does not correspond to civil rights history. Whereas academic theories of race have worked to undermine its ontological status via theories of social construction, environmental justice movements employ scientific data that track the material agency of environmental hazards, placing a new sort of materiality at the forefront of racial struggles. At the same time, however, biomonitoring techniques, which yield categories of vulnerability other than those of recognized racial groups, reveal how the maelstrom of risk culture mixes peoples, places, substances, and forces, disclosing new distributions of harm.

The second part of the book addresses environmental health, beginning with chapter 4, "Material Memoirs: Science, Autobiography, and the Substantial Self." Environmental health, which rejects conventional medical models, asserts that the human body is permeable and thus vulnerable to particular locations and substances. Environmental health, as a burgeoning scientific, political, cultural, and consumerist movement, is one approach to reckoning with contemporary risk society, in which ordinary citizens are compelled to take on scientific expertise and epidemiological projects in order to contend with the dangers of everyday life. This cultural landscape has fostered a new genre of autobiography— what I'm calling the *material memoir*. The strange, disturbing memoirs of Audre Lorde, Candida Lawrence, Zillah Eisenstein, Susanne Antonetta, and Sandra Steingraber dramatize life in risk society by showing how profoundly the sense of selfhood is transformed by the recognition that the very substance of the self is interconnected with vast biological, economic, and industrial systems that can never be entirely mapped or understood. Working as a form of "counter-memory," these works mix science writing, activism, genealogy, and autobiography, interdigitating objective scientific knowledge with subjective autobiographical rumination, the external material environment with the inner workings of the self. The self becomes unrecognizable in the material memoir, not because of its discursive construction, but because self-knowledge in risk society demands "scientific" understandings of a vast, coextensive materiality.

Chapter 5, "Deviant Agents: The Science, Culture, and Politics of Multiple Chemical Sensitivity," explores the puzzling condition known as *multiple chemical sensitivity,* or *environmental illness,* in which ostensibly harmless chemicals provoke extreme physical reactions. Drawing upon recent theories in science studies, I analyze a range of scientific and cultural texts, arguing that environmental illness offers a particularly potent example of trans-corporeal space, in which the human body can never be disentangled from the material world, a world composed of emergent, entangled biological creatures as well as a multitude of xenobiotic, humanly made substances. Oddly, whereas scientists debate whether MCS is a physical or a mental phenomenon, and thus whether it is material or immaterial, social theorists who are immersed in models of social construction become compelled by MCS to formulate models of material agency and corporeal modes of knowing. Todd Haynes's film *Safe,* activist websites, and Rhonda Zwillinger's photography invent ethical ways to represent invisible material agencies and "deviant" human bodies. Within the now-standard genre of MCS autobiography, for example, the body becomes something akin to a scientific instrument, in that daily life becomes a sort of experiment: what happens when I go there, breathe that, touch this? Thus, the bodies of those with MCS demonstrate that some material agents—in this case, the xenobiotics that interact in unpredictable, uncontrollable ways—demand new ethical, epistemological, and political strategies and, above all, new material practices that "deviate" from the norms of the early twenty-first-century chemical/industrial society.

Bodily Natures concludes with chapter 6, "Genetics, Material Agency, and the Evolution of Posthuman Environmental Ethics in Science Fiction." At a time when popular understandings of genetic engineering assume that humans can manipulate and control the passive codes of matter, Greg Bear's Darwin series dramatizes that materiality, as such, can transform the human. The premise of these novels is that an endogenous retrovirus—lurking within human DNA—provokes a monstrous fetus-ovulator inside women, which then creates a new species of child, one with flashing "squid cheeks" who can say "hello" after drawing her first breaths. Drawing upon Evelyn Fox Keller, Bonnie Spanier, and Donna Haraway's critiques of popular and scientific conceptions of "the gene," I argue that predominant understandings of genetics—"gene fetishism"—are hostile to an environmental ethos. Reading Bear's Darwin series against the science fiction of Slonczewski, Atwood, and Octavia Butler, I propose, instead, a posthuman environmental ethics that denies to the "human" the sense of separation from the interconnected, mutually constitutive actions of material reality. Through a series of parallel "enfoldings," Bear's novel *Darwin's Radio* reconfigures the commonsensical landscapes of figure and ground, human agent and material resource, civilization and wilderness, presenting instead a kind of in-habitation, in which what is supposed to be outside the delineation of the human is always already inside. This stuff of matter generates, composes, transforms, and decomposes: it is both the stuff of (human) corporeality and the stuff that eviscerates the very notion of human. By thrusting us into an evolutionary narrative, where there are no guarantees that humans will endure as a species, Bear enacts a powerful posthuman environmental ethics, in which human bodies—from the prehistorical past through unknown futures—are inextricably interconnected with material worlds.

Eros and X-rays: Bodies, Class, and "Environmental Justice"

> Evidently your body knows your class position no matter how well you have been taught to deny it.
>
> —Richard Lewontin and Richard Levins, *Biology under the Influence*

What does it mean for the body to "know" something as seemingly abstract as one's place within a class system? "Knowing" may not be the best term, as it poses "the body" as a facsimile of a rational human subject. Such an epistemology demands complication, especially when we consider that the most legitimized forms of knowing the human body require the instruments and institutions of science and medicine, neither of which is immune to ideology. Nonetheless, Lewontin and Levins's contention provokes us to question what the body of the worker can reveal and who is socially positioned to articulate those revelations. They alert us to the "codetermination" of biological and social causes, asserting that "[w]hereas human sociality is itself a consequence of our received biology, human biology is a socialized biology" (36):

> Racism becomes an environmental factor affecting adrenals and other organs in ways that tigers or venomous snakes did in earlier historical epochs. The conditions under which labor power is sold in a capitalist labor market act on the

individual's glucose cycle as the pattern of exertion and rest depends more on the employer's economic decisions than on the worker's self perception of metabolic flux. Human ecology is not the relation of our species with the rest of nature, but rather the relations of different societies, and the classes, genders, ages, grades, and ethnicities maintained by those social structures. Thus, it is not too far-fetched to speak of the pancreas under capitalism or the proletarian lung. (37)

Casting racism as environmental exposes how sociopolitical forces generate landscapes that infiltrate human bodies. Similarly, the "pancreas under capital-ism" and the "proletarian lung" testify to the penetrating physiological effects of class (and racial) oppression, demonstrating that the biological and the social cannot be considered separate spheres. And yet the images of the pancreas and the lung, displayed as in an autopsy, section workers' bodies, making them the object of scientific discourses and medical models of evidence that demand ex-pertise and legitimation. The oppressed, it seems, may be physically affected by economic and social systems and yet be unable to produce evidence for their biosocial conditions. Before considering how two leftist authors, writing pri-marily in the early twentieth century, addressed the material effects of economic systems, we should address the question of the worker's body more generally.

The image of the proletarian lung may give us pause. If ostensibly external social forces have transformed an internal bodily organ, does this movement across the social and the biological, the private body and the social system, sug-gest traffic among other personal, political, epistemological, institutional, and disciplinary domains? The lung certainly "belongs" to the worker, and yet it may also be scrutinized by experts in medicine, law, "industrial hygiene," occupa-tional health, insurance claims, and union organizing (as well as by the aca-demic writings of Lewontin, Levins, and myself). The proletarian lung illustrates my conception of trans-corporeality, in that the human body is never a rigidly enclosed, protected entity, but is vulnerable to the substances and flows of its environments, which may include industrial environments and their social/eco-nomic forces. Coming to grips with the biological/social condition of this lung may provoke new modes of literary production and analysis, which may be more jagged, or more hesitant, but also more permeable. It may be useful to consider the proletarian lung within the networks of nature/culture, which are "simultane-ously real, like nature, narrated, like discourse, and collective, like society" (Latour, We Have Never Been Modern 6).

The late twentieth-century framework of environmental justice offers potent avenues of approach to the sort of trans-corporeality exemplified by the proletar-ian lung. Indeed, environmental justice insists upon the material interconnec-tions between specific bodies and specific places, especially the peoples and areas that have been literally dumped upon. Environmental justice social movements and modes of analysis target the unequal distribution of environmental benefits and environmental harms, tracing how race and class (and sometimes gender and sexuality) profoundly influence material, often place-based inequities. Race, for example, has been well documented as the single most important factor in the placement of toxic waste sites in the United States. Thus, it is not surprising that most accounts of environmental justice activism trace its emergence from civil rights movements, pinpointing an African American community's protest against a toxic disposal site in Warren County, North Carolina, in the early 1980s as a pivotal moment.[1] And yet one could rewrite the entire expanse of the history of the United States from an environmental justice perspective, rethinking the grand narratives of, say, manifest destiny and noting that many of the forms of violence toward and subordination of Native Americans, African Americans, and Mexican Americans, in particular, could be understood as environmental justice issues: the slaughter of the buffalo and the genocide or "removal" of Indians from the environments essential for their cultural and physical survival; the institution of plantation slavery; Mexican-American farmworkers who, even still, bear disproportionately the harm caused by agricultural chemicals. Much of human history could be evaluated by assessing the environmental benefits versus environmental harms gained or suffered by different groups.

Even as U.S. history presents a multitude of ways in which social injustice is inseparable from physical environments, the environmental movements of the early twentieth century, devoted to conserving "natural resources" or to preserving aesthetic natures, were not just unconcerned by the plight of the poor or otherwise disenfranchised, but actively took up positions that articulated "conservation" with a white, middle-to-upper class. As I discuss in *Undomesticated Ground: Recasting Nature as Feminist Space,* William Hornaday, for example, elevated the worthy, responsible, middle- to upper-class white "sportsman" above the specter of the hordes of impoverished, darker races whose subsistence hunting he deplored.[2] What's more, despite the fact that labor movements and conservation movements were, by and large, worlds apart, workers and nature were subjected to similar regimens of control. Ted Steinberg explains that the "Progressive Era's" imposition of "scientific" management targeted both landscapes and laborers:

> Taylorism tried to help employers streamline production by eliminating the chaos present on the shop floor, prevailing on workers to use the most efficient set of motions necessary to complete any given task, to yield before the expert and his stopwatch. Conservation, meanwhile, at least in the form that [Gifford] Pinchot espoused, tried to rid not the shop floor but the forests of the very same disorderly tendencies, seeking the most efficient way of producing not steel, but crops of timber and animals. Taylorism controlled workers, conservation controlled nature, and both relied on the principles of scientific management to do so. (*Down to Earth* 141)

Subject to regimes of ever-increasing "efficiency," the body of the worker was managed like other "natural resources." Meridel Le Sueur, as we will see below, explicitly allied landscape and laborer by dramatizing their parallel plights. Certainly, it is anachronistic to use the term *environmental justice* for the early twentieth century. And yet, Cary Nelson, the foremost scholar of leftist American poetry, who is responsible for recovering a staggering number of poems from this era, insists that "what we 'recover' we necessarily rewrite, giving it meanings that are inescapably contemporary, giving it a new discursive life in the present, a life it cannot have had before" (*Repression and Recovery* 11). While I am by no means "recovering" the work of Le Sueur or Rukeyser (both are relatively well known by this point), I would like to explore the ways in which their work struggles with a nexus of forces that now resonate as nascent environmental justice concerns.

The principles of scientific management operated directly on the workers' bodies, often inflicting grave harm. John Rolfe's 1928 poem "Asbestos" eerily portrays a worker's body-become-deathbed: "John's deathbed is a curious affair: / the posts are made of bone, the spring of nerves, / the mattress bleeding flesh." Nelson observes that, in this poem, the "exploitation of workers . . . literally impresses itself on their bodies. Those bodies are the fulcrum, the point of application, of all the power relations in which their lives are embedded" (*Revolutionary Memory* 94). Extending Nelson's reading, we could say that the workers' bodies are not only the sites of the direct application of power, but permeable sites that are forever transformed by the substances and forces—asbestos, coal dust, radiation—that penetrate them. In the early twentieth century, the body of the worker also became a contested site for the institutionalization of industrial hygiene and occupational medicine, the site where businesses, the insurance industry, medicine, law, government, social reformers, labor organizations, and the workers themselves tussled for control. Claudia Clark, in *Radium Girls,* a study of New Jersey dial painters, notes that one of the debates sparked by their suits for compensation for radium poisoning "centered on whether industrial diseases should be considered primarily a labor problem (within the jurisdiction of labor authorities) or a medical problem (subject to the control of medical authorities)" (150). Medicine, as an institution, was often enlisted to protect the business owners, not the workers. Even something as seemingly progressive as offering medical care to employees may be a sinister management strategy. In a National Safety Council meeting of 1915, for example, Alice Hamilton, a pioneer in the study of occupational diseases, discussed how both workers and labor leaders fought the physical exams that were conducted in the workplace by company doctors because they believed that the exams were used to "weed out union sympathizers" or to deny work to those who were considered a "compensation risk" (Sellers, *Hazards* 118–119). Christopher Sellers notes that the labor leader Samuel Gompers was especially suspicious of company doctors because of the "parallels between the company doctor's exam and the time and motion studies of scientific manag-ers, through which workers surrendered their craft knowledge" (119). Gompers's rhetoric is notable. He exclaims that workers "want health," but "the health of free men and women, not that of work animals or slaves," condemning the "ef-ficiency fad as it prevails in industry" as a "vivisection experiment" (644–645). Although the installation of medical professionals within the workplace may signal the dangers of that environment as an environment, if medical scrutiny is restricted to the body of the worker, this scrutiny may not only objectify her but also obscure the trans-corporeal networks causing harm.

Scrutinizing the worker as an object requiring efficient management deprives her of "craft knowledge" as well as voice, perspective, and agency. Health itself is a situated knowledge (in Haraway's term) as well as a biological state, mean-ing that the condition of the worker's body can be ascertained only through particular, embedded, and partial perspectives, not the least of which would be those available to the worker herself. Katherine Shaub, a dial painter, for instance, was "the first to make the connection between the dialpainting [sic] and the dialpainters' illnesses" (Clark 12). According to Sellers, workers pushed for laws, governmental agencies, and research aimed at ameliorating workplace illness: "from the proliferating lead diagnoses of the 1910s to those of silicosis in the 1930s, it was the workers who, in alliance with their private doctors and lawyers, goaded corporations into sponsorship of disease research" (Hazards 230). More broadly, Clark contends that "much of the history of laboring people's politics can be reinterpreted as part of the history of occupational health and safety," and she cites the slogan "Health Is the Capital of the Laboring Man" (26).

Just as it has been crucial for environmental theorists to conceptualize the "agency" of nature so as not to subscribe to an ontology in which the material world is a passive resource for the exploits of the human, it may also be impor-tant to consider how the laborer resists the way her corporeality is utilized as a resource for industry. Sellers points out, for example, another sort of "worker resistance": "the extent to which their bodies were reacting to, rebelling against, the chemical and physical conditions of the workplace. Even the least organized and most submissive workers were not infinitely pliable; their own physiology set limits to their obedience" (Hazards 230). Occupational disease, then, can be seen as a corporeal mode of resistance to harmful labor practices.[3] Rather than separating bodily resistance from conscious action, however, we can imagine a multitude of intra-actions or trans-corporeal processes in which, for example, physiological responses to work environments spark lines of inquiry, paths of struggle, and even bodies of literature.

Several leftist women writers of the early twentieth century portrayed their concern for workers' health. As I discussed in *Undomesticated Ground,* both Fielding Burke and Tillie Olsen document the healthful benefits of natural environments: fields of dandelion greens provide vital nutrients for a family, country retreats revitalize workers for grueling strikes.[4] They prefigure an "environmental justice" insistence that working-class people should have access to environmental benefits, as their characters "trespass" on protected grounds. These writings are especially remarkable when read against the prevailing shift from nineteenth-century medical models that "acknowledged the interpenetration of body and environment" to "modern" medical models that focused on "pathogenic agents and the specific pathways of contamination" and separated human bodies from their environments (Nash 89). As Linda Nash argues, in the early twentieth century, "new ideas about health tried to erase the particularity of a given landscape in favor of an assumed homogeneity" (90). A cadre of leftist writers, along with certain strands of the industrial hygiene movement more generally, however, resisted the "modern" medicine that aimed to sever human bodies from their environments. Thus, focusing on the health of the worker forces us to consider all environments as areas of concern and encourages us to scrutinize economic systems; hierarchies of class, race, and gender; and the flows of potentially harmful substances and forces.

Meridel Le Sueur and Muriel Rukeyser wrote within this social/material landscape in which the relations between working-class bodies and their environments were under scrutiny from different institutions and interests. Their work manifests conceptions of "environmental justice," avant la lettre, exposing the relations among nature, capitalism, and the working class. While Rukeyser writes a poem of material documentation, Le Sueur resists the authoritative forces and institutions that would test, measure, and manage the body of the worker, moving instead toward an erotic connection between worker and world. Remarkably, both writers attempt to write bodies and natures in ways that emphasize their palpable interrelations; in so doing, they forge a sense of environment that counters the early twentieth-century conservationist and preservationist models of nature as a world apart. Rukeyser even anticipates more recent understandings of pollution, as she extends the hazards of the workplace across vast, peopled landscapes.

Meridel Le Sueur's Landscapes and Laborers

Remarkably vivid images of the earth as a human body and of the human body as vitally connected with the earth abound in Le Sueur's work. These places of connection, or "joints," between flesh and mountain, corporeality and landscape, serve as sites for cultural critique and transformation. Though Le Sueur has been largely ignored by ecocritics,[5] her writings offer illuminating accounts of how power structures mediate the human relationship to the natural world. Le Sueur's writings may be one of the richest sites in American literature for investigating questions of environmental justice, especially as they pertain to class and gender. Rather than idealizing a nature devoid of humans, she enmeshes the landscape and the laborer within a matrix of capitalist critique and utopian desire. By persistently linking the working class with the land, Le Sueur imaginatively infuses workers, predominantly rural whites, with value and vitality. Her insistence on the lively connections between these particular people and their environment may also challenge the public health concern that "like native bodies in the tropics and the poor and nonwhite bodies that inhabited American cities, bodies in the rural United States were not properly separated from the environment" (Nash 101). Nash explains that public health experts and physicians in the early twentieth century "openly equated certain rural diseases—especially hookworm and malaria—with the racial deteriorization [sic] of whites." They "blamed these diseases for breeding an inferior breed of whites that were plagued by poverty, low intelligence, and lack of vigor" (97). These fears provoked sanitation programs aimed at creating "fully modern and aseptic" landscapes that would then be "essentially irrelevant" (100).

Clearly, Le Sueur's utopia did not float in a sanitized, modern no-place. It may be particularly misguided, then, to ignore how her work registers the material agencies of place. Indeed, Le Sueur's fiction encourages us to consider what happens when we shift toward feminist theories of bodies and natures that push against the edges of discursive models in order to try to imbricate culture and matter. For Le Sueur's writings play out Deborah Slicer's important call for "environmentally concerned women" to "attend to their bodies as *materialized* starting points for theorizing similarly materialized nature" (70). Yet, while such matters are always as close as our own skin, the epistemological, ontological, and political question of how to conceptualize matter—be it the stuff of atoms, human bodies, or ecosystems—may be the most vexing question of early twenty-first-century theory, especially for the environmental humanities, science studies, and feminist theory. Le Sueur's innovative depictions of bodies and landscapes offer one intriguing avenue of approach to the question of matter, an approach that intertwines natural, generative forces with the potency of political struggle, posing people and the earth as "comrades of surge."

Le Sueur's short stories and reportage ally the landscape and the laborer, unveiling their parallel positions as fodder for the capitalist machine. The bodies of the laborers, however, serve not only as the site for a persistent critique of capitalism but also as a place of pleasure, beauty, value, and eros. For a strict social constructionist, such a double movement does not make sense; however, Le Sueur is willing to relinquish neither critique nor utopia. Instead, she braids together her condemnation of patriarchal capitalism with an alternative, utopian locus of value in which corporeality converges with the natural world. This sense of nature as palpably "at hand" contrasts with a more urban and more middle- to upper-class appreciation of the landscape as a pretty picture. The narrator of "American Bus," for example, muses that the "sight of the countryside to [rural women] is not pictorial, but touch and hunger and work and love" (99).

Those who pose nature as a place to escape to, as a place of psychic healing or transcendent moments, often gain these pleasures by objectifying not only the locales that they visit but the locals whom they hire. In "American Bus," Le Sueur satirizes the romantic escapism of rich city folk who want to live the "simple life" in the country. Honey, the new wife of the Lumber King, spends a fortune to procure an outdoor kitchen and hires two unemployed lumberjacks to make her a "woodsy bed." The wife of one of the lumberjacks mocks Honey's back-to-nature diversions, "Oh! I want to bake my bread outdoors in an oven—oh it's so picturesque—so woodsy" (64). The upper-class desire for the picturesque frames not only the woods but the workers, as one lumberjack realizes that he and his friend have been used as natural resources: "It's like when they come down to us we are like the birds or the stuff they planted, or the woodsy bed, as if they owned us like a dog or cow" (66). Le Sueur, aware that linking the working class to nature risks solidifying the sense that they, like the land, are mere resources to be mined, nevertheless insists upon this connection, but with a critical difference.

Le Sueur envisions nature and working-class bodies in a utopian manner, wresting them away from capitalist economies in which they are mere resources, granting them their own alternative economies of abundance and desire. Le Sueur thus echoes Emma Goldman's depiction of "Mother Earth" as an anarchistic mother who gives freely of herself to all of her children. In naming their journal *Mother Earth,* Goldman and Alexander Berkman posed both the journal—and Goldman herself—as an insurgent, abundant force. In many of the editorials, Mother Earth stands steadfast against the police who threaten the magazine and, more broadly, against the system of capitalist exploitation and state control. Goldman's sexual innuendos conflate the pleasures of the body and the delights of nature, posing the earth as an alternative site of value that disdains capitalist stinginess and Puritan reticence.

> Mother Earth, with the sources of vast wealth hidden within the folds of her ample bosom, extended her inviting and hospitable arms to all those who came to her from arbitrary and despotic lands—Mother Earth ready to give herself alike to all her children. But soon she was seized by the few, stripped of her freedom, fenced in, a prey to those who were endowed with cunning and unscrupulous shrewdness. (Goldman and Baginski 1)

This mythic tale makes capitalism seem profoundly unnatural, a perversion forced upon us by the few who benefit.[6] Interestingly, Mother Earth's "ample bosom" and "inviting and hospitable arms" pose her body as the locus of her riches and generosity. Le Sueur, who, for a time, lived with Goldman and Berkman in an anarchist commune, said that Goldman was the "only woman" she knew who "controlled her sexual life entirely" (quoted in Pratt, "Afterword" 226). Although Le Sueur, like Goldman, portrays an erotic, proletarian bodily nature, in Le Sueur's work the earth may be masculine and the desire feminine. In her tender and erotic poem "Nests," for example, the speaker, whose gender is not specified, luxuriates in the abundant pleasures of the lover's body:

> Your body is full of little birds moving in their sleep.
> My lips find them in the intimate nest of your neck,
> My lips startle them into flight beneath the marble arch of your arm.
> Your body is full of little birds singing as they fly. (ll. 19–22)

Desire, in this poem, does not emerge from lack nor does it concentrate on the phallus, but, more akin to a Deleuzian intensity, desire as a positive force seeks out the lover's body, which becomes a landscape replete with vibrant creatures.

Le Sueur's corporeal landscapes, rich with pleasures, contrast with the impoverishments of capitalism. In "Corn Village," which is perhaps Le Sueur's most complex meditation on the human relation to the land, Le Sueur asks: "What does an American think about the land, what dreams come from the sight of it, what painful dreaming? Are they only money dreams, power dreams? Is that why the land lies desolate like a loved woman who has been forgotten? Has she been misused through dreams of power and conquest?" (10–11). More elegiac than insurgent, and without the ironic edge, Le Sueur nonetheless echoes Goldman's fable of the conquest of Mother Earth. By demonstrating the connection between dreams and actions, Le Sueur insists on the social and environmental import of our terrestrial dreams. She contends, for example, that the "Puritans used the body like the land as a commodity, and the land and the body resent it" ("Corn Village" 20). Capitalism, likewise, devastates humans and nature alike, extracting economic value and leaving a wasteland behind: "Capitalism is a world of ruins really, junk piles of machines, men, women, bowls of dust, floods, erosions, masks to cover rapacity" ("The Dark of the Time" 122).

"Eroded Woman," first published in *Masses and Mainstream* in 1948—with the dustbowl crisis in recent memory—features a tough, gnarled woman who embodies the "abandoned lead and zinc mines," which "stand in a wasteland of ruined earth and human refuse" (83). The narrator, who is an outsider but who grew up poor, talks with the eroded woman about her experiences with unions, strikes, and the Klan. Although the story "documents" the eroded woman, listing visual evidence of her wretched condition—such as her flour sack garment and her "hulk of bones" (ibid.)— near the end the narrator empathizes with her: "I felt her deep exhaustion and her sorrow, wakened and warmed by unaccustomed talking, like soil stirred, the sorrow of its ruin reflected in her, the human and the land interlocked like doomed lovers" (89). The coupling of human and land cannot be understood except through economic relations and historical forces—specifically, capitalism, that "great beast" of "ruthless power" (ibid.)—yet an embrace, however "doomed," remains.

"Autumnal Village" counterposes two value systems, that of the bourgeois husband, who builds a house for "the looks of it in the world, for the bargains he would be making because of it," and that of his wife, who experiences the natural world as a space of freedom and plenitude. The woman, from whose perspective the story is told, laments: "O, it was a buckle to wear on his belt—the house, the children, and myself in fine clothes—a feather in his cap and bitter gall in my own mouth" (30). She revels in "the leaves falling, the bare trees and the warm, still golden and green hills, the russet oaks and the terribly blue sky, the frail golden-light sliver of the tan grasses, slanting down the stems" (ibid.). The woman embraces her rural environment as a place of beauty, abundance, and sensuality. She claims that "you might get filled up in the day," filled with the sight of red hens running, the fog rising, the "wild turkeys walking strong and gentle up the saffron slope" (36). She sees "the great mounds" of a village woman "offering her white globe of breast to the eager child" (32), she feels the "thighs of the hills alive and the milk from the breast of the wind," and she cries out to her daughters, "O *you are wild young daughters* . . . feeling [her] breast drive deep as the soil" (36). She relishes this fruitful "world of flesh and wheat and seed." Not unlike Luce Irigaray's "Commodities among Themselves," Le Sueur's lyrical imagery envisions an unbounded system of exchange, "without accounts, without end": "Nature's resources would be expended without depletion, exchanged without labor, freely given, exempt from masculine transactions: enjoyment without a fee, well-being without pain, pleasure without possession" (Irigaray 197).

Whereas Irigaray's women refuse to go to market, the wife in "Autumnal Village" has already been purchased. Despite her ecstatic roamings, she feels "outside the heart of this real happening" (35). Her marriage to the land's owner separates her from the community, if not from nature. The marks of ownership—the No Trespassing signs that he posts—signal separation from the land, rather than a genuine claim. She wonders: "Why are we intruders now who own it all, the mills, the land, the seed" (32). As the story ends, the woman anticipates her husband's return from hunting: "He will lift up the limp bodies of the rabbits and show me how he caught them square between the eyes, and the bright bodies of male and female pheasants with shot in the breast and their necks hanging broken and their eyes half open in the voluptuous death he loves. He will be a knife leaning above me as he kisses me" (37). This conclusion, stressing what the husband "will" do, haunts the story; the husband's mechanical predictability drops like a curtain, terminating the woman's wild excursions. Her "inordinate and terrible desire for the physical life, the forest, the garden" (36) is met by the cold blade of a knife, as she positions herself as one of the hunted animals. The narrative perspective is quite effective, since we glimpse the utopian possibilities of relishing the physical body and the natural world, but through the experiences of a woman who is caught in the system of commodification. Because the utopian moments are framed within patriarchal capitalism (the husband's hunt begins and ends the story), the woman's revelries arise as potent critiques. In fact, throughout the story, it is her ecstatic connection with nature that fosters her political consciousness. Just as utopian thinking "demands the continual exploration and re-exploration of the possible and yet also the unrepresentable" (Cornell 169), "Autumnal Village" imagines possibilities for ecstatic relations with nonhuman nature, yet frames these fragile moments within unrelenting economic systems.

Nature in Le Sueur's work may be understood in the context not only of Emma Goldman's work, but also that of Agnes Smedley, Tillie Olsen, Fielding Burke, and other leftist feminists of the early twentieth century, who engaged in a "contest of mapping" which aimed to align their interests with the socially potent category of nature.[7] During the early twentieth century, the pervasive "back to nature" movements and the desire to conserve natural resources were driven, in part, by middle- to upper-class anxiety about the right to determine the geopolitical territory. In different ways, Agnes Smedley's *Daughter of Earth* (1929), Tillie Olsen's *Yonnondio* (written in the 1930s), and Fielding Burke's *Call Home the Heart* (1932) respond to the middle- to upper-class claims on the American body politic by aligning nature with the working class. For Le Sueur, this alignment is often articulated through bodies, as female characters desire "natural" working-class men and sinewy male natures.

In "No Wine in His Cart," for example, Stella bemoans the fact that her upperclass husband's shrubs are not "natural" but "social," and his body is "white," "narrow," and unused: "Perhaps a woman never really could love the body of a money-making man" (30). The girl in "Spring Story," on the other hand, appreciates how her uncle Joe moves "as if the meaning of his life were in his body" (87). She awakens to her own heterosexual desire by probing a bed of canna, an unmistakably phallic figuration:

> Down on her hands and knees by the canna-bed she could see the white curved sprouts like scimitars just thrust from the earth. She put her finger on one of them and felt them hard and cold but with a moisture and this strong urgency, this upward thrust of power. They thrust upward, hard and single in the darkness, awaiting their day of flowering. (96)

The swooning repetition of "hard," "thrust," and "upward" drenches the canna with a musty maleness while divulging the girl's eroticism. Against a long history of portraying nature as female, as a mistress or mother for a desiring or needy male, Le Sueur puts forward remarkably fresh images of a robust male earth that women desire.

The most sustained version of this trope occurs in "The Girl," in which a priggish teacher drives through the Southwest and becomes, to her surprise, aroused by the landscape and a laborer. Nature and the body merge as she experiences the mountains as "fold upon fold of earth flesh" (66). Moreover, as she glimpses the "huge turn of the muscles" of the young man hitching a ride with her, her perceptions of the mountains and of his body fuse: "The earth seemed to turn on the bone rich and shining, the great mounds burning in the sun, the great golden body, hard and robust, and the sun striking hot and dazzling" (72). She desires what she fears, that his "big body would . . . lounge down upon her like a mountain," which would be as "frightening as some great earth cataclysm" (74). She considers lying with him in the hills, but denies herself this pleasure. The land, however, does not serve merely as an objective correlative or symbol of the teacher's desires, but is itself a force: "The great animal flesh jointed mountains wrought a craving in her" (77). By explicitly joining flesh to mountains, laborer to landscape, Le Sueur lends working-class bodies immensity and endurance. While it would be overreaching to read Le Sueur as promoting a consistently gender-minimizing position, her many depictions of male natures uproot the persistent binary in which women are aligned with nature and men are aligned with culture. Regrettably, her erotic landscapes are relentlessly heterosexual, and her celebrations of pregnancy seem oblivious to Marxist-feminist criticism of reproduction as a handmaiden to production.[8] Nonetheless, the proliferation of laboring and belabored, desiring and desired, eroded and ecstatic bodies overwhelms gender categories, leaving, in their wake, a potent sense of the vitality, energy, and diversity of bodies, natures, laborers, and landscapes.

Even as her enthusiasm for a kind of maternal, proletarian vitality betrays exactly the sort of essentialism that mires the (reproductive) female body within the relentless fecundity of nature, we may still investigate whether Le Sueur's sense of materiality, of the substance of flesh and world, may resonate in less predictable ways. Le Sueur produces original conceptions of wild matter, conceptions that urge a methodological turn from discourse to corporeality, from dichotomies to a spiraling imbrication.

Anthony Dawahare reads Le Sueur along a rather rigid Marxist axis, condemning her "irrationalism" and "essentialism," charging that her "response to modernity takes the form of what one might term a reductive 'materialism': what matters most in Le Sueur's vision of community are the workers' (and/or women's) bodies, experiences, and connections to 'nature'" (423). He states that her "attribution of a special, revolutionary knowledge to domestic and 'natural' labors ignores how even these 'enclaves' are permeated by the dominant culture" (414). The only worth he sees in Le Sueur's texts is that "they contain valuable lessons for theorizing some of the limitations for modern utopian thought then and now" (428). Dawahare would prefer that Le Sueur's texts depict "political theory," not the "working-class body," as the source of the workers' political consciousness (413). From a cultural studies perspective, however, one need not evaluate Le Sueur's writing from the standpoint of how well it represents the "correct" route to political revolution, but instead, it is possible, as I hope the analysis above has shown, to demonstrate that the laboring, desiring, blissful, and eroded bodies that Le Sueur presents manifest political "theories" and perform specific forms of cultural work. Yet, this sort of cultural studies analysis, in which the matter at hand here, namely, bodies and natures, gets taken up solely in terms of how it is represented, how it is articulated within a larger discursive landscape of political struggle, may diminish our ability to see Le Sueur reaching toward a radically different way of envisioning the places that we inhabit and the flesh that we are.

Dawahare's most pertinent critique, in this respect, is that Le Sueur engages in a "reductive materialism" when she valorizes "the workers' (and/or women's) bodies, experiences, and connections to 'nature.'" Le Sueur's texts do enact a sort of materialism, in that the landscape and various working-class male and female bodies are infused with value, meaning, and agency. Yet her imaginative materialism is rarely reductive. Not only does she represent the body as part of the social text, in that economic and political forces can be read there, but she insists that the natural world is also a semiotic realm. Though Dawahare contends that Le Sueur's "attribution of a special, revolutionary knowledge to domestic and 'natural' labors ignores how even these 'enclaves' are permeated by the dominant culture," many of her texts, such as "Eroded Woman," "Autumnal Village," and "American Bus," dramatize precisely how bodies, labor, and the relationship to the natural world are permeated with social and economic forces. In her introduction to the reprint of *Crusaders,* Le Sueur describes the miners who marched after the 1914 massacre in Ludlow, reading the bodies of the people in front of her: "I saw the bodies bearing the mark of their oppression, of their stolen labor, and now their holy dead. Their bodies were hieroglyphs of their exploitation, their blood and bodies taken, their lungs turned to silica stone" (xviii). Similarly, in "Iron Country," the bodies of the miners speak the symptoms of "silicosis"— against the authority of the Iron Range doctors who deny its existence. And in "Evening in a Lumber Town," Le Sueur observes the "distorted and swollen" faces of women, remarking that "[t]his life of excessive labor has marked them" (22). Le Sueur, who thought that political commitment that is restricted to belief or ideology is too disembodied to propel real social change, puts forth bodies that bear witness to their own oppression, teaching us to read corporeality as part of the social text.

One example of how the material is imbricated with the social occurs in "Women Know a Lot of Things," an article in which Le Sueur claims that women "don't read about the news" because they "pick it up at its source, in the human body" (172):

> In that body under your hands every day there resides the economy of that world; it tells you of ruthless exploitation, of a mad, vicious class that now cares for nothing in the world but to maintain its stupid life with violence and destruction; it tells you the price of oranges and cod liver oil, of spring lamb, of butter, eggs and milk. You know everything that is happening on the stock exchange. You know what happened to last year's wheat in the drouth, the terrible misuse and destruction of land and crops and human life plowed under. You don't have to read the stock reports in Mr. Hearst's paper. You have the news at its terrible source. (ibid.)

The ever-present body, "under your hands every day," is a more reliable, even if frightening, source of information than "Mr. Hearst's" paper. Though Dawahare claims that Le Sueur suggests that "the working class has an unmediated relationship with socio-economic and political knowledge: the working class reads itself to learn about politics and the world economy" (412), the entire import of this passage is that the bodies of the working class are themselves shaped by social and economic forces. This is, indeed, a more extensive sort of mediation, since it means that the body is not separate from the social. It is Dawahare, rather than Le Sueur, who imagines that reading the body implies a reductive materialism. Le Sueur's depiction of the body seems more in line with Elizabeth Grosz's notion of the body as a "threshold or borderline concept that hovers perilously and undecidably at the pivotal point of binary pairs. The body is neither—while also being both—the private or the public, self or other, natural or cultural, psychical or social, instinctive or learned, genetically or environmentally determined" (*Volatile Bodies* 23). Imagining the body as a pivot allows us to see how Le Sueur positions the body, paradoxically, as both a locus of value apart from capitalism and as a social text. The body pivots—or, like DNA, spirals—since it is informed by, but also informs, both natural and social processes. Indeed, this is putting it too simply, since the commonsensical divide between "nature" and "culture" has become more and more tenuous. As Karen Barad argues, "The point is not merely that there are important material factors in addition to discursive ones; rather, the issue is the conjoined material-discursive nature of constraints, conditions, and practices" ("Posthumanist Performativity" 823).

Rather than reading Le Sueur's materialism as reductive, it can be read as a corrective to the inability of most contemporary theory to engage with matter. Barad, for example, argues, "Language has been granted too much power. The linguistic turn, the semiotic turn, the interpretive turn, the cultural turn; it seems that at every turn lately every 'thing'—even materiality—is turned into a matter of language or some other form of cultural representation" ("Posthumanist Performativity" 801). Le Sueur's materialism can also be understood as a significant departure from predominant humanisms that employ an "illiterate and unthinking 'outside'" as the ground for human being (Kirby 5). As Kirby argues, considering the "question of corporeality" can lead us to confronting the "alien within—in the form of a very real possibility that the body of the world is articulate and uncannily thoughtful" (ibid.).

In "Annunciation," one of Le Sueur's most beautiful stories, the narrator, whose existence is otherwise pinched and bleak, experiences the vibrant activity of her pregnant body as similar to that of a newly planted field:[9]

> Suddenly many movements are going on within me, many things are happening, there is an almost unbearable sense of sprouting, of bursting encasements, of moving kernels, expanding flesh. Perhaps it is such an activity that makes a field come alive with millions of sprouting shoots of corn or wheat. Perhaps it is something like that that makes a new world. (91)

The narrator is tentative here, as elsewhere, about the connections she forges ("perhaps it is something like"), respecting differences, and remaining skeptical of her own concepts. The story spirals from fleshy experiencing, to questioning and rumination, to writing on "little scraps of paper." The story itself seems to come from the flesh, as the narrator states, "something seems to be going on like a buzzing, a flying and circling within me, and then I want to write it down in some way" (81). As she writes her lived body, the narrator suddenly becomes able to read the world around her; her pregnancy transforms nature into a communicative realm. "Everything is dead and closed, the world a stone, and then suddenly everything comes alive as it has for me, like an anemone on a rock, opening itself, disclosing itself, and the very stones themselves break open like bread" (90). The image of the stone suggests prevalent conceptions of nature as silent, static, and self-enclosed. The narrator, however, begins to hear the pear tree speaking with its "many tongued leaves": "The leaves are the lips of the tree speaking in the wind or they move like many tongues. The fruit of the tree you can see has been a round speech, speaking in full tongue on the tree, hanging in ripe body" (96). We should not read this story as a mystical union between woman and pear tree but instead as a meditation on how "word and flesh are utterly imbricated," because language and culture are not self-enclosed but are "emergent *within* a force field of differentiations that has no exteriority in any final sense" (Kirby 127). What the woman writes on "little scraps of paper," which resemble leaves, surfaces from her patient decoding of the semiotics of her body and the language of the pear tree; the story that we receive demonstrates the imbrication of word and flesh. The "speech" of the trees is not reducible to human language, however: "I listen to the whisperings of the pear tree, speaking to me, speaking to me. How can I describe what is said by a pear tree?" (97). Though "Annunciation" is rich with insights gained by listening to the pear tree, the narrator's ruminations are tenderly tentative. She repeatedly questions, "How can it be explained?" as she struggles to carefully *transcribe*—rather than simply *taking* the communications of the leaves and the flesh and putting them into words. The perceptive narrator seems, in N. Katherine Hayles's terms, to "ride the cusp" between the "flux, inherently unknowable and unreachable," and "the constructed concepts that for us comprise the world" ("Constrained Constructivism" 32).

Yet, as Hayles points out, riding the cusp may be the "hardest thing in the world" ("Constrained Constructivism" 30). The remarkably self-reflexive narrator of Le Sueur's "Corn Village" would agree, as she dramatizes how difficult it is to avoid overdetermined tropes:

> Oh Kansas, I know all of your trees. I have watched them thaw and bud and the pools of winter frozen over, the silos and the corn-blue sky, the wagon-tracked road with the prints of hoofs, going where? And the little creeks gullying with delicate grasses and animals, the prairie dog, the rabbit, and your country with its sense of ruin and desolation like a strong raped virgin. And the mind scurrying like a rabbit trying to get into your meaning, making things up about you, trying to get you alive with significance and myth. (24)

Knowledge, in this passage, begins as something stable and dependable; the subject's relation to discrete entities of the natural and social world—trees, silos, the road, hoof prints—seems unmediated. Yet once she mythologizes this collection of separate beings and objects, comparing the country to a "strong raped virgin," her musings collapse of their own cultural weight, leading her to a self-conscious epistemological critique: "the mind scurrying like a rabbit trying to get into your meaning, making things up about you, trying to get you alive with significance and myth." Just as Val Plumwood has insisted that an ethical human relation to the nonhuman world demands that we "recognise both the otherness of nature" as well as its "continuity with the human self" (160), Le Sueur suggests the difference between human understanding and "nature itself."

Even as we attempt to formulate new understandings that do not isolate the human from the flesh or from nonhuman nature, we need to mark the limits of our own ability to render the material world with language. Such a sense of limits does not pose nature as exterior to human language, but instead acts to ensure an awareness that the process of making meaning is an ongoing one, a process that includes nonhuman nature as a participant rather than as an object of inquiry. Rebecca Raglon and Marian Scholtmeijer, for example, insist that we "recognize nature's resistance to our stories," which "calls into question all the constructs we have built in our attempts to cement over the living earth" (261). Catriona Sandilands advocates an "ethics of the Real," which undertakes a "double movement": "in the search for new metaphoric relations in which nature can appear differently, there also needs to be a point in an ethical relationship at which the ill fit is explicitly recognized, preventing metaphoric closure and opening the need for ongoing conversation" (181).

An ethics of the real urges us to listen for wild matter, that which is neither overcoded nor silent. Sometimes, nonhuman nature becomes silenced in Le Sueur's work by overtaxed, constricting constructions. In the introduction to an excerpt of "Memorial," for example, Le Sueur explains that the novel includes three women, "mother, whore, and intellectual," who end up sleeping "in the true and mythical identity and cyclic return of all female nature" (272). This tidy and predictable formula relies upon a set conception not only of the female, but also of nature. It does not allow for nature's wily unpredictability, the kind of agency that Donna Haraway has characterized as that of the coyote trickster. "Memorial" also equates abortion to ecological plunder: "It's nothing they said mining me take it out take it all knife it out blast it out don't let them see the mined hole the blasted womb" (273). The heavy-handed repetition of the crude images of scraped wombs versus "the wilderness of ova" makes this almost unreadable, as the formal experimentation is drowned out by the roaring oppositional images. Yet Le Sueur's corpus is rich and varied. It would be a mistake to reduce her many rich, complex figurations of the fleshy world to one equation.

In her introduction to the reprint of *Crusaders*, a history of Le Sueur's extraordinary family, Le Sueur offers this unusual genealogy of her people, a genealogy that is as much biology as history:

> These people were like many pioneer crops, a great and wild root, vital travelers, through dark conceptions, wild migrations, like the wheat came to the prairie, multiplying like the people in a new and rich and deep soil, divergent seed, conduits of light and bread, and high vision of new crops. Traveling over continents they came for freedom, for the continuation of the new and shining human, bursting from inherited seed, herbal protein, all repeating and burgeoning into an abundance never before known on earth. The abundance is multiplied in genetic expectation. The abundance jetting from the seed, brought in sunbonnets and pockets from the Old Country, carbon from the air, oxygen making sugar, the raw materials of work and love—nitrate, potash, the leaf clasps, the stem pits, the blade clasps, the culm, grains enclose the bride encased. (xiii)

The passage ends by demonstrating that the "abundance" is no exaggeration, as she tells of an immigrant who planted five small grains of wheat, which eventually yielded enough wheat to feed 500 million people. The passage begins by spiraling like DNA, comparing people to crops and wheat to people, the images swirling together to demonstrate the utter imbrication of plants, land, and people. Agricultural practices, of course, exemplify the inseparability of natural and human agencies. Expectation becomes "genetic" not because it is inborn, but because genes in crops or people are the encoders that shape the process of generativity, a process in which wildly divergent and disparate elements and forces commingle and merge. The human activities of "work and love" are merely one part of the generative process, on par with carbon, oxygen, and potash.

Although this origin story echoes familiar historical accounts, it also defamiliarizes—radically rewriting the human subject by, in Kirby's words, unraveling it into "an interminable genetic debt" (157). "Converging, luminous, alive, we emerge out of the ancient seed" (Le Sueur, *Crusaders* xiii). Even though human and nonhuman nature intersect and coalesce in this experimental passage, there is nothing that can be disparaged as essentialist here, since nature is hardly an immutable, static essence. The swirling biological/agricultural/genealogical history insists that humans emerge from the same chaotic yet coded forces as other life forms. Indeed, Le Sueur's figure of the seed is not unlike that of Vandana Shiva, in which the seed embodies the inseparability of natural and cultural diversity: "In the seed, cultural diversity converges with biological diversity. Ecological issues combine with social justice, peace, and democracy" (*Biopiracy* 126). For Shiva, ideas and modes of life—as well as plants—sprout from seeds: "The diverse seeds now being pushed to extinction carry within them seeds of other ways of thinking and ways of living" (*Monocultures* 6). Writing a poetic biological history, Le Sueur envisions a posthumanism that is congruent with environmentalism. As Andrew Pickering puts it, this is a space "in which the human actors are still there but now inextricably entangled with the nonhuman, no longer at the center of the action and calling the shots. The world makes us in one and the same process as we make the world" (26).

Lest this sound too abstract, scientific, or apolitical, we need only consider that Le Sueur's experimental evocations of matter in "The Origins of Corn" are deeply infused with socialism. The corn, as the "green blaze of the promise and deliverance of abundance," quite literally fills empty stomachs. And, as it "shouts hosannas of abundance," it beckons as the "seed light of democratic races" (21). Le Sueur charts how capitalism exploits the land and the laborer, yet the revolution she proposes begins not in disembodied ideological critique nor even in conventional political struggle. Instead, she hails the people and the earth as "comrades of surge," interconnected in potent potential.

Muriel Rukeyser's *The Book of the Dead:* Tracing a Hazardous Trans-Corporeality

Meridel Le Sueur's sense of the vital links between the worker and the world counter the authoritative forces and institutions that would test, measure, and manage the body of the worker. Muriel Rukeyser, in her long poem sequence, *The Book of the Dead,* on the other hand, writes a modernist poem of material documentation, folding scientific, medical, and legal evidence into a literary form. In contrast to Le Sueur, who demonstrates that social forces can be read on bodies without any particular instruments or expertise, Rukeyser grapples with forces and substances more difficult to discern, those that cannot be adequately deciphered without access to specialized knowledges and technologies. While Le Sueur relishes positive, even erotic, relations between landscapes and laborers, Rukeyser depicts a more sinister trans-corporeality that arises from a particularly egregious moment in the history of occupational illness. Rukeyser based *The Book of the Dead* (1938) on the Hawk's Nest tunnel catastrophe of Gauley Bridge, West Virginia. According to Martin Cherniak in *The Hawk's Nest Incident: America's Worst Industrial Disaster,* in 1930 the construction firm Rinehart and Dennis, hired by Union Carbide, began work on a dam that would not provide electricity for local people but instead power the electrometallurgical complex in the town of Alloy, which was also owned by Union Carbide. A key component of this dam was a massive tunnel. Once the company discovered that the rock was silica, a valuable substance that could be used in the processing of steel, the tunnel was enlarged. It was well known at the time that silica dust caused silicosis. Ever efficient, the company sped up the drilling process by neglecting to use wet drilling methods and protective masks, both of which would have decreased the workers' silica exposure. Workers began to die soon after their exposure to the clouds of deadly dust, but the local papers, caring little about the predominantly African-American migrant workers, recorded no news of this for about eighteen months after the commencement of the work. The company's gag rule no doubt contributed to the silence surrounding the initial phases of this disaster. When the deaths began to be noticed, they were often attributed to the violent lifestyles of the "Negroes" and their "natural susceptibility to pneumonia." (Cherniak reports that many decades later some townspeople still blamed the African American workers, attributing their deaths to "pneumonia and too much alcohol and poker" [3]). Regional papers finally began to report the deaths as tunnel workers and their survivors took their cases to court. In 1935–1936, national newspapers and magazines—from *New Masses* to *Engineering News Record* to *Time*—ran stories on the Hawk's Nest incident. After having "exhausted all legislative or judicial remedies in their own state," the Gauley Bridge workers were granted national hearings which, alas, "did nothing to either relieve or to compensate for their suffering" (Cherniak 75, 80). The hearings did publicize the dangers of silicosis, but, as Sheldon Rampton and John Stauber state, industrialists met privately, a week after the congressional hearings convened, to form the "benevolent sounding" Air Hygiene Foundation, which warded off the threat of silicosis lawsuits by launching a propaganda campaign involving "partial reforms" and "reassuring 'scientific' rhetoric" (78, 79). It remains impossible to know exactly how many men died from this incident: 764 is Cherniak's conservative estimate.

According to Tim Dayton, nearly 3,000 men were exposed to silica while digging the tunnel (17). Some of these men were reported to have been secretly buried in a cornfield early on, others may have fled from this treacherous workplace, and many may have died years later, after the disease progressed. Thus, many deaths, like the tunnel itself, have been rendered invisible. As Cherniak notes, the road-side marker commemorates an "achievement in civil engineering," but "gives no hint of the undetermined number of men who died there" (1).

In 1936, Muriel Rukeyser, along with her friend Nancy Naumberg, traveled to Gauley Bridge, West Virginia, to investigate. Bearing witness to the suffering of the workers and to the corruption of authorities and experts of all stripes, *The Book of the Dead* remains faithful to its sources. Radically experimental, the poem draws heavily from the actual congressional hearings but also includes other reportage, letters, a clip from Union Carbide's stock report, a scientific equation for the energy of falling water, and the symbol for silica, SiO_2, thus mixing languages that are poetic, prosaic, technical, scientific, and colloquial. *The Book of the Dead* has received a great deal of critical attention, primarily from scholars of 1930s political poetry. Michael Thurston argues that the poem "sets out to imagine and construct a community of resistance to corporate power and its congressional apologists" (173). Tim Dayton's book analyzes Rukeyser's use of the lyric, epic, and dramatic genres, within a framework of Marxist theory. A few critics discuss silicosis and the body of the worker. John Lowney writes that Rukeyser "emphasizes the specific sociopolitical and sociohistorical contexts of silicosis" (45–46), while Stephanie Hartman argues, "Rukeyser moves from the specific occasion of the workers' deaths to a broader interrogation of how modernization itself refigures the body and, through it, the self, in ways that may be empowering to workers as well as destructive" (212). Interestingly, Hartman's reading parallels my reading of Le Sueur, arguing that Rukeyser "moves away from her emphasis on the individual ill body to celebrate the collective power of the working class" (220). Moreover, she notes that the body of Peyton, one of the workers, "becomes used up like a natural resource" (214). Although Hartman interprets some of the nature imagery in the poem, for example the power of the river, as a celebration of the "durability and strength of the worker," she notes that the ending celebrates the agency of workers in terms of how they have "made raw nature useful" (221). While Hartman presents a revealing analysis of the poem's depiction of the worker's body, she does not reconcile how the poem allies nature and the working class only to ultimately reduce nature to a raw material for the heroic labors of nation building. Furthermore, Hartman, like most critics, does not situate the poem in relation to environmental movements or traditions.[10] Leonard M. Scigaj, by contrast, contends that the poem fuses "the science of ecology with Egyptology and Marxist dialects," attempting to "rectify the degraded ecology, to offer a new whole" (n.p.). In an original, ecocritical reading of the poem, Scigaj argues that Rukeyser "begins to create a new ecological balance through allusions to an environmental dimension within the Egyptian Book of the Dead" (ibid.). Despite his thorough interpretations of the allusions to the Egyptian myth, I am not convinced that the poem "reinstates an ecology of the whole" through its final vision. The poem itself lacks references to ecological science, featuring instead medical science and X-ray technology. In my view, the poem does not reinstate a harmonious nature, but instead portrays hazardous industrial environments that extend across the landscape.

With its many images of eyes, glass, and X-rays, it is not surprising that several critics, including John Lowney, Michael Thurston, Walter Kalaidjian, Michael Davidson, and Shoshana Wechsler, have placed *The Book of the Dead* within the context of the popular as well as the specifically leftist 1930s documentary tradition. Davidson argues that the poem must be read "against the backdrop of the era's photojournalism and investigative reporting," noting that Rukeyser "was intimately connected to the worlds of photography and film through her participation in the Film and Photo League and Frontier Films" (140–141). The documentary, according to Paula Rabinowitz, was a politically mixed genre, as the "projects of state and capitalist regulation, reportage and fiction, documentary photography and feminism are thus curiously interwoven; each mode overseeing itself, its objects, and its others" (*They Must Be Represented* 59). Wechsler's reading of the poem investigates this sort of political complexity. Wechsler, noting that the now invisible Hawk's Nest tunnel serves as "the perfect objective correlative for Union Carbide's corporate obfuscation" and the "making invisible of human labor," argues that to render the "hidden artifact" visible "is in the 30s to aspire to the making of a wholly accurate picture or factual record" (123). The aim of documentary objectivity, however, inscribes a hierarchy "within the documentary gaze . . . the power dynamics between observer and observed," which, Wechsler argues, can be undone "by empathetic identification with the other" (134). Empathic identification, however, assumes a distance between the observer and the observed. It is possible to imagine that the poem is less interested in delineating distinct subjects and more interested in pursuing a network of interrelationships, or social/material environments, in which human subjects are immersed. Thus, I argue that Rukeyser documents the environment in two complementary ways: she critiques the aesthetic vision of a sublime, unpeopled nature, which is an impediment to seeing a place like Gauley Bridge, and she struggles to portray the material substance of the silica itself, marking how both industrial disease and what we would now call "air pollution" demand medical, scientific, and technical ways of seeing. Whereas Shira Wolosky presents a Foucauldian reading of the poem, arguing that Rukeyser "detects and exposes not only the complicity of medical, industrial, and legal institutions but also the ways in which this complicity takes place through specific modes of language" (157), I would argue that this sort of discursive focus risks losing sight of the materiality of human bodies and environments. I propose, instead, that even as Rukeyser includes a panoply of discourses, she struggles to map an ontology in which the body of the worker, the river, the silica, the "natural," and the industrial environment are simultaneously material and social, sites where institutional and material power swirl together. Specifically, Rukeyser presents what I call a transcorporeal landscape, as she traces the movement of silica dust from the rock to the body of the worker and even throughout the wider environment.

The emphasis on the camera and the rather self-reflexive critique of framing techniques may also contribute to the poem's critique of wilderness environmentalism, which was promoted by photographs of a pristine nature without humans. Finis Dunaway explains that the Progressive Era photographer Herbert Gleason "delivered visual sermons on the aesthetic power of nature"; Gleason's camera "heightened the spirituality of the natural world while also bringing it down to size, presenting it as both a source of salvation and an item for consumption" (13, 6). Rukeyser poetically captures nature as an aesthetic vision and sublime power, only to counter those images with depictions of peopled natures and, more compellingly, with the harmful material substances that "nature" can become. In the third poem of the sequence, "Gauley Bridge," Rukeyser chides the reader for desiring an unpeopled nature. The first line, "Camera at the crossing sees the city," promises us a picture, but human inhabitants obstruct our vision: doors are shut, a boy running with his dog "blurs the camera-glass." This city is not simply an object to be seen, but a place populated by other eyes: "[e]yes of the tourist house," "eyes of the Negro, looking down the track," "one's harsh night eyes over the beerglass" (78). With the word "and," Rukeyser places the ordinary person on par with the camera and, by extension, the poem: "the man on the street and the camera eye." Unlike landscape paintings or photos that give themselves up to the viewer's pleasure, the town looks back, and the poem confronts the reader's expectations:

What do you want—a cliff over a city?
A foreland, sloped to sea and overgrown with roses?
These people live here. (ibid.)

The long lyrical line, with its lulling "o" sounds—"A foreland, sloped to sea and overgrown with roses?"—soothes the reader, but it is followed by the accusatory, blunt, heavily stressed words: "These people live here." This moment occurs after several delicious lines that project the sublimity of the West Virginia landscape. Indeed, Rukeyser's poetic language itself seduces us with its verbal equivalence, as well as reference, to natural beauty and power. The second poem, "West Virginia," which documents the history of the state, includes the visually and aurally striking "gash of gorge and height of pine," an image powerful enough to be set as an imagist gem. Rukeyser, anticipating later debates about environmentalism versus environmental justice, shuttles back and forth between visually stunning depictions of nature and the insistence that these are not only peopled places, but places cut through by economic and political forces. The condensed history of West Virginia includes a recognition, for example, that the "found-land farmland" the Europeans ostensibly "discovered" had already been planted by native peoples. The poem leaves this environmental justice recognition behind, however, to revel in the beauty and force of nature:

> But it was always the water
> the power flying deep
> green rivers cut the rock
> rapids boiled down,
> a scene of power. (75)

This sublime scene frames nature as a place apart from the human, since the viewer, as well as any human inhabitants, are conspicuously absent. The lines describing the energy of the water "flying deep" and the imagistic precision of the rivers cutting and the rapids boiling pen a picture of elemental power and beauty. The brief lines encourage the reader to fully experience each image; the straightforward syntax suggests a "natural" aesthetic of clear-cut singularity.

The next section radically recontextualizes the power of nature, however, as social worker Philippa Allen presents her testimony in an unadorned language that undermines the earlier poetic reverence. As Rukeyser cuts to another scene entirely, nature is no longer an awe-inspiring realm distinct from the human, but a substance and force that both affects and is affected by human activities, institutions, and knowledge systems. Here, Rukeyser lays out the basic facts in the case:

> According to estimates of contractors
> 2,000 men were
> employed there
> period, about 2 years
> drilling, 3.75 miles of tunnel.
> To divert water (from New River)
> to a hydroelectric plant (at Gauley Junction).
> The rock through which they were boring was of a high
> silica content.
> In tunnel No. 1 it ran 97–99% pure silica.
> The contractors
> knowing pure silica
> 30 years experience
> must have known danger for every man
> neglected to provide the workmen with any safety device. (76)

Nature is no longer a force to be admired from afar nor a distinct entity, as the very substance of the rock threatens, with its "high silica content," to infiltrate the human body. As the rock becomes silica, it may be considered a "quasi-object" in Latour's terms: it is "real, quite real, and we humans have not made [it]" and yet it is also "discursive," "narrated, historical, passionate" (Latour, *We Have Never Been Modern* 89). Certainly, nature is agential here, since, if the rock were some other substance, the entire catastrophe might not have occurred; yet the silica is best understood as the stuff of nature/culture. Moreover, the dazzling power of the river is no longer isolated within the distinct realm of nature. Power, instead, shoots into divergent but colliding networks: the rhetorical power of the social worker's testimony, the political power of the subcommittee hearing, the physical power of the men drilling the tunnel, the economic powers that bought the men and subjected them to unnecessary harm, the racist and classist ideologies that discounted their suffering, and the ominous power of the silica itself. The bare facts here, such as "97–99% pure silica" and "30 years experience," disclose a complicated network of technical knowledge, politics, and economics, as they imply a more ethical sense of responsibility and legal culpability. Rukeyser suggests that silicosis, once it became public knowledge, eroded the public's faith in scientific neutrality, as people "began to see that the questions posed by scientists and technicians were framed by the larger social and political context" (Rosner and Markowitz 8). This section of the poem also reveals that the stunning power of the water is harnessed in economically unjust ways, as the energy from the hydroelectric plant was not distributed to local people but instead was diverted to the ugly-sounding "Electro-Metallurgical Co. / subsidiary of Union Carbide & Carbon Co." (76).

The vast networks of power, knowledge, and substance intersect in the bodies of the workers who dug the Gauley tunnel. Rukeyser begins "Absalom," a first-person account: "I first discovered what was killing these men" (83). The perspective is that of Mrs. Jones, the mother of three of the workers, who, Rukeyser notes, "was the first person . . . to bring the matter to court and to the attention of the country at large" (Rukeyser, radio interview 145). Even though Emma Jones witnesses material evidence—"I saw the dust in the bottom of the tub" (84)—she needs access to the X-rays for medical proof. Her testimony highlights the compounding economic injustices entangled with the need for medical authority:

> When they took sick, right at the start, I saw a doctor.
> I tried to get Dr. Harless to X-ray the boys.
> he was the only man I had any confidence in,
> the company doctor in the Kopper's mine, but he would not see Shirley.
> He did not know where his money was coming from.
> I promised him half if he'd work to get compensation,
> but even then he would not do anything.
> I went on the road and begged the X-ray money,
> the Charleston hospital made the lung pictures,

he took the case after the pictures were made
And two or three doctors said the same thing. (ibid.)

Her youngest son, who could not go to the doctor, "lay and said": "'Mother, when I die, / I want you to have them open me up and / see if that dust killed me'" (85). Wanting his mother to get compensation, he offers up the interior of his body for inspection. As poignant as this offering is, it also suggests the different sorts of evidence amassed by the actual Dr. Harless, who drew upon X-rays, chemical analyses of rocks, and chemical analyses of the workers' lungs (Sellers, *Hazards* 191). Sellers notes that, in one case, "the lungs contained 50% silica" (ibid.).

Emma Jones's aching account includes a few lyrical moments, most notably the following oft-interpreted lines lifted from the Egyptian Book of the Dead, where, according to Scigaj, they refer to the Nile floods and "their capacity to initiate a new growing season" (n.p.):

I have gained mastery over my heart
I have gained mastery over my two hands,
I have gained mastery over the waters
I have gained mastery over the rivers. (85)

The anaphoric refrain, "I have gained mastery over," allies the body and na-ture—heart, hands, waters, rivers—as forces that the "I" must rule. Scigaj claims that "mastery" signifies "an enlargement of perception" which results in an ethics of "responsibility for the West Virginia ecology." Such a sense of responsibility seems as distant a luxury as a trip to Egypt, however, as the workers are immersed in an environment that is already part and parcel of economic forces and politi-cal institutions that harm and degrade them. Given the mother's suffering and heroism, the reader may sympathize with this lyrical moment of triumph. Walter Kalaidjian, for example, interprets these lines as an example of "women's revi-sionary will to power, here mythically intoned through a divine poetic mask," ar-guing that women's "authority" "bestows mastery not only over heart and hands but, equally important, over the element of water as such," which is especially sig-nificant given that the river "drives the industrial forces of production" (174–175). But in what sense—other than in an utterly "divine" or imaginary realm—does this impoverished mother of dead sons have "mastery"? The lines preceding and subsequent to this refrain cast mastery itself as a rather romantic and individu-alistic delusion, given that the broader context here serves as a testimony to the nexus of legal, economic, medical, and scientific forces that make it impossible to separate out a coherent "I" that could gain mastery over one's body or over nature.[11] After the refrain, her testimony continues, "The case of my son was the first of the line of lawsuits. / They sent the lawyers and doctors down" (85). The doctors, probably paid by the company, "called it pneumonia at first," then they "would pronounce it fever" (ibid.). As the lawyers and the doctors are deployed to the area, the mother "hitchhike[s] eighteen miles" to pick up her $2. The mother has no doubt mastered survival skills, as she splits that $2, "one week, feed for the cow, one week, the children's flour" (ibid.), but the need for sustenance embeds her in networks that are simultaneously economic, political, and material. Although Thurston also reads Mrs. Jones in a mythical sense, as a "powerful female figure who bridges the all-too-earthly realm of tunnels, silica, and workers and the seemingly supernatural realm of waters, rivers, and air" (200), I would argue that the poem insists upon the materiality of water, air, and of course the silica-bearing rock itself. Mythical, spiritual, and transcendent readings escape the strong gravitational pull of the rest of the poem, which depicts a social/material landscape of substantial, all-encompassing networks of power and knowledge, substances and forces, environments and institutions. Rukeyser, asked to account for silicosis as an "unusual" theme for poetry, responded that the "actual world, not some fantastic structure that has nothing to do with reality, must provide the material for modern poetry" (quoted in Dayton 146). Perhaps the references to the Egyptian Book of the Dead lead us not upward to where spirit soars above matter, but instead downward (as if to the underworld) and across, traversing ostensibly distinct realms in order to map the entanglements of power and place.

The hope of spiritual transcendence from poverty and industrial disease is rendered impotent by the poem's vivid portrayal of a rather sinister trans-corporeality. The fact of silica invading the lungs highlights the substantial interconnections between worker and environment. Rukeyser poetically documents these connections, acting, in a sense, like an X-ray in that she renders the invisible strikingly visible. The image of the workers filling "their lungs full of glass" (79) effectively captures physical pain and harm, even as it faithfully records the literal, as well as poetic, metonymic slide between silica and the glass it can become. The glass also suggests the mechanism of seeing, as the poem both interrogates prevailing documentary perspectives and struggles to capture the material evidence of injustice. Moreover, in a rather postmodern formulation, the glass, which is a medium for seeing and knowing, is itself the material—as rendered by industrial/economic processes—that is to be seen. An immersed, rather than transcendent, epistemology materializes.

Interestingly, before the evidence of the X-ray is presented, first in "Absalom," the mother's account, and then in "The Disease," the poem employs the X-ray as a mere simile. The narrator's visual image of Mearl Blankenship interrupts the letter he is writing to a newspaper asking for help:

> He stood against the rock
> facing the river
> grey river grey face
> the rock mottled behind him
> like X-ray plate enlarged. (83)

Mearl Blankenship, who before working at the tunnel was certified to be "the picture of health" (ibid.), is struck with an illness that renders his body visually indistinct from the environment, as the actual rock eerily resembles a representation of the bodily harm its hidden substances will inflict.[12] Although the simile, signaled by "like," highlights the poetic license of the trope, the passage suggests the substantial, and in this case sinister, transit across human bodies and the environment. And, at the same time, it admits that discerning this materiality demands technical ways of seeing. A letter to a newspaper, however sincere, will not qualify as proof. Writing of the "correspondences" between art and science, Rukeyser explains, "[B]oth science and poetry are languages ready to be betrayed in translation; but their roots spread through our tissue, their deepest meanings fertilize us, and reaching our consciousness, they reach each other. They make a meeting-place" (*Life of Poetry* 162). In *The Book of the Dead*, the lungs, as represented by the X-ray, become a meeting place between poetry and science, as similes suggest medical knowledge and the medical expert creates tropes. As the expert points to the visual evidence on the X-ray, he states, "Now, this lung's mottled, beginning, in these areas. / You'd say a snowstorm had struck this fellow's lungs" (86). The "snowstorm" in the lungs is a particularly trans-corporeal trope, which, despite the word "struck," fails to capture the harm of silicosis. If poetry and science are both "languages," with "roots" that "spread through our tissue," they struggle to make the invisible visible, the unknown known, the material sensible. Although science is needed to make the illness visible, poetry, in this case, reveals how the X-ray technology, even as it is employed on the worker's behalf, renders him invisible, as the "lung" becomes a discrete object of inquiry. Rukeyser's rendition of courtroom testimony refers to examinations of "those sets of lungs" and questions "whether or not those lungs were silicotic" (92). As José Van Dijck notes, discussing the use of the X-ray in tuberculosis, "X-ray machines overruled [the] patient's own experiences" of disease, since "the patient's experience was inherently subjective, and hence unreliable" (87).

David Kadlec links Rukeyser's use of the X-ray in the poem to the practice of screening workers (and then dismissing those who had signs of disease), which, he argues, obscured racist labor practices:

> [The X-ray was] used to peel back layers of racial identity in order to provide an objective and essentializing ground for insulating industries against the very bodies that it had formerly been privileged to waste. Here the power of the X-ray to penetrate surfaces toward buried truths was deployed to conceal the practice of racial discrimination. (36–37)

Although Kadlec seems to argue that the X-ray conceals the fact that African American and immigrant workers would have greater rates of illness because they were more likely to work in the most hazardous jobs, the X-ray could, of course, be used to reveal that very fact. Kadlec charges that Rukeyser "linked silica clouds with X-rays as materials that could penetrate layers of 'false consciousness' to reveal the essential solidarity of the industrial workers" (37).[13]

Although Rukeyser was at pains to forge class solidarity across racial lines, as many leftists, including African American leftists, of the time period aimed to do, it seems odd to charge her with "reveal[ing an] essential solidarity," since the dust that covers the workers and penetrates their lungs is foreign matter that invades from the outside. Moreover, a class-based essentialism seems an odd concern, given that racial essentialisms, especially the belief that the African American workers were physically deficient, actually fueled not only their wretched treatment, but the course of the disaster itself. Cherniak explains that one of the reasons the deaths at Hawk's Nest were dismissed was because they were assigned not only to the African Americans' poor nutrition and climate but to their "unusual susceptibility to pneumonia" and "the general inability of the Negro to resist disease" (53).[14] As the X-ray has the potential to illuminate the effects of silica in the lungs of black workers, it also has the potential to demonstrate a sense of "race" that is substantial, yet not essentialist: it was not forces intrinsic to the bodies of the workers that spontaneously generated silicosis, but the racist labor practices that placed those workers in dangerous environments that forever altered their bodies. Indeed, this model is akin to Lewontin and Levins's model of "environmental racism" with which we began.

Why does Rukeyser alter George Robison's testimony, blanketing both white and black with white dust rather than black? For one, Rukeyser's documentary aims impel her to employ symbols that are also substantially literal. The silica was, of course, actually white. Moreover, as the paragraphs below will demonstrate, the poem abounds with images that associate whiteness with death, as the dust becomes symbolic of racist capitalism. Although the X-ray was being used as a mechanism of discrimination, that same technology can be employed on behalf of workers—black and white—to prove harm and seek remedy. This early twentieth-century industrial disaster was not unlike later twentieth-century instances of environmental racism, and both necessitated that activists use scientific knowledge and technologies in order to seek justice (as the next chapter will explore). Movements that would combat industrial illness, environmental racism, and environmental illness must draw upon the technologies—X-rays, maps, statistical modeling—that can trace the flow of substances and forces between people and places.

While the X-ray captures an image of a "snowstorm in the lungs," Rukeyser disperses this image across a wider geographical map. Take, for example, the first few stanzas of "Alloy," a poem that tracks the silica to the steel factory in the eponymous town:

This is the most audacious landscape. The gangster's
stance with his gun smoking and out is not so
vicious as this commercial field, its hill of glass
Sloping as gracefully as thighs, the foothills
narrow to this, clouds over every town
finally indicate the stored destruction.

Crystalline hill: a blinded field of white
murdering snow, seamed by convergent tracks;
the traveling cranes reach for the silica. (95)

Although its bullets can penetrate, the smoking gun is a distinct object, whereas
the deceptively enticing "hill of glass" flows into bodily images, with its "foothills" and graceful "thighs." The "white murdering snow" is "blinded," which
may mean that its hazards have been hidden from sight, but oddly the snow itself
is portrayed as the victim of bodily harm, again suggesting a sinister flow across
bodies and nature. What is most fascinating about this passage, however, is that
the trope of the silica as a snowstorm becomes nearly literal here, in that as the
silica is used in the production of steel, it is burned into "clouds," which threaten
"every town" with "stored destruction."

Indeed, Rukeyser extends what is, at first, an occupational hazard outward,
across the landscape:

Forced through this crucible, a million men.
Above this pasture, the highway passes those
who curse the air, breathing their fear again.

The roaring flowers of the chimney-stacks
less poison, at their lips in fire, than this
dust that is blown from off the field of glass;

blows and will blow, rising over the mills. (96)

The danger of silica extends from the "million men" who risk occupational illnesses to the generic "those" who "curse the air." As the dust blows over the
mills, it becomes the very stuff of air pollution in risk society, as described by
Ulrich Beck, in which imperceptible hazards usually affect some social groups
more than others, but eventually affect everyone, regardless of social position
(20–22). Furthermore, what was "considered unpolitical becomes political" (24);
as the dust disperses, it has the potential to enlarge the political struggles against
industrial hazards by recruiting *all* of "those / who curse the air."

My reference to Beck may be less anachronistic than it seems, in that Rukeyser's poetry manifests the link between occupational illness and an environmentalist sense of pollution. In "Factory as Environment: Industrial Hygiene, Profes-

sional Collaboration and the Modern Sciences of Pollution," Christopher Sellers argues that, from the 1910s to the 1930s, industrial hygienists, including Alice Hamilton, "forged the first modern environmental health discipline to focus on industrial chemicals and dusts rather than bacteria" by modeling the "industrial microenvironment, including its human inhabitants, in terms of measurable poisons and dusts controllable through quantitative monitoring aimed at safe concentration levels" (56). Just as Rukeyser extends the threat of silica as an "occupational" hazard, to a substance that "blows and will blow" across the landscape, the industrial hygienists, according to Sellers, extended their "toxicological approach beyond the workplace" (ibid.). In 1936, the same year that Rukeyser traveled to Gauley Bridge, the Harvard School of Public Health held a conference that "signaled the ongoing transformation of industrial hygiene into a science of environmental health." The conference included talks on "Air Conditioning in Normal Life" and "Atmospheric Environment and Its Effects on Man" (Sellers, *Hazards* 187).[15]

The Book of the Dead forges a geo-medical map of the effects of silica, thus positing occupational illness as the foundation for a broader sense of environmentalism. "The Disease: After-Effects" records a congressman's "bill to prevent industrial silicosis" and the testimony of a "gentleman from Montana," whose father was killed by being shot at a strike and from silicosis, a medically awkward, but politically useful, coupling. He testifies that copper, "limestone / sand quarries, sandstone, potteries, foundries, / granite, abrasives" all contain silica, thus harming many types of workers:

> Widespread in trade, widespread in space!
> Butte, Montana; Joplin, Missouri; the New York tunnels,
> the Catskill Aqueduct. In over thirty States.
> A disease worse than consumption.
>
> Only eleven States have laws.
> There are today one million potential victims.
> 500,000 Americans have silicosis now.
> These are the proportions of a war. (103)

The blunt, end-stopped lines of the last stanza, with their rough rhythms, stack the bare facts together until they suddenly arise as a declaration of war. The proportions of the disease become magnified as the camera-like eye of the poem attempts an aerial view, struggling to discern the dispersed effects of this substance:

> No plane can ever lift us high enough
> to see forgetful countries underneath,
> but always now the map and X-ray seem
> resemblent pictures of one living breath
> one country marked by error and
> one air. (ibid.)

Although transcendence affords forgetfulness, fortunately altitudes of igno-rance cannot be reached, even with an airplane. The enjambment, as well as the more melodious lines, encourage two different visions, the map and the X-ray, to flow together, intermingling the human body with the environment, forging a sort of trans-corporeal environmental nationalism of "one country marked by error and / one air." An ethical/political imperative emerges: it becomes es-sential to protect the "one living breath" from the air that is, audibly, nearly indistinguishable from "error," the wrongs of industrial, legal, economic, and medical institutions. As if to further materialize the body politic, Rukeyser of-fers an extended metaphor of the political obstructions that prevent reform as silicosis itself: "It sets up a gradual scar formation; / this increases, blocking all drainage from the lung, / eventually scars, blocking the blood supply." This sec-tion concludes: "Bill blocked, investigation blocked" (104).

In the final, eponymous section of the poem, "The Book of the Dead," Rukey-ser concludes with a mythic revision of American history, in which peoples and places intermingle and laborers risking occupational hazards emerge as heroic. Echoing the very first line of the poem, it invites the reader into the landscape: "These roads will take you into your own country," a country extending across a "landscape mirrored in these men" (106). The poem continues by interpellat-ing readers into a recognition of their own places, "your home river," but then develops a historical narrative of manifest destiny in which the pioneers "pushed forests down in an implacable walk / west" (107). As the poem moves through time and place, including fields, frontiers, rivers, wheatfields, deserts, moss, and lava, it confuses place with people, as the land is "peopled with watercourses" and the valleys are "planted in our flesh." This encompassing, seemingly celebratory geographic and historical vision concludes with "this fact and this disease" (108), enacting Rukeyser's own call never to "Forget" or "Keep silent" (107), as she in-jects the risks of industrial illness into the national myth of progress.

In the next section, Rukeyser praises striking workers and those who risk occupational illness: "These are our strength, who strike against history. / Those whose corrupt cells owe their new styles of weakness to our diseases" (109). Whereas the connection between landscape and laborer in Le Sueur's work was often one of vitality, here, even as Rukeyser honors the strength of the workers, she portrays them as succumbing to an ominous trans-corporeality. The miners drill not only the rock, but "their death" and those "touching radium" "glow in their graves" (ibid.). Although most critics read the conclusion as positive, which is not surprising, given the final phrase, "seeds of unending love," I see it as am-bivalent, in that Rukeyser tries to recast a manifest destiny myth of America, in which lands are mastered and tamed, with an acknowledgment of the sometimes hazardous materiality of these places—places that may well become the sub-stance of the people themselves. Moreover, for all of its heroic celebration of the workers, the ending of the poem may be more than a bit ironic, in that it echoes a sanguine article published in the *Fayette Tribune*. The article, entitled "Army of Workmen Drilling through Gauley Mountain," gushes: "But modern man came with his passion for mastering the works of nature, and seeing the hard and barren rocks, gashed everywhere with water courses, set about to put a bridle on the roaring, plunging, wild river" (quoted in Cherniak 54). When "mastery" appears at the end of Rukeyser's poem, it receives condemnation: "Down coasts of taken countries, mastery, / discovery at one hand, and, at the other / frontiers and forests" (110). These lines are followed by "fanatic cruel legend at our back" (ibid.), which, at the very least, casts aspersion on the march of progress. Perhaps the geo-social, material/discursive, natural/cultural landscapes that Rukeyser discovers through the Hawk's Nest tunnel incident are too complex to capture in a conclusion: multiple, interacting forces resist mythical teleologies.

Nature in *The Book of the Dead* is neither a debased wilderness nor a pristine image of the sublime, but instead a peopled place, a powerful force, and, significantly, a material substance that moves through human bodies, inseparable from networks of power and knowledge. This nature requires an environmentalism concerned with all environments—including the industrial workplace.[16] An environmentalism emerging from *The Book of the Dead* would employ both X-rays and maps, protecting human bodies and environments, tracing the flows of knowledge, power, and material substances. Although it concentrates on the Hawk's Nest tunnel incident, *The Book of the Dead* radiates a wider environmental vision, just as the contemporary paradigm of environmental justice, according to Robert Benford, "indicts not only individual companies, policies, and agencies," but also "constitutes a radical critique of entire social systems—at the local, regional, national, and global levels" (50). Entire social systems, as well as material substances, in fact, impact and possibly harm the "proletarian lung." Benford contends that one of the limitations of the environmental justice model is its "subordination of environmentalism to human justice" (37). Notwithstanding the tremendous achievement of Rukeyser's vision, which makes occupational illness the starting point for considering the effects of all environments on human health, *The Book of the Dead* fails to reconcile the competing aims of environmental justice and environmentalism. In short, the ethical and political vision she projects in this poem is profoundly anthropocentric, driven primarily by a concern for human health and well-being. Her documentary approach may have engendered this anthropocentrism since there was no environmental protest over the Hawk's Nest tunnel project, even though the Izaak Walton League was "attempting to prevent the damming of the Cheat River in the same region" during the same period (Cherniak 14). In any case, surely it is asking too much for Rukeyser to have resolved such conflicts in the 1930s, when neither environmental justice nor post–World War II environmentalism had developed. But it is, I hope, not impossible to imagine a trans-corporeal ethics that would include animals who are not human, and to visualize creatured, as well as peopled, environments in which the imperative remains to prevent silica dust and other forms of air, water, and soil pollution to permeate all sorts of bodies.

THREE

Invisible Matters: The Sciences of Environmental Justice

The waters of justice have been polluted.

—Percival Everett, *Watershed*

The Hawk's Nest tunnel incident discussed in the previous chapter illustrates how racism can materialize across bodies and places. Most scholarly contestations of race since the 1980s have employed social constructionist arguments to demonstrate that race is a social, not biological category, forged within a history of economic and political oppression, not simply found "in nature." Interrogating racism has, for the most part, meant shifting attention away from ostensible racial differences toward the social and political forces that have constructed these differences. It is useful to notice, for our purposes here, that these arguments divert attention from material bodies per se, toward the ideologies and discourses that constitute them.[1] Environmental justice science, literature, and activism, however, must to some degree focus on actual bodies, especially as they are transformed by their encounters with places, substances, and forces. Departing from the incisive philosophical analyses of the vast superstructures that support racial oppression, environmental justice activism needs to be rather literal, demonstrating material connections between specific bodies in specific places.

Whereas the predominant academic theories of race have worked to undermine its ontological status via theories of social construction, environmental justice movements must produce or employ scientific data that track environmental hazards, placing a new sort of materiality at the forefront of many of these struggles. The emerging sciences of biomonitoring and the particular forms of environmental activism that they enable capture the biochemical interchanges between body and place, but they also recast the categories of race and class, which have been at the heart of environmental justice movements.

This chapter explores the intersection of racially marked bodies, toxic environments, and the scientific mediation of knowledge within contemporary U.S. environmental justice activism and literature. Civil rights, affirmative action, and identity politics models of social justice—all of which assume that individuals are bounded, coherent entities—become profoundly altered by the recognition that human bodies, human health, and human rights are interconnected with the material, often toxic flows of particular places. Although Nikolas Rose, in *The Politics of Life Itself: Biomedicine, Power, and Subjectivity,* does not discuss environmental justice movements, EJ movements do create, in his terms, "biological citizens" "from below":

> Strategies for making up biological citizens "from above" tend to represent the science itself as unproblematic: they problematize the ways in which citizens misunderstand it. But these vectors "from below" pluralize biological and biomedical truth, introduce doubt and controversy, and relocate science in the fields of experience, politics, and capitalism. (142)

Activists, as well as ordinary citizens, struggle for access to "biological and biomedical truth" that captures the material interrelations between people and places in forms of knowledge that will be accepted as persuasive evidence of systemic harm. As Ulrich Beck asserts, however, the risks of modernization are difficult—if not impossible—for individuals to apprehend without access to scientific technology or institutions.[2] They require "the 'sensory organs' of science—*theories, experiments, measuring instruments—in order to become visible or interpretable as hazards at all*" (27; emphasis in original). Laypeople have contended with these difficulties by pirating scientific knowledges and developing their own scientific practices. Phil Brown, Giovanna Di Chiro, and Jason Coburn study the scientific practices of laypeople, terming the practitioners "popular epidemiologists" (Brown), "ordinary experts" (Di Chiro, "Local Actions, Global Visions"), and "street scientists" (Coburn). This "new species of 'expert'" results, Di Chiro argues, from "the everyday struggles of people striving to understand and negotiate their needs and desires in efforts to lead a decent life" ("Local Actions, Global Visions" 210).

Stephen R. Couch and Steve Kroll-Smith contend that environmental "groups and organizations are unhinging the languages of expertise from expert systems,

. . . taking these attributes of expertise into their communal worlds" (385). They mark a significant shift that has occurred in which environmental movements no longer rely upon "a rhetoric of civil rights or environmental justice": "they are also arming themselves with the lingual resources of toxicology, risk assessment, biomedicine, environmental impact inventories, nuclear engineering, and other instruments of reason" (384). As powerful as this sort of discursive contestation may be, however, many ordinary experts must first contend with the onto-epistemological shift effected by risk society, in which ordinary knowledges are rendered, to some extent, inadequate as the surrounding reality with which those knowledges have contended itself transmogrifies. For one thing, invisible matters and forces often require technological devices and scientific mediation; "lingual resources" are not enough. Indeed, the literature, photography, and oral histories discussed in this chapter dramatize how toxic chemicals and radioactivity rupture everyday modes of knowing. As risks disperse, they disrupt both indigenous knowledge systems and Western epistemologies as they mix science, politics, activism, and daily life. Percival Everett's novel *Watershed,* for example, charts how within an environmental justice crisis the notion of scientific objectivity becomes complicated by a political struggle in which the protagonist, unwittingly, finds himself entangled.

Environmental justice movements epitomize a trans-corporeal materiality, a conception of the body that is neither essentialist, nor genetically determined, nor firmly bounded, but rather a body in which social power and material/geographic agencies intra-act. If, as Rose argues, "biological citizenship" relocates science "in the fields of experience, politics, and capitalism," some of those relocations are both motivated by and magnify a sense of trans-corporeality—a recognition that one's bodily substance is vitally connected to the broader environment. Different scientific and popular-scientific accounts shuttle across bodies and places, often emphasizing one at the expense of the other, for varying political ends. New models are emerging, scattered throughout science, activism, consumerism, literary texts, and photography, that capture, contest, and reconfigure the relations between (raced) bodies and specific spaces. Percival Everett's environmental justice western, *Watershed,* dramatizes a scientific activism that is, in a sense, in the protagonist's very blood, as history, politics, and the substances of a particular place collide. One of the characters in Ana Castillo's magical realist novel *So Far from God,* the speaker in several of Simon Ortiz's poems, and the Diné people interviewed for the Navajo Uranium Miner Oral History and Photography Project's *Memories Come to Us in the Rain and the Wind* strive to perceive and represent invisible risks in order to survive ravaged landscapes. While new technologies such as biomonitoring may be employed by EJ activists in order to detect and battle environmental injustices, these very technologies may also reconfigure categories of vulnerability, provoking more questions about the ever-emergent interrelations of race and place.

Science, Politics, and Embodied Knowledges
in Percival Everett's *Watershed*

Even as environmental justice movements specifically, and risk society more generally,[3] generate nonscientists who must attain some level of scientific fluency for effective legal and political struggle—or merely for daily survival—the contemporary landscape of harm also generates scientists who must reconcile still-potent ideals of scientific distancing and objectivity with the recognition of their own ethical, political, or even material relations to the matter at hand. Steve Wing, an epidemiologist, explains that "the value and prestige of the sciences" result from their "perceived objectivity." Both scientists and laypeople believe that the "scientific method, by removing subjectivity and social influence, yields knowledge that is ostensibly trustworthy and objective" ("Objectivity and Ethics" 1809). His own professional experience and his knowledge of the history of radiation epidemiology, however, led him to become skeptical "toward official assumptions and logic" (1811). Moreover, he argues, the "naïve" approach to objectivity "conceals and reinforces" "existing inequalities" between social groups which have affected the production of scientific knowledge (1816). Thus, he advocates a version of Sandra Harding's "strong objectivity," in which "scientists critically evaluate how the knowledge they create is shaped at every point by historical social forces" (ibid.). Wing calls for a new "science of environmental justice" that would be "instituted not by scientists, but by the organizations they serve" ("Environmental Justice" 61). It would be "a science for the people, applied research that addresses issues of concern to communities experiencing environmental injustice, poor public health conditions, and lack of political power" (ibid.). Scott Frickel, in "Just Science? Organizing Scientific Activism in the U.S. Environmental Justice Movement," argues that, despite "continuing professional pressures to remain above the political fray, the emergence of new science-oriented organizations and the politicization of existing ones are strong indications that a culture of activism among environmental research professionals is emerging as a legitimate means of political expression" (464).

As environmental scientists become activists, the borders between science and politics erode. Beck argues that risks compel us to traverse many "carefully established" borders:

> Risks lie *across* the distinction between theory and practice, *across* the borders of specialties and disciplines, *across* specialized competences and institutional responsibilities, *across* the distinction between value and fact (and thus between ethics and science), and *across* the realms of politics, the public sphere, science and the economy, which are seemingly divided by institutions. (70)

Risks traverse seemingly separate spheres of human activity, forcing us to contend with them in ways that may jumble our conceptual maps. More specifically, EJ activist science and scientific activism—whether performed by "scientists" or "activists"—suggest that, by the early twenty-first century, we can no longer take refuge in a vision of science as an objective, separate sphere of knowledge making, but rather we must recognize and grapple with its entanglements. For feminist epistemologists, postcolonial epistemologists, and others who have long critiqued Western scientific models of objectivity, this shift may be an opportunity to transform science into something more accountable, more just, and more democratic.

Sherman Alexie introduces Everett's 1996 novel, *Watershed*, by explaining:

> [It] fictionalizes the 1970s political battle on the Lakota Sioux's Pine Ridge Indian Reservation in South Dakota, combines them with fictional and real events during the 1960s civil rights battles for African Americans, and sets it all on a contemporary and fictional Indian reservation where a Native American dwarf and an African American hydrologist struggle to save themselves and the tribe from evil corporate bastards. (ix–x)

Alexie describes the novel as a "wonderful political thriller, love story, murder mystery, and literary novel seasoned with interracial politics, parody, and comedy" (ix), but it could also be termed an environmental justice mystery or a postmodern western. We should note that Everett's many novels include the bitingly satirical environmentalist *Grand Canyon Inc.* and the progressive early twenty-first-century western *Wounded*. Although several of Everett's novels are ripe for environmentally-oriented analysis, *Watershed* is particularly pertinent here, as it grapples with how an environmental justice mystery corrodes the boundaries between science, activism, and even one's own corporeal integrity. At the start of the novel, the protagonist assumes sturdy borders between his work as a hydrologist, his family history in the civil rights movement, and his romantic life, even as the form of the text itself mixes these domains. The first words of the novel, "My blood is my own and my name is Robert Hawks," entice us to wonder why his blood would *not* be his own, as the opening scene juxtaposes a (fictional?) epigraph from 1873, asserting that an "Indian War can never occur in the United States," with Hawks, M-16 in hand, holed up with several other armed people in a church on an American Indian reservation, with 250 police officers, FBI agents, and National Guard troops outside, as well as a few dead bodies within.

By juxtaposing family memories of the civil rights movement with Hawks's contemporary situation as a black scientist-become-activist for Indian lands, Everett questions not only the political relations between African Americans and Native Americans,[4] but also the relations between the civil rights movement and contemporary environmental justice struggles. Most histories of environmental justice trace its emergence from the civil rights movement, citing an African American community's protest against a toxic disposal site in Warren County, North Carolina, in the early 1980s as the origin. Indeed, the NAACP declares: "Environmental justice is fundamentally a civil rights issue. It is defined as the fair and equal treatment of all people regardless of race, color, national origin or income level in the development, implementation, and enforcement of environmental laws, regulations, and policies" (National Association for the Advancement of Colored People website). The NAACP situates EJ in the "legal" section of its website, but does not mention it on the "health" page even though many nascent EJ activists may first suspect an injustice based upon the ill health of themselves, their children, or their neighbors. Oddly, science is not mentioned by the NAACP as a means for advancing environmental justice: "The Program seeks to eradicate environmental disparities by advancing judicial precedent, legislative initiatives, and community education and empowerment in the area of environmental justice." Although the NAACP positions EJ as a subset of civil rights law, Everett's novel tangles these unproblematic lines of descent by concocting a turbulent brew of science, activism, and armed struggle.

The protagonist, who ponders the civil rights activism of his family and his own encounters with racist police, attempts to distance himself and, especially, his work as a hydrologist from political entanglement:

> I had done so much to remove all things political from my life. Even in my work as a hydrologist I seldom involved myself in the use of my findings for any kind of agenda promotion; rather I saw myself as an objective hired gun. . . . Terrace formation and sediment evaluation were simple, observable things and meant only what they meant. (152)

At the start of the novel, Hawks believes that scientific practice, grounded in objective observation, can and should be distinct from politics. The fragments of hydrological reports scattered through the text were presumably penned by Hawks, though the technical style and the passive voice obfuscate their authorship: "High-water marks and flood debris *were observed*. . . . Flow *was* estimated using standard equations approximately seven miles from the confluence with Plata Creek" (86; emphasis added). Although Hawks sees himself as merely an objective "hired gun," who would work for anyone, the phrase itself suggests the impossibility of transcending political engagement or culpability as such "objective" scientific weapons are usually aimed *by* someone *at* someone. A hired gun does not escape the shoot-out. When Hawks discovers that a creek was dammed in such a way that the toxic runoff would harm the Indian—but not the white—residents of the town, his scientific observations immediately become political:

> I studied the land there, the terracing, looking up toward the tree line down the mountain and then it hit me. Here the drainage was into the Silly Man Creek. I

was in Silly Man Canyon and from here the water would feed down into the Plata,
which ran through the Plata Creek Indian Reservation and not into Hell-hole
Lake, which held water for both Indian and non-Indian ranchers. (167)

The terrace formation is no longer "simple" and "observable" as it has become
bound up in a potential environmental crime. Although Hawks tells himself that
his curiosity alone compels him to become involved with the American Indian
revolution, his curiosity is no mere intellectual pursuit but is instead overdetermined by personal and historical forces, as it is motivated, in part, by his
"personal quest to understand" his grandfather (153). His grandfather, a physician who risked his career by treating, but not reporting, the gunshot wound of
a Black Panther, but who did not want Dr. Martin Luther King Jr. to visit their
family because civil rights talk was equivalent to "Santa Claus" and "Christian
bullshit" (112), provides a model of skeptical, pragmatic "activism." As a physician, he employed his science as a political act when the need arose. In the end,
Hawks's rather solitary, scientific, yet physically heroic action—he escapes from
the armed standoff, hiking through the mountains to deliver evidence of the
crime to an environmental organization—echoes the solitary heroic acts of his
grandfather.

The postmodern structure of the novel, in which the plot is interrupted by
random bits of discourse—chemical diagrams, medical texts, descriptions of
fishing lures, hydrological reports, letters, a barrage of treaties and other legal
documents pertaining to American Indians—is consonant with the mystery plot,
in that it impels the reader to decode the fragments, searching for clues. The
postmodern structure of the narrative clashes, however, with the old-fashioned
sense of scientific objectivity upon which the protagonist insists. Perhaps the
disjunction between the postmodern narrative form and the business-as-usual
model of objective scientific practice that the protagonist espouses suggests that
playful postmodernism may inhabit its own discursive universe, segregated from
material practices, such as hydrology. The novel doubles back on itself, as it becomes skeptical about postmodern skepticism, articulating a politically engaged
quest for (scientific) truth. Hawks insists, for example, that hydrology requires
accurate modes of visual representation, rather than aesthetically interesting but
murky photos:

"These are for work," I said to the pony-tailed man.
"These are not art shots. I have to be able to read these."
 "I don't see what the problem is," he said.
I took another photo from my case. "Look, this is a good print. See here. That's a
creek. Now, look at this piece of shit." I put his work in front of him. "Somewhere in
this mess is a river. Would you show it to me?" (92)

Since this incident occurs in a flashback and is unrelated to the present mystery,
the river could be anywhere. However, near the end of the novel, when Hawks is

documenting the environmental crime, which, it turns out, is probably a secret anthrax dump leaking onto Indian lands, representational accuracy is crucial: "I took out my camera and snapped pictures of the clearing and of the dead elk, then marked the spot on my map" (180). Despite the fact that both the protagonist in particular, and environmental justice struggles more generally, require representations that can, to some extent, capture material realities, the novel as a whole does not embody a simple (scientific) realism, in that Hawks's scientific practice becomes inextricably entangled with personal, political, and historical narratives.[5] Thus, the epistemology of this scientific quest, which is inseparable from historical and political forces, roughly corresponds to Sandra Harding's "strong objectivity" or Donna Haraway's "situated knowledges," both of which insist upon the positioning of the knower. Even as Hawks imagines himself as a detached observer, near the end he is marked by his bodily immersion in this place.

As *Watershed* morphs into an environmental justice mystery, or even a western showdown, it alters its register from ironic, detached play toward a troubled, yet determined quest to document the environmental justice harm. One wonders, along with Beck: Is it "at all possible to create and maintain a critical distance towards things one cannot escape? Is it permissible to abandon a critical distance just because one cannot escape it, and to flee to the inevitable with scorn or cynicism, indifference or jubilation?" (41). *Watershed* concludes with neither scorn nor cynicism, occupying, in the end, the territory of a traditional western, an ethically principled standoff in which the African American hydrologist allies himself with the Native American tribe, gun loaded, canister of film in hand, in pursuit of (environmental) justice.

Since a very short Indian woman running about in the cold and the deaths of two FBI agents do not exactly point to a secret anthrax dump, the EJ mystery seemingly appears out of nowhere. The plot, in fact, mimics a fundamental sense of risk society, in which the unseen, unknown hazards may be more perniciously "real" than what is perceived: "What escapes perceptibility no longer coincides with the unreal, but can instead even possess a higher degree of hazardous reality" (Beck 44). Perhaps the three puzzling chemical diagrams, dropped into the narrative early on, suggest these sorts of imperceptible risks that may lurk within this place (Everett 76–77). But the fact that the "real" plot and the "real" hazard seem to appear out of nowhere suggests, more disturbingly, that they were always already there, surrounding Hawks at every turn. As a hiker or as a hydrologist, he may already have been exposed to anthrax in his excursions near the dump. He has in fact, already been an inhabitant of a landscape of trans-corporeality, where people and place are substantially interconnected. Early in the novel, Louise, the mysterious small woman, suggests that the Indians see themselves as linked to the land: "You should come to the reservation and meet my people. They're part of this land. I didn't grow up here, so I'm not. But my mother is as much a part of this land as Silly Man Creek. . . . Our way tells us that when the river dies, so will our people" (19). In response, Hawks merely nods blankly at her, but much later, when told that "the army has been illegally storing anthrax bombs and other kinds of biochemical agents on the north edge of the reservation" (140), he confronts his own misguided trust in his country: "The government was doing secret experiments, like the Tuskegee thing, all the time, and I realized that that was the scariest part of all, that in spite of knowledge of past transgressions, I still resisted belief in a new one" (ibid.). The historical example of Tuskegee propels Hawks's reflections on the significance of an anthrax dump, as his heretofore "objective" hydrological analyses suddenly become a political matter:

> "If what you're saying is true . . ." I stopped and pictured the terrain in my head. "It depends on where the stuff is. Any leaks would be carried by the groundwater to Silly Man creek right into the Plata or down the Dog into the lake or simply into the aquifer. It's all wells on the reservation."
> Tyrone Bisset was nodding.

> Each and every cranial nerve is attached to some part of the surface of the brain, but these fibers also extend deep into the nucleus of the brain, the center of the gray matter. The nerves emerge from the brain, pass through tubular prolongations in the dura mater and leave the skull through foramina at its base, on the way to their final destination. (ibid.)

The medical discourse about the brain, which traces the path of the nerves, mimics the movement of the water across the landscape, charting paths within bodies and places. Although Hawks holds a "picture" of the terrain in his mind, making a material place a mental image, the medical text, conversely, maps the brain itself as a material place, casting being and knowing, liquids and nerves, within substantial networks. More generally, the fragments of medical texts in the novel register particular captures of bodily materiality, insisting upon the substance of the human.

Hawks can conjure a picture of the terrain in his mind because he has been there; he practices hydrology out in the field, not in a laboratory. When the Indians in the revolution ask Hawks to help them investigate, they admit that Hawks knows their land better than they do. When he hikes up the mountain to search for the dump, ice forms on his mustache, and he must camp during a blizzard. He discovers a dead elk, which "startled [him] a little and disturbed [him] greatly" (179) and then spots the dump, photographing it and marking it on the map. His transformation from a detached gun-for-hire into an activist/scientist is now complete. Disturbed by the dead elk, he dreams of becoming elk:

> I was crying in the dream, following the zig-zagging path of the elk. I looked at the clear blue sky and thought what a beautiful day it was, how warm and glorious, and I found my feet falling effortlessly into the tracks of the elk. I staggered with him, my shoulders slumping, my breathing beginning to race. I felt my heart

hot in my chest. And then I was outside of myself and looking into my own big, glassy, elk eyes. (181)

The dream betrays Hawks's passion for both the stunningly beautiful landscape and the wild animals. As his feet fall into the elk tracks, he begins to stagger, slump, and breathe heavily, suffering from whatever the elk is suffering from, becoming elk. The dream of becoming animal dramatizes Hawks's deeply empathic environmental ethics, which is no longer abstract or merely aesthetic, but provoked by the recognition of his own risky, bodily immersion in this place. As contact with or proximity to infected animals can infect people with anthrax, it makes sense that he would wonder "how long it would be before the symptoms of anthrax would begin to appear" (198). Anthrax can produce toxins that travel in the blood, linking Robert quite literally to the elk, a material metonym for this beautiful but toxic place.

The blood that Robert Hawks asserted at the start of the novel "was his own" has long been the stuff of racial categorization for both African Americans and Native Americans. Such racial essentialisms are too simplistic for this novel, however, in which the protagonist's blood connects him to his family (which is linked to both the civil rights and black power movements), to his own bloody encounters with racist police, and to the environmental racism manifest in the military's degradation of this particular place, a degradation which may now be, literally, coursing through Hawks's very blood. History also pulses through the narrative: in the infamous syphilis experiments at Tuskegee, the 339 black men were told that they were being treated for "bad blood." In these horrific experiments, as in this novel, blood is neither merely social nor merely natural. As Nancy Tuana explains, there is "no sharp ontological divide" between "social practices and natural phenomena," but rather "a complex interaction of phenomena" ("Viscous Porosity" 193). Everett places his protagonist within a landscape of interactions, as the hydrologist's scientific apprehensions of material reality become embodied, historically entangled pursuits. As Hawks risks his life to deliver photographic evidence to the "Naturalists Conservancy," his blood is no longer simply "his own."

Capturing Invisible Matters

Robert Hawks, scientist-turned-activist, manages to capture evidence of environmental racism through both his hydrological analyses and, more simply, by photographing the expertly constructed concrete dam, the pipeline, and the dead elk. At the novel's conclusion, Hawks is no longer a "hired gun" for someone else's struggle. Instead, the photographs and the maps arm him for an environmental justice battle. Although the novel is, of course, a fiction, photography has been employed in environmental justice campaigns, most potently perhaps as a form of evidence. Our most basic sense of the material world is that it is self-evident, apparent, substantial, and visible. One definition for *evidence*, in fact, is "evident." Commonsensical tautologies circle around the real, the visible, and the true, as "seeing is believing." Significantly, within this everyday epistemology, everyone has access to these truths, as no technical or scientific mediation is required. Photojournalism and documentary depend—even, somehow, in an age of photoshopping—on the photograph as factual evidence—clear visual testimony. Photographs, according to Susan Sontag, "are a species of alchemy" and yet "they are prized as a transparent account of reality" (*Regarding the Pain of Others* 81.). The internet has made it much easier to disseminate photographs and videos as evidence of wrongdoing. The women described as the "Head Start mothers" of Detroit, for example, employ visual evidence to document environmental injustices. An article about the Photo Voice project, which was instigated by faculty in the University of Michigan's School of Social Work and School of Natural Resources and Environment, appears on the university's web page with the headline "Detroit Mothers Reveal Environmental Abuses through Photography" (Wadley). The article stresses the evidentiary nature of the photographs: "The photos captured many cases of illegal dumping in their neighborhoods by trucks with covered license plates. Some photos show air pollution from factories, as well as abandoned, unsafe buildings" (ibid., n.p.). A video about the women's activism adds another layer of documentation, as it visually surveys the neighborhood's conditions. Some, but not enough, of the photographs are featured in the video, along with interviews with a few activists and some University of Michigan faculty, including the EJ scholar Bunyan Bryant, who were involved in the program. Interestingly, although the project began, in part, because Michael Spencer and other social work faculty at the university were concerned about the high levels of lead in the local Head Start children—something that can only be documented via blood tests—the women who participated in the Photo Voice project envisioned a broader sense of environmental justice, as they photographed such things as abandoned buildings, garbage, and children wearing protective face masks. Even as the article and video testify to the determination of the activists to improve their environment, the account fails to grapple with the children's lead poisoning or with air pollution; these issues, which do not lend themselves to photography, remain undocumented. Worse, neither culpability nor solutions are discussed.[6]

The Environmental Justice Foundation, which is based in London but works for the "global south," seeks to "combat environmental and human rights abuses" by training individuals around the world to use video cameras:

The single aim of this program is to share skills and empower environmental advocates to document, expose and peacefully resolve threats to their natural environment and basic human rights. New technologies and media are invaluable tools for successful advocacy and the resolution of abuses. Modern communications can send images from an isolated community to the world's power centres instantly. A trained video operator can document and expose abuses, telling the truth as it really is on location. Powerful video evidence and compelling filmed testimonies from those suffering from environmental destruction can reach targeted audiences and elicit positive change from the public, policy-makers and corporations nationally and internationally. (Environmental Justice Foundation website)

The EJF website features PDF training manuals on "The Internet for Activists" and "Photography," outlining the political potential for photographic activism: "Photographs can provide irrefutable proof of a problem—such as illegal logging or fisheries or illegal actions against local communities. They can help to show who is causing a problem and how, as well as what the impact is on people, wildlife and the environment." The training manual offers several compelling examples of how photography has provided evidence of environmental wrongdoing. The EJF campaign against illegal pesticides in Cambodia, "Death in Small Doses," includes photos of illegal but widely available pesticides piled high on store shelves; abandoned pesticide containers contaminating the fields; baskets of pesticide-laden greens for sale; people who eat the contaminated food; and birds who are harmed by the illegal chemicals. One photo shows a farmer mixing pesticides in food containers, without any protective equipment. The Sprite bottle signals a serious problem: "Food containers are used for mixing pesticides. This can lead to confusion and serious domestic accidents, especially for children" ("Death in Small Doses" n.p.). (See figures 3.1 and 3.2.)

Notwithstanding the significant environmental justice work accomplished through the savvy use of photography and video, many EJ problems cannot be visually discerned nor photographically documented. The quintessential difficulty of life in risk society, according to Ulrich Beck, is that "the risks of civilization today typically escape perception" (21). The paradigmatic risk for Beck is radioactivity, "which completely evades human perceptive abilities," but also "toxins and pollutants in the air, the water, and foodstuffs, together with the accompanying short- and long-term effects on plants, animals, and people" (22). Even though such risks may "induce systemic and often *irreversible* harm," they remain "*invisible*" and thus "initially only exist in terms of the (scientific or anti-scientific) *knowledge* about them" (23; emphases in original). Several works of contemporary U.S. literature depict the struggle to know the invisible risks that travel across bodies and landscapes. Ana Castillo's novel *So Far from God* and Simon Ortiz's poetry, for example, dramatize the onto-epistemological ruptures that occur when people must contend with the invisible dangers of risk society.

Castillo's wildly funny, deeply tragic, magical realist novel *So Far from God* relates the adventures and deaths of the four daughters of Sofia, the matriarch.

Figure 3.1. "Mixing pesticides in Cambodia." 2009. From the "Death in Small Doses" album of the Environmental Justice Foundation website.

Figure 3.2. "Pesticide packages abandoned near fields are an important
site of environmental contamination." 2009. From the "Death in Small
Doses" album of the Environmental Justice Foundation website.

Fe, the daughter who had faith in a capitalist, consumerist American dream,
does not enjoy a life after death, unlike her sisters, who are resurrected, return
"ectoplasmically," or disappear "down, deep within the soft, moist dark earth . . .
to be safe and live forever" in a place reminiscent of a Pueblo emergence tale.
Catholic, New Age, and Native American beliefs happily cohabit in this rollick-
ing novel, perhaps because they all provide some sense of hope in a materiality
that is, in a positive sense, infused with cultural traditions. Near the end of the
novel, the loquacious, indomitable narrator, who has already related all manner
of wild and sometimes tragic happenings—a retreat to a cave, a rape by a bizarre
(colonialist) creature, faith healings—halts at Fe's story, which she says is "hard
to relate" because "Fe just died. And when someone dies that plain dead it is hard
to talk about" (186). Fe's death produces an irrecuperable moment, a rupture in
an otherwise hopeful ontology in which even the dead carry on. The ironically
named Fe (her name means "faith" in Spanish) is all realism, no magic—cold,
dead facts cannot be alchemized into madcap comedy.

Unlike the other sisters, Fe disappears from the text, becoming as invisible as the substance that killed her. Fe's husband, Casey, may be her comic counterpoint in that his bleating (like a sheep) is an instantiation of a trans-corporeality that links person and place in vital, though peculiar ways. Although Fe was rather surprised when she heard her husband make a "soft but distinct ba-aaa sound," the narrator explains that, "after three hundred years of sheepherding and a long line of ancestors spending lifetimes of long, cold winters tending their herds," he had an "inbred peculiarity that couldn't be helped" (175). A bit awkward in social contexts, the bleating nonetheless suggests a kind of coevolution between shepherd and sheep, as well as the tenure of a people on the land. The bleating echoes a Mexican-American pastoral tradition that persists even though Casey himself had to become an accountant after the "familia lost it[s] profits" and "gave up big chunks of land" (174). Fe, living in the late twentieth century, does not become a shepherd's wife, but instead searches for the American dream within an industrialized New Mexico. The narrator chides Fe's consumerism,[7] dismayed that she bought "an automatic dishwasher, a microwave, Cuisinart," etc., with "the bonuses she earned at her new job." And, she adds, dramatically granting the sentence its own paragraph: "It was that job that killed her" (171). Fe, praised by Acme International as the "queen" of "utilization and efficiency," dies from cancer after having efficiently utilized the residual chemical in the fluids she was using to "clean" parts of military weapons.[8] After she intially poured the extra chemical down the drain, because she had been told it was "harmless," Fe is ordered to "just let what is left in the pan evaporate" instead (184). The FBI arrives, concerned that Fe has been using the chemical illegally, but "not the least bit concerned" that she "was dying in front of their eyes because of having been in contact with it" (187). Like other citizen-experts in the making, Fe is transformed by her experience. She is no longer the "manicured, made-up bride of a few months before but a Fe without even the nice insides she had when she started at Acme International" (189). Fe reads a manual that says the chemical "should not be left to evaporate" "because, in fact, it was (and this last part really got to Fe) *heavier than air*." Fe, her voice damaged in an earlier episode of love gone bad, screams urgently, where did this chemical go if it did not evaporate? "'WHERE DID _____, GO PENDE_____, SON-_____-A. . .' She screamed again, 'IF NOT IN _____ ME?'" (189). To her horror, Fe realizes that the invisible chemical fumes were unspeakably substantial—heavier than air. They were not apparent, but they did not disappear. She concludes that they must be dwelling inside her.

Despite the industrial setting, Castillo frames Fe's story as an environmental justice tale, rather than an occupational health story alone, as her world, not just her workplace, becomes "incomprehensible":

[M]ost of the people that surrounded Fe didn't understand what was slowly killing them, too, or, didn't want to think about [it], or if they did, didn't know what to do about it anyway and went on like that, despite dead cows in the pasture, or

sick sheep, and that one week late in winter when people woke up each morning
to find it raining starlings. (172)

Dropping down dead, the birds, like Fe's chemical, are heavier than air. Once
Fe does comprehend her incomprehensible world, she realizes her own uninten-
tional but harmful actions. She recollects how she had "more than once dumped
[the chemical] down the drain at the end of the day," which meant that it "went
into the sewage system and worked its way to people's septic tanks, vegetable
gardens, kitchen taps and sun-made tea" (188). In this work of marvels, mysteries,
and myths, it is the invisible yet substantial, mundane yet brutal flow between
bodies and places that makes life in risk society a most difficult matter to comprehend. The dazzling magical realism[9] that provokes readers to wonder what is
"real" in this fictional universe parallels the confounding everyday experience
of life in a world where risks are, "in a fundamental sense, both *real* and *unreal*"
(Beck 33). The harm inflicted by the unseen chemical is already apparent in Fe's
body, even as its effects on the plants, animals, and people in her region may go
undetected.

Another contemporary southwestern U.S. author, Simon J. Ortiz (Acoma),
has written compelling poems and essays about the destruction of Indian lands,
particularly in the case of uranium mining. In the prose poem "Our Homeland: A National Sacrifice Area," Ortiz sketches the history of uranium mining
on Navajo and Pueblo land from the early 1950s, describing the assaults on the
land and the people: the drilling and blasting that turned the land into "just so
much rubble" and the work that exposed people to brutal accidents, dangerous
dust, and radon gas (355–356). Ortiz himself went into the uranium mines several times, though he usually worked at the mill site in "crushing, leaching, and
yellowcake" (357). He states that, in 1960, "there was no information about the
dangers of radiation from yellowcake, with which I worked," and yet, "at moments," "I got paranoid about my own health" (358). Such "paranoia" is obviously
justified, when the government and the mining companies neglect to protect or
even inform workers.[10]

Concern about one's physical self may be exacerbated by the weird transformations of material reality that routinely occur during the mining and production of uranium. In the poem "Stuff: Chickens and Bombs," Ortiz ponders a mysterious materiality[11] that is simultaneously biophysical, scientific, and social. The
poem describes in straightforward language how "I," presumably Ortiz, "usually
worked in Crushing / where the uranium stuff / was just rocks and dirt" (320).
The "stuff" which begins as "just rocks and dirt" becomes a "yellow powder":

we packed the processed stuff
which is a yellow powder
into fifty-five gallon drums

and wheeled them out
to waiting trucks
bound for where we didn't know. (320)

The clear, orderly sequence of tasks and the seemingly ordinary stuff itself belie
a wider tangle of uncertainty, risk, and perhaps even fear of culpability as the
yellow powder proceeds toward an unknown destination. The next two stanzas
move rapidly from an assertion of knowledge embedded within the ironic voice
of the speaker to an utterly confounding moment of perplexity:

Once,
thinking I knew something,
I told Wiley
that the government used
the yellowcake for bombs
and reactors and experiments.
Wiley studied my face a minute,
then he spat on the ground
and said, "Once I worked
in a chicken factory.
We plucked and processed chickens
so people could eat 'em.
I don't know what the hell else
you could do with them." (ibid.)

This strange moment, which leaps from nuclear bombs to plucked chickens,
stuns with the ontological incompatibility of the stuff the workers process. The
uranium, which begins as simple, seemingly knowable rocks, somehow ends up
as experiments, reactors, bombs. The chickens may seem a sort of solid ground,
stuff that is safe, understandable, and put to good use.[12] Yet the transformation
of rocks to yellowcake shifts the ground so dramatically that we are left wondering even about chickens—"what the hell else" *could* you do with them?[13] The
seemingly innocuous, seemingly evident stuff of the title disperses into networks
of unknowing, shaped by government, industry, and science. Perhaps an unstated knowledge of danger lurks, invisibly, in this poem, as the recognition that
chickens are food, and thus enter human bodies, circles back around to the "yellowcake," which sounds like food and which penetrates the workers' bodies as
radiation.

Other poems in Ortiz's collection *Fight Back: For the Sake of the People, for
the Sake of the Land* (republished in *Woven Stone*) posit a Pueblo alternative to
the extreme form of alienated labor shown in "Stuff: Chickens and Bombs." "We
Have Been Told Many Things but We Know This to Be True" begins by declaring
foundational truths:

The land. The people.
They are in relation to each other.
We are in a family with each other.
The land has worked with us.
And the people have worked with it.
This is true:

> Working for the land
> and the people—it means life
> and its continuity. (ll. 1–9)

Ortiz proclaims, in straightforward diction, a sense of work in which people and the land cooperate and continue.[14] This proclamation takes on a new urgency within the context of the collection as a whole, which documents how the U.S. government has not only stolen land from indigenous peoples but assaulted those lands. And yet, urgent as they may be, the truths that Ortiz outlines may no longer be sufficient for survival within the now-ravaged environment. The penultimate prose poem, "Our Homeland: A National Sacrifice Area," tells of the Aacqu's extensive knowledge of plants, as well as their historical sense of "war, crisis, and famine" captured in the oral tradition, which promoted "important lessons, values, and principles" (345). Ortiz asserts that, before "Mericanos" came, the people possessed the knowledges needed for survival: "there was a system of life which spelled out exactly how to deal with the realities they know. The people had developed a system of knowledge which made it possible for them to work at solutions. And they had the capabilities of developing further knowledge to deal with new realities" (349). American capitalism, culminating in uranium mining, ruptured the traditional ecological knowledges, robbing the people not only of their land, labor, health, and political sovereignty, but of their intellectual sovereignty[15]—their ability to make sense of the place that had long been home.

Memories Come to Us in the Rain and the Wind: Oral Histories and Photographs of Navajo Uranium Miners and Their Families, compiled in 1997 by the Navajo Uranium Miner Oral History and Photography Project, documents the struggle to survive within a "national sacrifice area." Dan N. Benally, analyzing the devastating landscape that he inhabits, explains how radiation may be traveling across mines, landscapes, animals, and people:

> Well, the mines are still open. I wonder if radiation is going all over the communities among the residents. Waste was dumped outside the mines, the rain and snow thaws wash the ore into the washes and the people blame this for contaminating their animals from the watering places. It is true that waste was dumped off the hill sides and the water carried it into the main washes. Meat from these animals is consumed, and contamination continues to affect humans. Forty-three of the people I worked with have died now. Some time ago, I counted this. (26)

Although he begins by "wondering," rather than asserting, Benally's account testifies to what he, with his knowledge of the landscape, the environmental processes, and his culture's practices, can demonstrate, offering compelling evidence of extant harm. Whether or not one considers Benally's practices "scientific" depends, of course, on how the term is defined. Sandra Harding promotes the potential benefits of recognizing indigenous and other non-Western "effective knowledge systems" as "sciences," thereby "conceptualizing on a single map humanity's attempts to understand and effectively interact with themselves and the environments they encounter" (*Science and Social Inequality* 11). She notes, however, that even as this framework attempts to "level the playing field," it may itself be Eurocentric, since the concept "science" may not be employed by the people creating these knowledge systems.[16] Western notions of scientific practice, of course, assume a vast gulf between science and other ways of knowing the world as well as between science proper and the practices of everyday life.

The Diné Natural Resources Protection Act of 2005 declares, "*No person shall engage in uranium mining and uranium processing on any sites within Navajo Nation Indian Country*" (emphasis in original) and asserts an intellectual sovereignty that subsumes "science" within Diné beliefs, framing the declaration within the "Diné medicine people's interpretation of the 'Natural Law,'" in which legal, medical, scientific, and religious knowledges are inseparable:

> The Navajo Nation Council finds that the Diné medicine people's interpretation of the Diné Natural Law [*Nahasraan doo Yadilhi Bitsaadee Beehazraanii*], which is codified in Title 1 as 5 of the Fundamental Laws of the Diné, mandates respect for all natural resources within the four sacred mountains and is symbolized by the Sacred Mountain Soil Prayer Bundle [*Dahndiilyee*], to maintain harmony and balance in life and a healthy environment, and their recitation of the ceremonies and stories that have been passed down from generation to generation warn that the substances of the Earth [*doo nal yee dah*] that are harmful to the people should not be disturbed, and that the people now know that uranium is one such substance, and therefore, that its extraction should be avoided as traditional practice and prohibited by Navajo law. ("Resolution of the Navajo Nation Council" 2)

Interestingly, the document envelops the recently acquired knowledge of the dangers of uranium within a more encompassing system of knowledges and principles, thus subordinating the specific understanding of the dangers of uranium to a more vast vision of natural law.

While this document asserts a scientific as well as political sovereignty, emphasizing the authority of Diné natural law, other accounts of uranium mining on Navajo lands reveal an understandable frustration with the fact that many people—through no fault of their own—do not possess the expertise needed to live within this irrevocably altered landscape. As Giovanna Di Chiro explains, "Native communities' battles for sovereignty over their ancestral territories and traditional knowledges" continue to be thwarted by "the economic and ideological apparati of colonialism" ("Indigenous Peoples" 252). Floyd Frank, in his interview in *Memories Come to Us in the Rain and the Wind*, suggests a complicated epistemology in which the legacy of uranium mining casts the Diné as both the knowers and the known:

> There are many things we could talk about regarding uranium mining on our land. Some of our animals have been affected; calves have been born defective and sheep had lung problems, these we learned about ourselves. Uranium is really dangerous, we learned, and that is how it is. Why did they not tell us this? Perhaps we were just experimental subjects to them, I wonder. "How will it affect them, and what will it do to them in the end," perhaps this was what they thought. Were these the reasons they did not tell us? (Navajo Uranium Miner Oral History and Photography Project 8)

Like Benally, Frank testifies to the experiential knowledge gained by witnessing the effects of the uranium on their animals. Unlike models of scientific objectivity, however, which separate the knower from the known, Frank's account underscores how he and his community are immersed within this same landscape, becoming experimental subjects, perhaps, for those experts at liberty to remove themselves from this dangerous experimental site. Even if, as Beck argues, in the broader global landscape "there is no expert on risk" and thus ordinary citizens must muddle through many a "scientific" decision about their daily lives, the history of uranium mining on native lands warns that this generalized axiom may obscure particular, and particularly egregious, incidents in which individuals and institutions must bear the blame for knowingly harming peoples and places. Intellectual sovereignty, in this instance, is not just lost, but stolen.

Ordinary individuals may pay dearly for the expertise they are forced to gain. George Lapahe notes in his interview that uranium, when refined into yellowcake, looks like corn pollen. For the Diné, corn pollen is a ceremonial, life-giving substance, which is sometimes touched to one's head and tongue. Lapahe explains that it is "better to just leave [uranium] alone" until "they know of an effective medicine," because "it is not good for my children, who came back from school to play in the piles. Whatever they brought home from the piles they used as toys. Corn pollen and uranium are the same color and they ate some uranium. This is true, they put them on their window sills" (Navajo Uranium Miner Oral History and Photography Project 22).

The harrowing, thoughtful perspectives in this collection portray the need for new forms of expertise, as indigenous peoples' knowledges and cultural practices take place in landscapes that are suddenly foreign. Although the difference between uranium and pollen cannot be discerned by the naked eye nor by photographic methods, the horror of the suffering nonetheless calls out for some sort of documentation. The photographs in this collection bear an unsettling witness to that which they cannot portray: the invisible hazard of radioactivity. The photos of the people, their animals, their homes, and their lands, when read intertextually with the interviews, ask us to somehow see that eerie invisibility that is endemic to risk culture. By contrast, Peter Eichstadt's *If You Poison Us: Uranium and Native Americans* provides one exceptional photo as visible evidence of radioactive harm. This book includes many photos of the messy remains of uranium mines left uncovered, with piles of rocks, rotting wood, and desert plants that are strikingly beautiful. Lest that beauty lull the viewer, however, Eichstadt includes one shot that insists upon danger: a "scintillometer on a pile of mine waste" that "shows high levels of radioactivity" (n.p.). This single image of technologically registered knowledge—the exception to the limits of photographic testimony—bears a heavy evidentiary weight.

Emergent Models or Category Confusion in the Sciences of Bodies and Places

Simon Ortiz and the Diné people interviewed for *Memories Come to Us in the Rain and the Wind* struggle to capture invisible risks. They epitomize the loss of intellectual sovereignty that Beck described, even as they work to become "ordinary experts" (Di Chiro, "Local Actions, Global Visions") engaging in everyday "scientific" practices that mix traditional knowledges with new apprehensions of material reality. While many environmental justice activists seek evidence of the often invisible risks that surround them, new technologies of biomonitoring[17] direct attention to human bodies, charting the substances that linger in particular people. Human biomonitoring mixes the scientific analyses of people and places, as "environmental field sciences meet concepts and methodologies from epidemiology and biomedicine" (Bauer 2). Such technologies have the potential to reveal the damages of environmental racism, especially when they link bodily harm to particular substances in particular places. Thomas McKone, a researcher at the Berkeley Center for Environmental Public Health Tracking, is undertaking a project that will combine biomonitoring data with geographical tracking of hazards in order to "characterize populations with respect to hazards":

> To improve methods to assess and characterize environmental hazards and exposures, we will merge biomonitoring data with geographically based emissions and environmental sample data to increase the relevance of hazard indicators; and develop new approaches to combine the geographic distributions of environmental factors with information on human population distributions and activities. This is important because biomonitoring data alone do not always capture exposures to environmental hazards. (McKone n.p.)

Seeking to capture exposures that may not be detected by biomonitoring alone, McKone's project brings together data gathered from both human bodies and geographic locales. Despite the potential for environmental justice movements to benefit from initiatives such as these, the EJ activists interviewed by Sara Shostak see the new biotechnologies as not only potentially beneficial, but potentially dangerous:

> Some environmental justice activists are interested in the possibility that molecular genetic/genomic technologies, particularly those emerging from the field of toxicogenomics, might enable activists, in collaboration with scientists, to ascertain the chemical body burden of individuals living in exposed communities, and measure and document the effects of those chemicals within the human body. ("Environmental Justice" 551)

Shostak explains, however, that activists are concerned about the "post-hoc nature of body burden testing." In the vivid words of one activist, biomonitoring means that "you are using a child as a monitor for lead" (553, 554). More effective environmental health practices and policies would actually *prevent* exposure rather than merely document it after the fact. Activists are also concerned that molecular genetics/genomics "could lead to a future in which environmental health and illness" are "individualized" and "biomedicalized" (556), shifting the responsibility away from those who produce, disseminate, or fail to regulate toxic substances and to the individuals whose bodies harbor those substances. Environmental justice activists chart the material connections between particular places and particular communities, whereas medical models circumscribe individual bodies as such.

Even as race and class have been cited as the most important determinants of potential environmental harm, large-scale biomonitoring projects may yield categories of concern other than race and class. As this chapter has drawn upon the work of Ulrich Beck to analyze activist and literary renderings of environmental justice struggles, it may be fitting to conclude with one of the paradoxes in Beck's theory—the idea that everyone now inhabits risk society, and yet, at the same time, particular groups bear an unequal share of the risks. Whether, when, and how to emphasize the harm done to "everyone" versus that done to particular groups remains an open question for activists, scientists, environmental (justice) organizations, environmental health movements, and other inhabitants of risk society. Even as the evidence gleaned from body burden testing may offer compelling evidence of environmental harm, the categories that emerge from this testing may not correspond to expected racial categories, but may instead focus attention on other kinds of groups.

Race, for example, is invisible on the Physicians for Social Responsibility website, which responds to the question "Who do chemicals affect?" by answering

"Chemicals affect everyone." The site, however, does emphasize three specific categories: "children," "pregnant women and developing fetuses," and "rural communities." The last category includes the "large rural population of 56.4 million people" in the United States, "of which nine million work in agriculture." The category of "rural communities," which is not specific regarding race or class, then morphs into the category of "farmworkers": "Despite federal laws designed to protect farm workers from the effects of pesticide exposures, farm workers and their children continue to be exposed to dangerous toxins at levels higher than the general population" ("Toxics and Health" n.p.). Although "farmworker" denotes class, PSR's campaign on toxics and health does not mention race, and the large font of "Rural Communities" emphasizes geographic, rather than class, boundaries. The Pesticide Action Network North America (PANNA), in "Chemical Trespass 2004," finds that "children, women and Mexican Americans" shoulder the heaviest "pesticide body burden." This result is based on "an analysis of pesticide-related data collected by the Centers for Disease Control and Prevention in a study of levels of chemicals in 9,282 people nationwide" (n.p.). The categories of concern include one recognizable environmental justice category, Mexican Americans; the majority of humans, who are women; and children, who, of course, are dispersed across race, gender, and class lines. The term *chemical trespass*, which is also used by PANNA, evokes trans-corporeality as a space of intrusion; the chemicals enter the body "without consent." The degree to which different sorts of bodies have suffered these invasions will, no doubt, continue to be a matter of debate and concern, as various social and geographic groupings emerge from the practices of government institutions, scientific activists, and activist scientists. The specific interrelations of bodies and places will continue to be potent ethical and political matters, even though the specific categories of risk and vulnerability may differ. The maelstrom of risk culture will no doubt, continue to mix up people, places, substances, and forces, with unforeseen consequences and as yet uncharted patterns of harm.

The next two chapters will continue to discuss the implications of body burden testing, as well as considering how race and class materialize in sometimes unpredictable ways across the geo-social landscapes of risk society. It is fitting to conclude this chapter by noting that a colonialist history lurks behind the metaphor of chemical trespass. For American Indians, this invisible form of invasion is the most recent mode of assault in a long history of colonialism. Moreover, the loss of intellectual sovereignty throughout risk culture, broadly defined, takes on a particularly bitter resonance within indigenous peoples' cultural landscapes, given their many struggles to maintain or reclaim cultural and political sovereignty.

Material Memoirs: Science, Autobiography, and the Substantial Self

I do believe not until every woman traces her weave back strand by bloody self-referenced strand, will we begin to alter the whole pattern.

—Audre Lorde, *The Cancer Journals*

It is clear to me the nineteen aliens have a much better story, one that does not require twenty years to mature, to reveal its nature. They have provided instant death, multiple ministories, countless funerals, many hundreds of father- or motherless children. No one has to sit at a typewriter and try to prove something.

—Candida Lawrence, *Fear Itself*

In Audre Lorde's poetic language, the strands of the self can be understood as part of the weave of history, culture, economics, and power; tracing those strands constitutes an act of black feminist consciousness-raising. But Lorde's account in *The Cancer Journals* is, appropriately, much more visceral than the term *consciousness-raising* would imply. The "bloody self-referenced" strands testify that the self is corporeal, woven into a larger fabric of history, culture, and power. In fact, Lorde's famous call to transform silence into "language and action" may be much more substantial than is usually presumed. She asks: "What are the words you do not yet have? What do you need to say? What are the tyrannies that you swallow day by day and attempt to make your own, until you will sicken and die of them, still in silence?" (21). Notwithstanding the potent metaphorical resonance of "swallowing" tyranny, the swallowing—and the death that results—is also quite literal, since it alludes to the ingestion of carcinogenic foodstuffs. This particular chapter from *The Cancer Journals,* which appears in many women's studies anthologies, is often read as a generalized call to refuse to be silenced. (I have taught the essay that way myself.) Even as this refusal endures as a political principle, transforming it into an abstraction disentangled from the context of Lorde's breast cancer deflects attention from the pernicious practices of agribusiness, making her struggle more personal and psychological and less political and systemic. Fixing upon an accepted abstract principle may detract attention from "the words [we] do not yet have." Some of the words that we still do not have, I contend, are the words that can evoke the materiality and trans-corporeality of the human self.

Memoirs of Unrecognizable Subjects

Lorde's unflinching memoir, published in 1980, is the predecessor of what I'm calling the "material memoirs" of Zillah Eisenstein, Susanne Antonetta, Sandra Steingraber, Candida Lawrence, and others, which were published roughly ten, twenty, and twenty-five years later. Rather than dismissing Lorde's insistence on the actuality of her own flesh as essentialist, it may be more revealing to examine how she traces her bodily immersion within power structures that have real material effects. As Marcy Jane Knopf-Newman contends, Lorde's politicization of breast cancer takes "bodies and the environment into account. Cancer is political not because either subject—bodies or environment—is inherently political, but rather because of the silence and secrecy surrounding the overlapping intersections of these subjects" (134). Lorde's *Cancer Journals* is remarkably prescient in its insistence on the interconnections between body and environment, which poses cancer as a feminist, antiracist, and environmental justice issue. She refuses to make breast cancer a merely "cosmetic" problem, scorning that infamous puff of lambswool in the process; she condemns the American Cancer Society for not "publicizing the connections between animal fat and breast cancer" (58); and she excoriates the psychological theories of cancer, noting, "It is easier to demand happiness than to clean up the environment" (74). Against the cancer establishment, which continues to downplay the environmental causes of cancer,[1]

Lorde displays her scars: she sees them as "an honorable reminder that I may be a casualty in the cosmic war against radiation, animal fat, air pollution, McDonald's hamburgers and Red Dye No. 2, but the fight is still going on" (60). Against the American Cancer Society's focus on treatment rather than prevention, she contends: "We live in a profit economy and there is no profit in the prevention of cancer; there is only profit in the treatment of cancer" (71). As part of the larger feminist health movement that generated *Our Bodies, Our Selves,* Lorde urges women to do their own research, to amass "an arsenal of information" (72). She herself cites the *British Journal of Cancer,* as well as less mainstream sources. In short, epitomizing the feminist maxim that the personal is political, Lorde takes on sexism, racism, capitalism, and the medical establishment within a genre—the "journal"—that has been a site for private self-reflection.

Such genre bending is indicative of the contemporary material memoir, which incorporates scientific and medical information in order to make sense of personal experience. Whereas Joan Scott argues that "experience" cannot be understood apart from the discourses that constitute subjects, thus making "the question" "how to analyze language" (34), in the material memoir, the question becomes how to understand the very substance of the self. In other words, material memoirs emphasize that personal experience cannot be directly reckoned with, not only because discourse shapes experience, but also because an understanding of the self as a material, trans-corporeal, and always emergent entity often demands the specialized knowledges of science. If, as Susan Squier, explains, genre "regulates and it brings into being; it shapes how we can enter and engage in a preexisting social practice, and it constitutes that social practice, giving us ways of understanding it, as well as the conventions that make such practice possible" (262), then material memoirs forge new ways of knowing our bodies and our selves. Squier explains that "genre's regulatory function collaborates with a major strategic function of reflexive modernity: the construction of 'expert' knowledge, as distinct from nonexpert, 'lay,' or popular knowledge" (265). Material memoirs critique such divisions, offering up personal experiences as "data," as the author examines her own life story through a scientific lens. Departing from the quintessentially American, quintessentially Enlightenment life story of Benjamin Franklin, in which "man" is free to create himself through acts of principle, intention, and will, and, departing as well from Maxine Hong Kingston's postmodern masterpiece, *The Woman Warrior,* in which the self, à la Judith Butler, is constituted by the tangle of (in this case, multicultural) discourses, these trans-corporeal autobiographies insist that the self is constituted by material agencies that are simultaneously biological, political, and economic.[2]

Such material agencies are not easy to capture, discern, or unravel. Although *The Cancer Journals* is a predecessor to more recent material memoirs, the differences between the Lorde epigraph above and that of Lawrence are striking. Candida Lawrence, who was exposed to radiation and lost a breast to cancer, is worlds apart from Lorde's confident proclamations. Lamenting that "nineteen aliens" have a better story than she does, Lawrence worries that the "twenty years" it can take for cancer to result from an exposure may make her story seem not only dull, but unbelievable. Why, indeed, should one write such a memoir, when "[n]o one has to sit at a typewriter and try to prove something"? She herself is "all too aware of hidden, unseen, unsmelled, unproven, lurking dangers denied so often by those who claim knowledge" (185). And yet, the very invisibility of these threats impels her to illuminate them: "I must *see* the invisible and conjure up signs of environmental damage from repeated above ground bomb tests" (169). Lawrence emphatically doubles the material embeddedness of her epistemological quest by self-reflexively addressing the two "selves" of her memoir, each of which is strikingly corporeal:

> When I left Candida the year was 1956 and she was thirty-one. She was slowly—in first person, present tense—trudging through the years, and she'll continue advancing towards us, but at a much faster pace now. I must accelerate her dogged pursuit of information about her egg pouch because I have been arm wrestling with Mother Mortality: a chaotic thyroid, a raging pulse, a rock-and-roll heart beat. (116)

Both Candida, the subject of the memoir, and Lawrence, the writer, pursue an understanding of the substance of their selves by investigating books and articles, some of which are included in the memoir itself, such as the long excerpt that follows the quote above, entitled "U.S. Acknowledges Radiation Killed Weapons Workers Ends Decades of Denials" (117). The image of the personal—and oddly phrased—"egg pouch" reminds us of the enduring material effects veiled by the sweeping journalistic language of the sources she interrogates.

The most important difficulty for the material memoir, a difficulty that is simultaneously political, epistemic, and generic, is that autobiography by definition surfaces from one individual person, yet at present it is not feasible to trace the exact causes of cancer or other environmentally generated illnesses within an individual. There are no shortages of epidemiological studies and animal studies that demonstrate the carcinogenicity of various substances. The science exists, and it is staggering. But there is a chasm, a vast lack of proof, between these scientific facts and the murkier realm of the individual case history. (Even the new and prohibitively expensive biomonitoring techniques, which quantify the levels of many different toxins in an individual's blood and tissues, do not usually determine the source[s] of the chemicals.) Thus, material memoirs manifest the epistemological/political difficulties with what Lawrence Buell terms "toxic discourse." Buell argues that, although toxic discourse "rests on anxieties about environmental poisoning for which there is often strong evidence, it is a discourse of allegation or insinuation rather than of proof. Its very moralism and intensity reflect awareness that the case has not yet been proven, at least to the satisfaction of the requisite authorities" (*Writing* 48). Buell contends that the "climate of scientific and legal complexification calls toxic discourse into question even in advance of its utterance, yet also calls it into being and argues for both its social and ethical import" (ibid.). Buell exposes a sticky quandary: how does toxic discourse retain a potent sense of "social and ethical import" if its truth is always in question?

Conjuring material memoirs from within this miasma of skepticism requires that one risk writing a self that is barely recognizable as such. Judith Butler, discussing Foucault, argues, more generally, that critique "cannot take place without [a] reflexive dimension," since "any relation to the regime of truth will at the same time be a relation to myself" (22). The reflexive dimension of critique, then, involves risking oneself:

> [S]elf questioning of this sort involves putting oneself at risk, imperiling the very possibility of being recognized by others, since to question the norms of recognition that govern what I might be, to ask what they leave out, what they might be compelled to accommodate, is, in relation to the present regime, to risk unrecognizability as a subject or at least to become an occasion for posing the questions of who one is (or can be) and whether or not one is recognizable. (23)

As a mode of critique, the material memoir undertakes this sort of self-questioning, which risks unrecognizability. But what makes these selves even less recognizable is the extent to which they undertake investigations not only of norms, principles, and genealogy but of their own materiality—a materiality that must often be understood via scientific knowledge. The self of the material memoir—a self that is coextensive with the environment, trans-corporeal, and posthumanist—is a self that epitomizes the larger scientific and popular movements of environmental health that have arisen in what Ulrich Beck terms a "risk society."

Environmental Health, Risk Society, and the Ordinary Expert

Conevery Bolton Valencius, in *The Health of the Country: How American Settlers Understood Themselves and Their Land*, discusses the surprising emphasis on "the health of the country" in nineteenth-century settlers' writings:

> Assessments of the health of places fill newcomers' letters and journals, the columns of local newspapers, the reports of physicians and scientific observers, the adventure stories of hunters and trappers, the tall tales of regional humorists, and the floridly written pages of the myriad travel and emigration

guides that promised to interpret the Far West to American and European migrants. (7)

Linda Nash, in *Inescapable Ecologies: A History of Environment, Disease, and Knowledge,* argues that the predominant conception of the body in the nineteenth-century United States was the "ecological body," though she notes that the term is anachronistic, in that what she terms the "ecological body" preceded the science of ecology. This body is characterized by its "permeability," "a constant exchange between inside and outside, by fluxes and flows, and by its close dependence on the surrounding environment" (12). She argues, for example, that nineteenth-century settlers in California used their own physical health as "a powerful way of understanding local environments": "In their discussions of miasma and other endemic diseases settlers acknowledged that they could not fully control or even predict the results of their environmental interventions; those interventions, moreover, would be registered in their own bodies" (5, 50). Whereas "body and land were intimately intertwined" in nineteenth-century medicine (Bolton Valencius 19), the modern medical sense of the body severs these links. Nash describes the "modern body" as "the body of Western allopathic medicine and American consumer capitalism, the body that is defined in medical textbooks, the body that is composed of discrete parts and bounded by its skin; in other words, the idea of the body that most of us take as so self-evident that it requires no comment" (12). In the modern body, "'health' comes to connote primarily the absence of disease; it implies both purity and the ability to fend off harmful organisms and substances" (ibid.).

After having been eclipsed by the modern body, the ecological body comes forward again, in the mid-twentieth century. In the late 1950s, before the 1962 publication of Rachel Carson's articles that would become *Silent Spring,* Mexican American braceros, "in response to *other* questions" (Nash 137; emphasis in original), tell an interviewer that the pesticides used in the fields are making them sick. As Nash puts it, the workers "read their bodies as a kind of instrument whose limits and illnesses measured the health of the land"; their knowledge emerged not from official discourses, but from embodied experiences (138). One unnamed worker says, for example, "While I was working for _____ Farms, I got sick. My mouth puffed up and swelled. I think it was because of the poison they put on the plants. It hurt a lot" (quoted in Nash 137). By the end of the 1960s, not only farmworkers, but also "consumers, and public health officials all acknowledged that human health was linked to environmental conditions, that bodies were porous, often helplessly so—even if they envisioned those connections in somewhat different ways" (168). Carson's *Silent Spring,* a book often credited with sparking the modern environmental movement, was to a large extent responsible for the reemergence of the sense of the body as ecological. As Nash explains, Carson powerfully links "the quality of soil, water, and air to animal and human physiology," thus crossing the divide separating "the study of human bodies from the study of nonhuman environment" (157).

As illuminating as it is, this sweeping historical survey may obscure how various groups and forces have struggled to promote and contest different models of the body. The popular success of *Silent Spring*—to take just one example—was met by a vociferous backlash, much of which was spearheaded by chemical manufacturers. More generally, despite the reappearance of the permeable body in the late twentieth century, the medical model of the enclosed modern body still stands, as powerful social and economic forces continue to prop it up. The pharmaceutical industry profits from the modern medical body; those companies would not benefit from more attention to the environmental causes of disease. Moreover, halting or just minimizing the production and dissemination of toxic substances would have staggering economic results for chemical companies.[3] As a backlash against the reemergence of an older sense of permeable bodies, then, particular industries work to manufacture not only products and their often toxic by-products, but a state of uncertainty. As Robert N. Proctor explains in *Cancer Wars: How Politics Shapes What We Know and Don't Know about Cancer,* many areas of ignorance have been socially constructed:

> The persistence of controversy is often not a natural consequence of imperfect knowledge but a political consequence of conflicting interests and structural apathies. Controversy can be engineered; ignorance and uncertainty can be manufactured, maintained, and disseminated. (As one tobacco company privately put it: "Doubt is our product.") (8)

Skepticism, doubt, ironic detachment—some of the very qualities that intellectuals and leftists value—have been produced in such a way as to minimize and obscure the medical and political ramifications of the ecological body.

Nonetheless, at the start of the twenty-first century, environmental health sciences, movements, organizations, and businesses proliferate. Current definitions of environmental health vary as to their level of specificity and sense of urgency. The World Health Organization defines environmental health rather broadly, including "all the physical, chemical, and biological factors external to a person, and all the related factors impacting behaviours. It encompasses the assessment and control of those environmental factors that can potentially affect health. It is targeted towards preventing disease and creating health-supportive environments" (World Health Organization). The Centers for Disease Control of the U.S. government include a National Center for Environmental Health, the mission of which is to "promote health and quality of life by preventing or controlling those diseases or deaths that result from interactions between people and their environment." The European Union's statement is, not surprisingly, stronger than that of the United States, noting disturbing percentages of deaths and illnesses that can be attributed to environmental factors:

> Certain environmental factors, such as exposure to pollutants through water, food or air, are important determinants of health. For example, it has been estimated that up to one sixth of all child fatalities and disease can be attributed to environmental factors. Individuals can make certain choices that affect their lifestyle and health on their own, but they also rely on public authorities for protection from health threats.[4]

Since environmental health involves both individual decisions and public policy, regulations, and enforcement, it requires the involvement of a great many professions other than medicine, although "ecological medicine" is also taking root. The Science and Environmental Health Network defines *ecological medicine* as "a new field of inquiry and action to reconcile the care and health of ecosystems, populations, communities, and individuals" stating that the "health of Earth's ecosystem is the foundation of all health" (n.p.). While environmental medicine is not in the mainstream of U.S. medicine,[5] certainly, the popularity of Dr. Andrew Weil and many of the practices and philosophies considered "alternative medicine" attests to a growing sense that medicine should not exclude the environment from consideration. Groups such as Breast Cancer Action and the Silent Spring Institute publicize the environmental causes of disease, especially cancer. Even more striking is the rapid growth in stores, websites, and products devoted to "green living," including food chains such as Whole Foods, online stores such as Gaiam, the *Green Guide* (originally a small newsletter called *Mothers and Others*, now taken over by *National Geographic*), and a proliferation of air filters, water filters, organic cotton bedding and clothing, natural pesticides, and other products. The things-you-can-do-at-home-to-save-the-earth movement has become, in part, things-you-can-do-at-home-to-save-yourself. Sadly, many of these things involve the consumption of more products and more energy, thus contributing to further environmental degradation and climate change. These things also demand the resources to ferret out information and the finances to purchase an arsenal of protective devices. As Timothy W. Luke puts it:

> Without any clear strategy for mounting a more powerful collective response, liberal society mostly puts the responsibility for assessing the risks and managing the threats of toxics onto the individual, turning the containment of unreasonable ecological costs in the marketplace into a personal health benefit created by private responses at home. (241)

On one end of the spectrum, green living becomes just another consumer choice, as individuals are made responsible for threats they cannot possibly subdue. (Home air filters, for example, can minimize particulate matter but can do nothing about dangerous ozone levels.) On the other end, the recognition that human health is undeniably affected by the health of the environment impels global environmental justice movements. As Giovanna Di Chiro contends, "women grassroots environmentalists from around the world" "argue that the health of humans and the 'health' of the environment are profoundly linked" ("Local Actions, Global Visions" 203).

Contemporary environmental health and environmental justice movements have developed as modes of surviving within as well as critiquing and transforming risk society. Ulrich Beck defines "risk" as "a *systematic way of dealing with hazards and insecurities induced and introduced by modernization itself.* Risks, as opposed to older dangers, are consequences which relate to the threatening force of modernization and to its globalization of doubt" (21; emphasis in original). The risks of late modernity include radioactivity

> but also toxins and pollutants in the air, the water and foodstuffs, together with the accompanying short- and long-term effects on plants, animals, and people. They induce systematic and often *irreversible* harm, generally remain invisible, are based on *causal interpretations,* and thus initially only exist in terms of the (scientific or anti-scientific) *knowledge* about them. (22–23; emphases in original)

Beck explains that "knowledge gains a new political significance" in risk society (23), revising the Marxist dictum that class determines consciousness into the formulation that "in risk positions *consciousness determines being*" (ibid.). Dwelling in a landscape of perpetual risk, where even the most benign-seeming substances—bread, water, a sofa—may harbor danger, the subject within risk culture confronts not only a barrage of conflicting information and disinformation but the specter of a dangerous lack of information that should guide the most commonplace—yet potentially deadly—actions and choices. As Beck explains, the subjects in risk culture are struck with their own inability to assess danger: "Unlike news of losses in income and the like, news of toxic substances in foods, consumer goods, and so on contain a *double shock.* The threat itself is joined by the loss of sovereignty over assessing the dangers, to which one is directly subjected" (54). In her application of risk theory to contemporary novels, Ursula K. Heise argues that the chemical toxins in Don DeLillo's *White Noise* and Richard Powers's *Gain* "blur the boundaries between body and environment, the domestic and the public spheres, and beneficial and harmful technologies. It is in the territory between these realms that the uncertainties of risk perception and risk assessment play themselves out" ("Toxins, Drugs, and Global Systems" 748). A profound sense of uncertainty, emanating not only from this sort of trans-corporeal boundary blurring, but also from the necessity of engaging with scientific accounts, emanates from material memoirs as well.

Citizens within risk society not only experience their own inability to properly assess danger, but they suspect that even the authorities do not, in fact, have everything under control. More broadly, risk society renders the Enlightenment quest to master nature an absurdity:

> Ironically, the more culturally mediated the environment, the more volatile and mysterious it becomes. Enlightenment thinkers, of course, promised just the opposite. Human knowledge and intervention would tame nature, harness it to social ends. Environments do increasingly serve social ends, but they appear anything but tame. A key problem in a postnatural world is the considerable lag between the rapid changes taking place in environments and the limited capacity of experts and their systems for making coherent sense of the changes. (Brown, Kroll-Smith, and Gunter 16)

The recognition of the "limited capacity of experts and their systems" encourages—or forces—people to cobble together their own forms of expertise. Environmental justice movements, for example, have been led by citizen-experts, usually women, usually people of color, who undertake their own crash courses in chemistry, nuclear physics, biology, and other specialized fields in order to protect themselves, their families, and their communities from harm. Activists also research the health of people within their communities, often going door to door. Phil Brown has termed these practices "popular epidemiology," "in which laypeople detect and act on environmental hazards and diseases" (18). Di Chiro argues that "a new species of 'expert' has emerged—one that is constructed from the everyday struggles of people striving to understand and negotiate their needs and desires in efforts to live a decent life" ("Local Actions, Global Visions" 210). She contends that the knowledge arising from "struggles for environmental justice on the border is *more* than local, more than anecdotal, more than just personal experience. It is the outcome of shared observation, careful research, and the forging of syncretic assemblages of 'experts' of all stripes" ("Living Is for Everyone" 129). Stephen R. Couch and Steve Kroll-Smith explain that ordinary people "now know that environmental dangers require technical solutions, but they are increasingly distrustful of the experts" (385). In response, laypeople take the "attributes of expertise into their communal worlds" where they "tinker with them sufficiently to make rational sense of their miseries and appeal to significant institutional others to change, based on a rhetoric of communal, or what we might call, moral rationality" (ibid.). Couch and Kroll-Smith contend that these knowledge practices mark not a "postmodern" "demise of science" but a "strikingly new phase in its development," which "challenge[s] traditional methodological assumptions, constructing an alternative epistemology based on immediate, practical concerns" (388, 387). Whereas green consumerism privatizes our response to widespread environmental degradation, the practices of the citizen-expert may foster political awareness of the relations between power and knowledge as well as between science and capitalist enterprise.

The Science and Politics of the Self

The material memoir develops from the trans-corporeal landscape of risk society, environmental health, and the knowledge practices of "ordinary experts."

It epitomizes life in risk society, mirroring the epistemological urgency that is not undermined by its concomitant incertitude, as it dramatizes the compulsion to undertake "scientific" investigations of one's daily life. Material memoirs complement the studies of risk culture, popular epidemiology, and the ordinary expert by revealing how profoundly the sense of selfhood is transformed by the recognition that the very substance of the self is interconnected with vast biological, economic, and industrial systems that can never be entirely mapped or understood. Material memoirs, like the literature that Susan Squier discusses in *Liminal Lives,* are positioned "between knowledge and unawareness" (22), but rather than serving as an "alternative to the expert discourse" (ibid.), they enact new forms of expertise that are, to greater or lesser degrees, dependent upon scientific knowledges. In this sense, the material memoir may be a form of "counter-memory," as described by Ladelle McWhorter, drawing on Foucault: counter-memory is "an important ethical practice—first of all because it helps us escape from the cage of official truth and start thinking again and second because it is the very stuff of alternative matrices of knowledge and power, because it can function as the building material of alternative systems of meaning" (199). The material memoirs of Audre Lorde, Candida Lawrence, Zillah Eisenstein, Susanne Antonetta, and Sandra Steingraber forge "alternative matrices of knowledge and power" by refusing the oppositions between objective scientific knowledge and subjective autobiographical rumination, between the external material environment and the inner workings of the self. These works, which mix science writing, activism, genealogy, and memoir, depart not only from the genre of autobiography but, even more strikingly, from science writing as well. Rachel Carson, as Michael A. Bryson notes, suppressed information about her breast cancer, fearing that "it would compromise the objectivity and argumentative force" of *Silent Spring.* Bryson adds that such a strategy was warranted since "*Silent Spring* was subsequently attacked as unscientific and even hysterical by some representatives of the chemical industry" (172). Steingraber, by contrast, "ventures into territory where Carson did not take us—that personal space where the author confronts disease and comes to terms with the tangled ecological roots of her childhood home" (ibid., 173–174). Whereas Bryson focuses primarily on the rhetorical strategies of Carson and Steingraber, I would like to propose that the striking difference between the "objective" scientific writing of Carson and the more recent material memoirs reflects a sea change of sorts—a broad consciousness or, at least, an anxious, nearly conscious awareness—that late twentieth- and early twenty-first-century citizens may not imagine ourselves as separate from the risky environments we inhabit. Material memoirs arise from feminism's long history of attending to body politics and asserting that the personal *is* the political. Material memoirs do not, however, forge a solid identity politics of gender oppositions, but instead dramatize the miasma of uncertainties and interconnections in risk society. Joni Seager has warned that when activist groups enter the "environmental 'big time' through the portal of mainline science, feminists risk losing their distinctive stance of oppositionality and their insistence that environmental knowledge comes in many forms" (963). Material memoirs portray many forms of environmental knowledge, but their political critique does not emerge from an oppositional stance; instead, it emerges from a trans-corporeal space that demands some sort of engagement with science, as scientific knowledges are invaluable at the crossroads of body and place.

Zillah Eisenstein, in *Manmade Breast Cancers,* begins with a "political memoir" (4), telling her family's stories of breast cancer. She shares "pain and suffering not simply to authenticate this way of knowing, but to push elsewhere" (ix), insisting that theory is a "way of seeing connectedness" (ibid.). Her focus on the breast radiates in multiple directions, due to the "fluidity of borders between the breast and all else" (ibid.). She critiques the cancer establishment, global capitalism, and the unequal distribution of cancer risk and treatment due to racial and economic inequities. Writing feminist theory in the late 1990s, Eisenstein struggles to write about "female place-consciousness and its materiality." Contrasting her project with Marx's materialism and Irigaray's female body, she attempts to find a way of capturing the "materiality of the female body": "I cannot find the right phrasing because no language quite fits my purpose" (41). The book may never find a language adequate to its purpose, and it may never quite weave some of its more disparate topics together in a compelling way—the critique of Bill Clinton's affair with Monica Lewinsky seems a bit irrelevant today, for example—but it does contain compelling, manifesto-like moments:

> Let me reimagine the breast. Connect it to the body systematically and to its complex environments cyclically. Define our environments with open yet connected boundaries between air, water, soil, economic and racial hierarchies and the female body.
> Interrogate the cause/effect scientific model for its linear blindness. Supplant this model with an interactive and multistage model of malignant growth that recognizes the interstices between bodies, genes, and environments. Such an *episteme* will need to critically address the conflicting messages about women's bodies, their socially and environmentally constructed genes, and the role of genes in breast cancer. (76)

Reimagining the breast demands an epistemology that can encompass cultural and political critique, as well as a more complex science of cancer that accounts for the interactions of genes and environments. It is no wonder that Eisenstein struggles to pull together personal narratives; social, political, and economic critiques; and scientific explanations. As a Marxist, antiracist, anticolonialist feminist, she is driven to understand her own personal experience through multiple critical frameworks that expand outward, positing a trans-corporeality that sees the breast, the body, the self as coextensive with the physical environment. Breast cancer, she argues is "truly manmade" because the "science we need is squashed by this capitalist, masculinist, and racialized frame of reference that naturalizes and neutralizes ecological and bodily devastation" (76). Eisenstein's memoir calls for broad social, political, scientific, and medical changes.

Although I hesitate to fault this important and ambitious text, its arguments and positions stand clear of epistemological quandaries and confusion, even when contending with complicated matters such as the debates about environmental versus genetic causes of cancer. Paradoxically, perhaps, what makes this book less gripping than the work of Lawrence, Antonetta, or Steingraber is that Eisenstein does not mark the difficulties of becoming an ordinary expert in a risk society. We don't see her wading through popular journalism, medical textbooks, epidemiological data, biochemistry handbooks, or other scientific studies. The scientific information is rendered as immediate, as close at hand, as the traditional materials for autobiographical consideration. The messy, perplexing, maddening process of sorting through conflicting, sometimes opaque scientific accounts seems to have been shelved.[6]

In contrast, even though Sandra Steingraber is a scientist, her memoir suggests the challenges of understanding the material self within a scientific matrix. *Living Downstream: A Scientist's Personal Investigation of Cancer and the Environment* presents an interwoven account of the astounding number of chemicals that circulate through the world and, in particular, through the agricultural county in Illinois where she grew up, and thus through her own body. Steingraber's book is a scientific exposé, a political call to action, and a scientific autobiography that uncovers the many probable environmental causes of her own bladder cancer. Her memoir frequently calls attention to how difficult it is to uncover reliable scientific data. She explains how the data in cancer registries are compromised (34–39), she notes that the EPA's Toxics Release Inventory "is about the size of an average phone book" (103) and the National Institute of Health's *Biennial Report on Carcinogens* is "473 pages long and features 200 entries" (126), and she frequently describes herself as being surrounded by "bulging files" of scientific studies. We witness her laboring to grasp the world. What is most compelling about her account, however, is that the scientific data that initially appear as inert, arm's-length facts about an external world become vividly transformed into the very substance of her self. Knowing this sort of self poses astonishing challenges. For example, Steingraber explains that the best way to test body burden (a measure of one's cumulative exposure to dangerous substances) is by "sampling each and every fluid and compartment of tissue," which is best done after the person is dead (236). This procedure would, of course, be of little benefit to autobiographers. One could, however, have one's "[b]lood, urine, breast milk, exhaled air, fat, semen, hair, tears, sweat, and fingernails" (ibid.) tested to assess body burden. Wisely, Steingraber segues from this highly individual assessment of toxicity—which risks becoming merely a high-tech form of navel gazing—toward a wider sense of trans-corporeality, which is epitomized by her phrase "ecological roots." Although realizing that one's own body is marked by all of the toxins it has absorbed over a lifetime may be a stunning illumination, it is the movement *across* human bodies and the wider environment that fosters an environmental and environmental justice ethic. Furthermore, the pursuit of a trans-corporeal genealogy is, in itself, a politicized knowledge practice that catalyzes further environmental activism:

> Going in search of our ecological roots has both intimate and far-flung di-
> mensions. It means learning about the sources of our drinking water (past
> and present), about the prevailing winds that blow through our communities,
> and about the agricultural system that provides us food. It involves visit-
> ing grainfields, as well as cattle lots, orchards, pastures, and dairy farms.
> It demands curiosity about how our apartment buildings are exterminated,
> clothing cleaned, and golf courses maintained. It means asserting our right
> to know about any and all toxic ingredients in products such as household
> cleaners, paints, and cosmetics. It requires a determination to find out where
> the underground storage tanks are located, how the land was used before the
> subdivision was built over it, what is being sprayed along the roadsides and
> rights-of-way, and what exactly goes on behind the barbed-wire fence at the
> end of the street. (267–268)

"Intimate" and "far-flung," personal and scientific (in the broadest possible sense), this quest is made possible by the assumption that the individual has the "right to know." Indeed, the epilogue catalogs useful sources under the title "Exercising Your Right to Know." But the search for ecological roots also implies that we can or should *do* something with the information we dig up. What would be the point of each of us undertaking similar investigations, uncovering different (or similar) sorts of carcinogenic exposures for different regions and life stories? Even though each of us *could* investigate our ecological roots and discover the probable origins of toxins (some of which might, eventually, contribute to our demise), it may be that Steingraber's convincing demonstration of how "all the material that is us—from bone to blood to breast tissue—has come to us from the environment" (*Living Downstream* 267) impels readers not to look back toward origins, but to embrace an environmental ethic that understands world and self to be coextensive. Steingraber may motivate her readers to take on the work of becoming ordinary experts who fight against risks that they must fight to even know. Similarly, Chip Ward, in his memoir, *Canaries on the Rim: Living Downwind in the West,* envisions "millions of ecodetectives, investigating the hazards and risks in their backyards and making the connection between poor health and environmental degradation" (148).

Susanne Antonetta undertakes a similar quest, digging up her ecological origins. Her bold memoir, *Body Toxic,* works as a form of epidemiological counter-memory as it foregrounds the struggle to understand the substance of the self within a risk society that encourages ignorance and denial. Antonetta counters the official truths and the predominant modes of forgetting that sail over the stunningly toxic landscape of the Pine Barrens in southern New Jersey. Although her parents vividly remember the film *Psycho* (her dad calls it "that bastard movie"), which was released during the summer of 1960, they have forgotten about the nuclear warhead that caught fire that same year, just fifteen miles from their house, which sprayed radioactive particles over the area. Twelve years later, "the government, answering cries for protection, installed a chainlink fence to protect civilians" (15). Along with forgetting that the family is multiracial and that it includes people with severe psychological problems, the family forgets the dangers of the landscape they have made their home: "We forget our thrown-together shore cottages lie on polluted land licked by polluted water. When we reminisce about the fruitberries, droll fruit the color of seasickness, we forget we picked them walking along a chainlink fence guarding a nuclear power plant" (54). Against the pervasive denial of the dangers lurking in the landscape, a landscape that becomes a body, Antonetta presents a counter-memory that emerges not only from personal reflection but from historical, journalistic, and scientific research into the place that shaped her. In true activist form, she names names: the BOMARC bunker fire, the Oyster Creek nuclear reactor, Ciba-Geigy chemical corporation, Denzer & Schafer X-Ray, Union Carbide, Nicholas Agricola, DDT.

Undertaking autobiography as a form of popular epidemiology, Antonetta notes that her childhood home, the Toms River/Beachwood area, was, in the 1970s, 1980s, and 1990s, "wracked by childhood cancers—particularly of the brain and nervous system—leukemias, breast cancers, many times higher than normal. My family was not. We've been wracked by infertility, tumors, organs malformed at birth and manic-depression" (27). Antonetta flatly states the disjunction between the epidemiological data and the evidence from her own family. Frustrated with her inability to pin down the facts, she struggles to make the knowledges of science and self align:

> I choked facts but they choked me back; they stuck, like Legos—clingy but hard to build into anything real. I can know what hung in the water, nested in the soft tissues of the fish. I can't look into the novel of my body and go to the end, where it tells what happened. I have or have had one spectacular multiple pregnancy, a miscarriage, a radiation-induced tumor, a double uterus, asthma, endometriosis, growths on the liver, other medical conditions like allergies.
>
> Here are tales of cause and effect:
>
> After low-level radioactive releases in Hanford, Washington, exposed women developed double the rate of thyroid disease and spontaneous abortion (miscarriage).

In a medical study of workers exposed to low-level radiation the majority
of the workers developed thyroid tumors.

After exposing female laboratory monkeys to dioxins and PCBs, those
monkeys more often than not develop endometriosis.

Liver tumors like mine can be induced by too many industrial chemicals
to list.

Low-level exposure to many pesticides causes kindling in the brains of
laboratory mice—electrical misfiring, spikes and bursts of activity, like the
firing you'd see in the brain of a manic depressive. (27–28)

The list of "tales of cause and effect" continues, reading like an epic catalog, a
late twentieth-century version of Walt Whitman's "Song of Myself"—diagnostic
rather than democratic, listing disparate medical facts, rather than coherent persons. Although Antonetta tries to "choke facts"—positioning herself as a knower
in the predominant model of scientific mastery—they choke her back, dramatizing that she cannot imagine herself as a transcendent knower, removed from
the material realities that have caused her tumors, asthma, and miscarriages.
Antonetta dramatizes Beck's sense of the "loss of sovereignty" of the citizen as
well as Couch and Kroll-Smith's "alternative epistemology based on immediate,
practical concerns." Most tellingly, perhaps, the disjunction between Antonetta's
own corporeal state and the disjointed list of scientific conclusions dramatizes
the "problem of uncertain science." As Brown, Kroll-Smith, and Gunter explain,
it "is almost impossible to document conclusively that a specific disease is caused
by exposure to specific environmental toxins," since individual bodies have been
formed and affected by myriad substances and forces (10). The uncertainty of the
science may have fostered the disorganized, almost random, form of the book,
in which people are awkwardly reintroduced in later chapters and topics are repeated seemingly without cognizance that they've already been discussed. One
could easily call the book postmodern, self-reflexive, and metafictional, all of
which it is. We could also see it as a "chaos story" of a "wounded storyteller," in
that it "represents the triumph of all that modernity seeks to surpass" (Frank 97).
In such stories, as Arthur W. Frank explains, "the modernist bulwark of remedy,
progress, and professionalism cracks to reveal vulnerability, futility, and impo-
tence," as well as "how easily any of us could be sucked under" (ibid.). But neither
the predominant characteristics of postmodernism nor even the wounded storyteller's critique of modernity capture the sense that Antonetta, like other popular
epidemiologists, is driven not only to critique metanarratives of scientific progress, but to uncover material realities that impinge upon her very survival. Like
Latour, she does not aim to "get away from facts but closer to them, not fighting
empiricism but, on the contrary renewing empiricism" (Latour, "Why Has Critique Run Out of Steam?" 231). For Antonetta, "matters of fact" are always already
"matters of concern."

Material Environments, Material Selves

In the midst of right-wing denials of global warming, in which "dangerous extremists are using the very same argument of social construction to destroy hard-won evidence that could save our lives" ("Why Has Critique Run Out of Steam?" 227), Latour urges us to develop new critical methods that cultivate a "stubbornly realist attitude" toward "matters of concern" (231). Rather than "debunking," Latour's critic would "assemble," "offering participants arenas in which to gather" (246), multiplying rather than subtracting, cultivating "care and caution" for our fragile constructions (ibid.). Latour's call to develop new critical methods that can address matters of concern seems appropriate for material memoirs, which must come to grips with trans-corporeal materialities that are staggeringly difficult to grasp.

Timothy W. Luke, in "Rethinking Technoscience in Risk Society: Toxicity as Textuality," argues that "scientific facts of toxicity and broad risk to human health are turned into contestable texts":

> Because a more sophisticated science of analyzing toxicity is not yet at hand, our understanding of toxics often is much more explicitly textual than it is technical. A text is whatever can be read or reinterpreted beyond some recognized conventional meaning, and textuality marks anything that evokes, or is seen as capable of generating, many successive rereadings and interpretations. . . . To see toxicity as textuality is to admit to the contested, unknown, and indeterminate qualities of toxic effects. (239)

Notwithstanding the serious limitations of scientific understandings of toxicity, to transplant the entire enterprise from the "technical" to the "textual" seems a dangerous move, especially given the last several decades of critical theory in which material reality has, to a great extent, been cordoned off from language, discourse, and textuality. Ironically, although Luke plays off the sense of textuality as extensive, interwoven, and able to "disclose much larger social forces" (240), when textuality is invoked within the context of global environmental degradation, it may seem a domain of relief, a space for words rather than substances, culture rather than nature. Moreover, when Luke contends that, for "almost any substance in the environment, toxicity becomes an open-ended textual question rather than a purely closed technical one" (244), he assumes that texts are "open" whereas technical or scientific knowledge is "closed," which is a strange way of depicting ongoing scientific practices. Interestingly, despite his emphasis on textuality, Luke offers one of the most tangible and disturbing depictions of what it is to live in risk society. After explaining that environmental risk management routinely calculates such things as "for every A, B, or C benefit of this chemical or material, X people per 10,000, Y people per 100,000 . . . will be harmed by ill health, genetic mutation and/or death," he states: "[i]n modern society, everyone tacitly consents to the crippling and painful execution of many of their fellow consumers every time they spray herbicide on lawns, fill their gas tanks with high-test, buy pressure-treated lumber, and purchase plastic housewares" (248). This devastating realization will probably not be embraced by many. Luke concludes by arguing that his sense of toxicity as textuality will be useful for ordinary citizens: "textualizing the understandings of toxicity leaves every citizen and consumer more aware of their roles as lay readers struggling either to decipher useful information from public toxic advisories or to decode the final meaning in scientific hieroglyphics about environmental hazards" (252). And yet "textualizing" the understanding of toxicity may also exacerbate the ontological divide between nature and culture, world and ideas, in which skepticism provokes simple dismissal, as with the many conservatives who simply choose not to "believe" in global warming or any other form of environmental degradation. The emphasis on textuality may detract from, rather than contribute to, the sense that we are all materially interconnected with the rest of the world.

Antonetta's memoir is a richly literary text that portrays the struggle to account for a self who is coextensive with a wider materiality. Autobiography becomes profoundly biological as bodies and selves are constructed from the very stuff of the toxic places they have inhabited. As various toxins take up residence within the body, the supposedly inert "background" of place becomes the active substance of self. Antonetta reveals how the substance of place, in this case, one of the most toxic places in the United States, is not separable from her biological body, her psychology, or her self. Her 2001 memoir unwittingly mirrors nineteenth-century understandings of the interrelations between health and place as described by Nash and Bolton Valencius. Antonetta notes that Barnegat Bay, near where she grew up, "tends to stagnate and grow what look like floating molds and mildews. Rather than sand beaches we have marshes and weeds spreading up to the water" (11). This area in New Jersey is or was home to radioactive particles, DDT, and hazardous landfills leaking lead, arsenic, chromium, mercury, and a multitude of other xenobiotic chemicals. Antonetta herself is home to manic depression, infertility, tumors, and a deformed uterus. Emerging from this diseased place, Antonetta imagines a medical "test" for this environment: "If there were blood tests for place all I can see is a brackish test tube with a kelp strand, moss bunkers like fat minnows on their sides, and frogs with ova and testes, both useless" (30). As place becomes blood, blood becomes landscape: "I have blood drawn all the time to monitor various things. I like to daydream while the vials rush and color about what's in there. Salt water, red cells, ancestors braided and escaping. A bony geography" (28). Antonetta insists upon the biological substance of her body, unlike her grandmother who combats horrific memories of the amputations that she witnessed as a nurse in World War I by becoming a Christian Scientist and refusing to believe in matter, except as an "error" (62). By contrast, Antonetta's lurid images crowd her text with biological entities (kelp, minnows, frogs) and corporeal substances (blood and bones), immersing us in a defamiliarizing zone where place becomes self becomes place.

In *Having Faith: An Ecologist's Journey to Motherhood,* Steingraber also writes her body as an environment. Pregnant, she realized, "with amazement" that she had "become a habitat," her womb an "inland ocean with the population of one" (ix). Her investigation into the many substances that could potentially harm her developing child transforms her desire for a safe pregnancy into a wider environmental stance: "protecting the ecosystem inside my body required protecting the one outside" (ibid.). Steingraber presents a staggering indictment of how physicians, pregnancy handbooks, even the March of Dimes—which is devoted to the prevention of birth defects—downplay or ignore the many environmental threats to fetuses and babies. While women are everywhere exhorted to abstain from alcohol during pregnancy, despite the lack of evidence that small amounts of alcohol pose a threat, "there is no public conversation about environmental threats to pregnancy" (107). A March of Dimes publication, for example, "does not mention solvents or pesticides or toxic waste sites or Minamata or Vietnam" (105). Against this manufactured ignorance, Steingraber exposes the many common household substances that are known to be teratogens and, perhaps more disturbingly, explains how little we know about the prevalence or the causes of birth defects. For one thing, many of the surveillance systems only "count birth defects among live-born infants," not those who were miscarried, aborted, or stillborn (87). Moreover, "[m]ost chemicals have not been tested for their ability to have teratogenic effects," including three-quarters of the "high production volume" chemicals (88). Although Steingraber often fails to interrogate the specific forces behind this socially constructed ignorance, maintaining instead the dual voices of the objective scientific researcher and the softer, concerned mother, it is impossible to read the book without a sense that science, medicine, and government have failed to provide the rudimentary knowledges necessary for healthy human reproduction.

Steingraber's central conceit in this interdigitated personal and scientific exploration is that her body, the habitat for her developing child, is inextricably connected to the wider world. During amniocentesis, the obstetrician fills vials with amniotic fluid while urging Steingraber to drink more water. In a long, poetic rumination, Steingraber traces the amniotic fluid to its many worldly origins:

> I drink water, and it becomes blood plasma, which suffuses through the amniotic sac and surrounds the baby—who also drinks it.
>
> And what is it before that? Before it is drinking water, amniotic fluid is the creeks and rivers that fill reservoirs. It is the underground water that fills wells. And before it is creeks and rivers and groundwater. Amniotic fluid is rain. . . . The blood of cows and chickens is in this tube. The nectar gathered

by bees and hummingbirds is in this tube. Whatever is inside hummingbird eggs is also inside my womb. Whatever is in the world's water is here in my hands. (*Having Faith* 66–67)

Significantly, Steingraber imaginatively transforms a medical test for genetic "abnormalities" into a poetic exploration of how the substances of the vast world flow through her body as well as her daughter's body. Brilliantly, Steingraber evokes an aesthetic, beloved nature of creeks, rivers, cows, chickens, bees, and hummingbirds—painting a utopian nature that we cannot help but desire—even as we already know that pernicious substances run through these waters and these creatures. Amniocentesis, intended only to ensure the emergence of a genetically proper human, is eclipsed by a broader environmental ethics that would protect the water, the farm animals, the bees, and the hummingbird eggs from harm. Moreover, standard prenatal medical precautions are overwhelmed by environmental precautionary principles, which state that it is impossible to attain human health and well-being without securing the health and well-being of the broader environment of which we are a part.

Steingraber's text dramatizes trans-corporeal processes, as various toxins flow through the environment into water, air, and food, through the mother's body, and finally, into the developing fetus and the nursing infant. Even as Steingraber's vision is utterly compelling, this particular form of trans-corporeality is a bit worrisome for gender-minimizing feminists, since the potent category of "mother" threatens to engulf the entire range of identities that women inhabit. The pregnant female body is an ideologically hazardous terrain due to the centuries-old articulations of woman/body/nature as passive matter, a resource for active human minds and cultures. An entire constellation of pernicious practices and assumptions emanate from the melding of woman as nature, nature as woman.[7] Steingraber does mention how the "toxicology of semen is an emerging area of study that may eventually shed more light on the question of paternal exposures and birth defects" (*Having Faith* 95), but it is the reproducing female body that is at the center of this book. (In her defense, however, she cannot discuss scientific evidence about semen if it does not exist.) Despite the ideological risks of calcifying the female body as a reproductive body and of eroding reproductive choice by focusing on fetal health, it is impossible to deny the devastating consequences that environmental toxins have on developing fetuses and on infants who are ingesting human milk, which is, as Steingraber discusses at length, simultaneously the best food for infants and terribly toxic. Feminism, even gender-minimizing feminisms, cannot turn away from matters of reproductive health and bodily politics. Moreover, Steingraber's text itself subtly contends with epistemologies that pose man as knower and woman as known by reiterating that she writes, at once, as an ecologist and a pregnant woman, as a scientist and a mother (to be), as someone who searches for information about teratological effects and someone who submits her body to amniocentesis. Both the knower and the known, alternating rational scientific facts with intimate, emotional revelations, Steingraber oscillates between gendered polarities, dramatizing perhaps an epistemological "everyman" of risk society who must contend with puzzling scientific matters that penetrate the substance of the self. The pernicious formulation of mother as matter is overwhelmed by a more complex, less gendered understanding of ourselves as material selves, embedded in processes that are simultaneously biological and social, scientific and personal.

Steingraber makes a convincing case for expanding prenatal care to include environmental ethics, policies, and practices and, simultaneously, for environmentalism to embrace reproductive health as part of its domain. Steingraber's solutions are never merely consumerist or personal but sharply political. It does not diminish the impact of her text, however, to advocate that it be complemented by other accounts lest its particular form of white, economically privileged reprosexuality be naturalized or even romanticized. Obviously, racism, poverty, and the lack of universal health insurance threaten prenatal as well as postnatal health and must be attended to. Furthermore, the heteronormativity of Steingraber's narrative needs to be countered by a diverse array of "queer ecologies"[8] that resist the naturalization of sex as primarily reproductive and heterosexual.

Genomes and "Toxomes": The Environmental Politics of Toxic Bodies

Insisting upon the trans-corporeal substance of their selves, Antonetta and Steingraber depart from the popular and scientific fixation on genetics as the key to human health. In *Living Downstream,* Steingraber questions what caused her bladder cancer. She notes that a great deal is known about the "sequential genetic changes that unfold" throughout the course of this particular cancer. But, "sadly, all this knowledge about genetic mutations, inherited risk factors, and enzymatic mechanisms has not translated into an effective campaign to prevent the disease" (257). Despite the fact that each new discovery in genetic research is reported by the media as a promising breakthrough, she notes rather commonsensically that, since we "cannot change our ancestors," "[s]hining the spotlight on inheritance focuses us on the one piece of the puzzle we can do absolutely nothing about" (260). Worse, Steingraber contends that this "obsession with genes and heredity" deflects attention from environmental carcinogens. The material memoirs of Lorde, Lawrence, Steingraber, and Antonetta, as well as the activist accounts of "toxomes" and "chemical fingerprints," which will be discussed below, counter the scientific and popular obsession with genetics by emphasizing the ongoing material interchanges between body and place.

Even as Antonetta's memoir mixes family histories, her own memories, diary entries detailing her teenage drug use, the history of the toxic contamination of her home, medical research, and epidemiology, her physicians take a narrower approach, focusing on her genetic rather than her environmental heritage: "My doctors loved my family history. . . . Though there's a lot written about the neurological and physical effects of chemicals and radiation, I've never met a doctor who liked to talk about that" (203). In the standard medical paradigm of the modern body, as Nash calls it, the human body is sharply delineated from the background of the environment—magically sealed, impermeable, isolated. Genes have become the prime movers of the modern body. Genes—imagined as discrete, mechanistic, agential entities, as Evelyn Fox Keller, Donna Haraway, and others have argued—have become invested with the power of life itself. Haraway contends that, in the sociobiology of Richard Dawkins, "living flesh is derivative; the gene is the alpha and omega of the secular salvation drama of life itself. This is barely secular Christian Platonism" (*Modest_Witness* 133). We rarely consider, for example, that an environmental inheritance of sorts is passed along to one's progeny, along with one's genes. Steingraber, in *Having Faith,* critiques the "narrowness" of the now nearly standard practice of amniocentesis. Noting that "the majority of birth defects are not attributable to inborn genetic errors," she cites the "thousands blinded by rubella and the legless ones exposed to thalidomide": "And yet we put legions of geneticists to work looking for [genetic errors], and we ritualize amniocentesis as a rite of passage for pregnant women, as though chunks of DNA were the prime movers of life itself. As though pregnancy took place in a sealed chamber, apart from water cycles and food chains" (74–75). The unpleasant matters of environmental health, which radiate outward, exposing culpable industries, institutions, and government agencies, are supplanted by "the gene." Whereas an environmental history of birth defects would include such things as thalidomide and Minamata disease, which raise uncomfortable questions about who is to blame and which forms of knowledge can be trusted, the spotlight on the gene raises no such ethical or political questions.

Giovanna Di Chiro argues in "Producing 'Roundup Ready®' Communities? Human Genome Research and Environmental Justice Policy" that the Environmental Genome Project "claims to be on the path to solving environmental health problems at their core by zeroing in on the innate flaws in the human genome" (141). The EGP "intends to uncover these defects, which may show up disproportionately in particular subgroups of the population and which are associated with an increased susceptibility to a range of environmental illnesses" (ibid.). Di Chiro and the environmental justice activists she interviews offer cogent critiques of the implications of this project. Tellingly for our purposes here, Di Chiro reveals that, even though "EGP's stated focus is interaction between genes and environment," "[e]nvironment consistently falls out of the picture in EGP documents, except as the naturalized substratum on which genetic variation operates" (155). Some of the most important cultural work that the material memoir performs is to spotlight what may be considered a "naturalized substratum," bringing it to the foreground in often defamiliarizing ways.

Although she does not focus on the EGP per se, Sara Shostak presents a more optimistic assessment about the potential for the emerging sciences of genetic epidemiology, molecular epidemiology, and toxicogenomics to focus our attention on gene-environment *interactions*. She contends that this research may "transform both bioscientific and popular understandings of the relationship between bodies and environments" by "making exposure(s) visible at the molecular level" ("Locating Gene-Environment Interaction" 2338). She explains that the "environmental genetic body is porous; it absorbs what it touches in the air, soil, and water and is changed at the molecular and morphological level by these absorptions. The body itself becomes a molecular archeological site revealing the past history of exposures and potential future harms" (ibid.). As I will discuss below, environmentalists, including Bill Moyers and the Environmental Working Group, have seized upon these sciences to dramatize the immediacy of environmental concerns. These sciences make it possible to imagine prenatal tests that "inquire about environmental problems as well as genetic ones" (Steingraber, *Having Faith* 75). Imagine what sort of environmental politics and practices would develop if obstetricians (or "environmental screeners," parallel to "genetic screeners") routinely discussed teratological toxins with pregnant women.

Like Shostak, Antonetta insists on the interplay between genes and environment in a chapter called "Double Helix": "Genes create tendencies the environment can activate, as doses of radiation and toxic chemicals alter body and brain chemistry and also attack the chromosomes helping recessive traits come forward" (175). Against the current tendency to overemphasize the power of genes, she vividly emphasizes the material agencies of place: "Radiation breaks chromosomes, like a woodchopper flailing at logs" (202). Or, "[a]s children, even in the womb, we [were] changed, charged, and reformed by the landscape. I may have pummeled away at my central nervous system and organs and drifts of ganglia but what did it was the small white fish and the blackberries and the air itself" (148). The "small white fish" and the "blackberries" exist not only as childhood memories but as the conveyers of substances lurking within, forming, and harming the body and the mind that Antonetta finds herself to be.

Condensed versions of the material memoir have been proliferating throughout the various media of popular culture and environmental activism. Take, for example, the October 2006 issue of *National Geographic*. The cover displays a rugged "wilderness" area, a tall mesa rising up from the desert—with three ominous smokestacks behind it—announcing, in a large font, "Places We Must Save." Accompanying this traditional environmentalist cover is the story "The Chemicals within Us" in which David Ewing Duncan, a writer "engaged in a journey of chemical self-discovery" (120), has himself tested for "320 chemicals I might have picked up from food, drink, the air I breathe, and the products that touch my skin—my own secret stash of compounds acquired by merely living" (ibid.). He receives a "chemical report card" stating that, of the 320 chemicals for which he was tested, 165 were detected. Like Steingraber and Antonetta, Duncan goes in search of where "those toxic traces came from," mentioning that he played in an EPA Superfund site as a child and grew up near both pesticide-laden agricultural areas and factories that spewed noxious clouds. The article provides information about the pervasiveness, origins, and health effects of several common and potentially dangerous categories of chemicals, such as PBDEs and phthalates. It also includes disturbing information about how little we know about the safety of the chemicals that pervade us. For example, "only a quarter of the 82,000 chemicals in use in the U.S. have ever been tested for toxicity" (122). Despite these unsettling data and the comments of a Swedish chemist, who notes that Duncan's concentration of PBDEs is "very high" (120), parts of the article are oddly upbeat. The box along the side of the "report card," for example, announces in a large font: "Duncan can go toe-to-toe with a Midwestern cornfield for pesticide variety—16 of the 28 tested for were found. Don't try to set him on fire either, as his blood is rich in BDE-47, a common fire retardant that is now being phased out" (126).

Whereas the toxic bodies of Antonetta and Steingraber exhibit vulnerability, Duncan arises as tougher, scrappier, more impervious, even "richer." Like sci-fi heroes made more powerful by radiation or a mysterious toxic brew, Duncan is fortified. The essay concludes with Duncan showing his tests to his internist, who "admits that he too knows little about these chemicals," but confirms that Duncan is "healthy" ("The Chemicals within Us" 133). The essay could have concluded with recommendations for medicine to acknowledge the dangers of xenobiotic chemicals, or for more extensive tests and regulations, or for greener domestic practices. But despite the inset that tells the reader "how to avoid" various chemicals in "our toxic homes," the article ends with business as usual: "So I'll keep flying, and scrambling my eggs on Teflon, and using that scented shampoo. But I'll never feel quite the same about the chemicals that make life better in so many ways" (ibid.). The biochemical realities of Duncan's exposure fade into immateriality, as feelings become the focus. What an expensive affective adventure this was, costing $15,000 for the testing alone.

National Geographic surrounds this masculine, privileged toxic body, which reconstitutes itself as strong and healthy, with the bodies of the less fortunate ones who fail to rise above their exposures. Photos of three women with breast cancer, posing in front of a horizon lit up by factories and oil refineries, precede Duncan's essay; the article itself includes photos of children at risk from flame retardants and lead as well as a woman wearing a gas mask as she heads through the laundry detergent section of a supermarket. The only other photo of an adult male is that of John Moore who, smiling, enjoys a detox procedure at a spa. Turning the pages, the reader may be stunned by the sight of a baby with a blur where the eyes should be, the introductory photo to the story "A World of Hurt." In this suspiciously brief article, Duncan discusses how "chemical 'hot spots' expose people to pesticides, heavy metals, and other substances at levels many times higher than most of us experience" (139). Noting that "the victims are often the world's poor and powerless," he explains that, although "tragic in themselves," "these high exposures also raise troubling questions about the much smaller, parts-per-billion traces we all pick up in daily life" (ibid.). The "we" here rests on an uncomfortable, shifting ground of relative risk and security. "We" are all both like and not-like the "world's poor and powerless" in that, as Beck formulated, toxicants may be concentrated in certain areas, but they ultimately transgress social and economic sectors. Most disturbingly, the vivid examples of people seriously harmed by toxic exposures are said, by someone from the National Center for Environmental Health, "to provide us with information that comes from people" (ibid.). As the essay does not discuss environmental justice activism nor popular epidemiology, it casts these people as objects of knowledge, not knowers in their own right, and, more disturbingly, as lab rats who ultimately provide information for "us": "While science searches for answers, one thing is certain: The known horrors inflicted by high doses of chemicals make the small amounts inside each of us even more unsettling" (140).

Bill Moyers also underwent body burden testing, as part of his PBS television program *Trade Secrets,* which "reveals how the public's right to know the truth about the thousands of chemicals that surround us has been compromised" ("Trade Secrets" website). The astoundingly detailed and comprehensive website lists Moyers's test results, grouping them by eleven different types of toxicants. The twenty-five brain and nervous system toxicants that were detected in Moyers, it states, may cause the following symptoms: "muscle weakness, tremors, dizziness, eye pain, blurred vision, confusion, numbness, twitching, paralysis, and death." Furthermore, "[l]earning, memory and other higher brain functions may also be affected" (ibid.). Even as it offers evidence of how we all harbor a fleet of toxicants, Moyers's body burden testing is downplayed on the website, which notes that most people could not spend the $6,000 to be tested; it concludes, significantly, with a link to *Scorecard: The Pollution Information Site.* At Scorecard.org, people can type in their zip codes and find lists of the toxic chemicals currently being released in their neighborhoods, along with the health effects of these chemicals. Moreover, this easy-to-use site names names. After typing in 75208, I was only one click away from discovering the "top polluters" in my county: Lasco Bathware Inc. emitted 141,721 pounds of toxins in 2002, and Dal-Tile, ranking second, emitted 131,210 pounds. (Since I'm writing in 2010, the information is a bit dusty.) Even though Moyers offered up his body for testing, the site resists a medical or consumerist model of the health of individual bodies and encourages a broader sense of environmental health that is concomitant with political activism. Lest the activism become merely that of the not-in-my-backyard variety, the site also includes an image of the earth, which maps how PCBs could have traveled all the way from Alabama to the Arctic Circle. The home page for "Trade Secrets" clearly delineates "the problem," "the evidence," and "the options." The evidence includes a database of 37,000 pages of chemical industry documents and a rollover chart that shows how chemical industry money flows into the government. The options include both "the right to know" and "protecting yourself." The site provides ample resources for popular epidemiologists, citizen-experts, environmental activists, and green consumers. One's own personal health becomes a matter that demands knowledge and activism.

The 37,000-page archive that accompanies the "Trade Secrets" site is provided by the Environmental Working Group (EWG), which has undertaken the Human Toxome Project. The Human Toxome Project uses "cutting edge biomonitoring techniques to test blood, urine, breast milk and other human tissues for industrial chemicals that enter the human body as pollution via food, air, and water, or from exposures to ingredients in everyday consumer products" (EWG website). Brilliantly, the Human Toxome Project presents an environmental alternative to the Human Genome Project; bodies become coextensive with place as the project's subtitle suggests: "Mapping the Pollution in People." Clicking on the world map brings up a list of people who have been tested. Clicking on their names reveals the now-familiar lists of chemicals found in their blood and urine. An eerie disjunction arises between the smiling portraits at the top of the page and the long, disturbing chart that graphs the levels of particular toxicants, their health effects, and probable exposure routes. Andrea Martin, for example, looks so happy, but her levels of at least two different carcinogens are "high." One worries for her. Indeed, her brief bio further down on the site tells us that she is a cancer survivor—but also that she has climbed Mount Fuji with 500 other survivors. These web pages defamiliarize our conceptions of the human, as the modest photos and bios are dwarfed by the charts of toxicant levels and their dangers, as if we are all floating in vast landscapes of invisible threats. But then again, we are.

A Cautionary Note on Environmental Health, Environmentalism, and Animals

The Human Toxome Project puts forth a less literary version of the material memoir, using biomonitoring to disclose the material interconnections among people, places, and industries and urging stronger regulations, fewer toxic emissions, and more citizen and community control. The Human Toxome Project, however, neglects to mention the body burdens of nonhuman animals, who absorb the full array of humanly produced toxicants. Just as material memoirs reveal the interchanges between the human and more-than-human worlds, we can imagine all creatures existing as part of their own corporeal crossroads of body and place, provoking an ethics of concern for a multitude of creatures and their habitats. It would be bitterly ironic to erode the foundations of human exceptionalism, as trans-corporeality does, only to reinstate a narrowly humanist ethical sphere. As someone devoted to environmental health practices, I am often dismayed that human health may be purchased at the expense of nonhuman creatures, as environmental health movements, practices, and products sometimes seem to be cordoned off from environmentalism as such. Switching on my home air filter, for instance, is a selfish act in that it contributes to global climate change, which will harm plants, animals, habitats, and ecosystems. Despite their green wrappings, environmental health practices at their most solipsistic are reminiscent of a bomb shelter mentality in which we, the fortunate few, attempt to save ourselves. A recognition of the risks of trans-corporeal interchanges can, in short, motivate an array of psychological, political, and material boundary practices aimed at protecting individuals from the world. On the other hand, understanding the world and the self to be coextensive, as the material memoirs do, can also inspire a trans-corporeal, posthuman environmentalism that builds connections rather than boundaries and that undertakes ethical actions from within global systems, interchanges, and flows. Karen Barad advocates an ethics of "mattering" and "worlding," which is "about responsibility and accountability for the lively relationalities of becoming of which we are a part" (*Meeting the Universe Halfway* 392–393). Barad's theory of intra-action supplants the human subject as the locus of both "knowing" and "ethicality": "We (but not only 'we humans') are always already responsible to the others with whom or which we are entangled, not through conscious intent but through the various ontological entanglements that materiality entails" (393). Attending to our ontological entanglements and "lively relationalities," which cannot be circumscribed or defined in advance, is a rather formidable ethical/epistemological enterprise that reconfigures commonsensical conceptual landscapes. A glimpse of just such an ethics appears in material memoirs, as their narrators grapple with what it means to know, to be, and to act, when one is literally part of the emergent material world.

I will conclude by mentioning one relatively new environmental organization, BlueVoice, which is dedicated to dolphins, whales, and the oceans. A document on its website entitled "A Shared Fate" states that the "contaminated ocean food web threatens the health of humans and marine animals alike." Another brief report on this site, authored by Brian G. M. Durie, a hematologist/oncologist, and Hardy Jones, a documentary filmmaker with the BlueVoice organization, states that studies "are now underway to correlate recent bioaccumulations in dolphins and humans": "Probability calculations for risk of developing myeloma will support interventions to reduce both contamination of the marine environment and elimination of human toxin exposures." Perhaps similar modes of activist science will help to unite environmental and environmental health movements, fostering a trans-corporeal ethics that links human and nonhuman animals in networks of advocacy and concern.[9] This sort of science, activism, and ethics may travel along with the "pilgrimage" that Steingraber imagines, in which "people with cancer [travel] to various bodies of water known to be inhabited by animals with cancer" to undertake "an assembly on the banks and shores of these waters and a collective consideration of our intertwined lives" (*Living Downstream* 145).

FIVE

Deviant Agents: The Science, Culture, and Politics of Multiple Chemical Sensitivity

The classical medical advice is avoidance, but if any place on this planet is chemical- and pollutant-free, I haven't found it.

—Jacob B. Berkson, *A Canary's Tale*

There is no expert on risk.

—Ulrich Beck, *Risk Society*

Whether it is a syndrome, illness, disability, disease, allergy, or psychosomatic condition, whether it is called multiple chemical sensitivity, environmental illness, chemical injury, chemical intolerance, total allergy syndrome, universal reactor syndrome, chemically induced immune disregulation, or even twentieth-century disease, the terminological maelstrom suggests that this medical, scientific, political, subcultural, and economic terrain is fiercely contested. Even as the National Institute of Environmental Health Sciences declares that the "preferred medical term is Idiopathic Environmental Intolerance (IEI)" ("idiopathic" marking uncertainty), a 2005 essay in *Chemical and Engineering News* asserts not only that "chemical intolerance" is the standard term, but that there is now a "widespread recognition that the vast majority of these patients are indeed sick and that their symptoms have something to do with chemical exposures" (Hillman 25). Multiple chemical sensitivity (MCS) or environmental illness (EI)[1] is a condition in which exposure to "normal" twenty-first-century environments and substances causes a range of reactions, including rashes, tremors, convulsions, breathing difficulties, headaches, dizziness, nausea, joint pain, "brain fog," and extreme fatigue. Multiple chemical sensitivity overlaps with Gulf War illness, sick building syndrome, and food intolerance syndrome. The scientific, medical, and popular accounts of this syndrome multiply and diverge; minoritizing accounts see it as a distinct illness, whereas universalizing accounts see it as something that afflicts us all, in various degrees. Some believe it causes, or is related to, cancer, autoimmune diseases, and other diseases, while others dismiss it outright as a psychosomatic, hysterical condition. There is no standard medical test for MCS/EI, nor even an established definition. The etiology is unknown. Various experts cited in Peter Radetsky's *Allergic to the Twentieth Century* posit that EI is caused by the trigeminal nerve, the limbic system, allergic reactions to chemicals, immune system disregulation, or a disturbance of cholinergic processes in the brain. Most provocatively, Radetsky cites one scientist, Claudia Miller, who claims that "toxin-induced loss of tolerance" (TILT) may well be an entirely new category of diseases (in the plural) on par with infectious diseases.

The "treatment" for MCS, which entails avoiding all offending substances, suggests how this condition epitomizes a trans-corporeal conception of the human and, at the same time, demonstrates how attention to the flows and interchanges between body and environment catalyze new modes of thinking about and being within the emergent material world. "Avoidance" requires no drugs, no surgeries, and no hospital stays—in fact, each of these standard medical treatments would only increase the patient's "toxic load."[2] Metaphorically "weighed down" by toxins, the bodies of the chemically reactive—which are extreme examples of the substantial selves discussed in the last chapter—have more in common with the permeable corporealities of nineteenth-century medicine than they do with the "modern bodies" of twentieth-century allopathic medicine, which are "composed of discrete parts and bounded by the skin" (Nash 11). And yet, environmental illness is a particularly twentieth- and twenty-first-century phenomenon, in part because of the avalanche of xenobiotic chemicals produced and disseminated in recent years. Moreover, the treatment for environmental illness thrusts the patient into the onto-epistemological terrain of contemporary risk society, where the ordinary citizen must assess a multitude of potential dangers—confronting vertiginous sources of information, colliding with objects and substances that seem to morph from benign to malignant. Since commonplace products and substances, such as pesticides, perfumes, vehicle emissions, fabric softeners, clothing, magazines, and carpeting, may trigger symptoms, a truly effective treatment for MCS would not be an individual matter but instead would entail a staggeringly thorough overhaul of nearly all military, industrial, manufacturing, agricultural, domestic, and consumer practices. As Radetsky contends, a "disease based on the contention that chemicals are bad for us threatens to unravel the fabric of our civilization—and the enormous profits gleaned from it" (167). Or, as Steve Kroll-Smith and H. Hugh Floyd put it, MCS may be nothing less than a "somatic indictment of modernity" (xi).

As a radical challenge to business as usual and as a corporeal condition that does not fit predominant medical models, EI presents potent possibilities for rethinking the boundaries of human bodies and the territory of "health." When Susan Sontag attempted to release illness from its service as a cultural metaphor, she contended not only that "illness is *not* a metaphor," but that "the most truthful way of regarding illness—and the healthiest way of being ill—is one most purified of, most resistant to, metaphoric thinking" (*Illness as Metaphor* 3). Whereas Sontag would like us to peel off the cultural overlay of metaphor to see the reality of disease, I propose that we dwell on the possibilities for a metonymic slide, a chain of material significations in which *"environmental* illness" extends the body outward into a trans-corporeal space. Such a body (or mind) cannot be distinguished from that which surrounds it, since various substances may provoke pain, illness, disability, confusion, and fatigue. As Kroll-Smith and Floyd put it, a "person with MCS examines points of intersection between her body and those places and things it is encountering. She is interested in the surface of her body and its points of contact with material culture" (104). Rhonda Zwillinger's collection of photos of people with MCS captures this sense of trans-corporeality by creating portraits that merge person, domestic space, and environment. Thus, environmental illness offers a particularly potent example of trans-corporeal space, in which the human body can never be disentangled from the material world, a world of biological creatures, ecosystems, and xenobiotic, humanly made substances.

Karen Barad's *Meeting the Universe Halfway: Quantum Physics and the Entanglement of Matter and Meaning* and Andrew Pickering's *The Mangle of Practice: Time, Agency, and Science*—in quite different ways—conceptualize the world as an emergent place of entangled material agencies. Pickering, for example, arguing against the notion that scientists "represent" the world, contends that the world "is continually *doing things,* things that bear upon us not as observation statements upon disembodied intellects but as forces upon material beings. Think of the weather" (6). Clearly, this is the world—a world that is constantly "doing things"—that those with MCS inhabit. The theories of Barad and Pickering are invaluable not only for making sense of how ordinary people experience this condition, but, more broadly, for developing the theoretical, ethical, and political ramifications of environmental illness in particular and bodily natures in general.

One of the most surprising things that emerges from an exploration of MCS is that, like xenobiotic chemicals, people deviate from their proper places: cultural critics seek material agencies rather than textual contestations, scientists dissolve materiality into metaphor, and ordinary people engage in the practice of "science." Chemically reactive people continually negotiate the intra-acting material agencies of every place, every stream of air, every food and personal care product that they encounter, experiencing their bodies as scientific instruments. Ironically, even as MCS is denounced as "immaterial" by the scientists who claim that it is a psychological not a medical problem, it has incited cultural theorists immersed in social constructionist paradigms to insist upon its unruly materiality. This unruly materiality can be understood as a kind of deviance, in the sense that bodies and human substances may depart from norms, standards, and models of prediction. This sense of deviance, which is put forth by Ladelle McWhorter, bears both utopian and dystopian dimensions, both biological and political force.

This chapter begins by considering whether or not MCS can be understood within the frameworks of environmental justice, which were explored earlier in this book. The rest of the chapter develops the theoretical positions outlined in chapter 1, regarding emerging models of materiality and the possibilities for trans-corporeal conceptions of the human, by exploring MCS as it is revealed and portrayed in science, cultural theory, autobiography, photography, and film. Multiple chemical sensitivity may well be the quintessential example of what I'm calling trans-corporeality, as those who are chemically reactive experience their selves as coextensive with the material world—an ever-emergent world of risky knowledges, mangled practices, and disturbing, potentially deviant material agencies.

Sex, Gender, Race, and Class: The Question of Environmental Justice

Environmental illness, because of the literal slide between substance and person, is, perhaps, the condition that epitomizes the paradigms of the environmental health movements discussed in the previous chapter. As we have already discussed, Linda Nash explains that the "ecological body" of environmental health movements is characterized by its "permeability," "a constant exchange between inside and outside, by fluxes and flows, and by its close dependence on the surrounding environment" (12). While the relationship between environmental illness and environmental health movements is clear, it is more difficult to determine whether or not it makes sense to consider environmental illness as an environmental justice issue. The standard rubrics of environmental justice—race, class, and sex—do not correspond in predictable ways to the distribution of environmental illness. According to an epidemiological study by Barbara A. Sorg, about 4% of the people in the United States suffer from severe MCS, while as many as 15–30% experience less severe symptoms.[3] Some claim that the majority of those with MCS are female.[4] Fiona Coyle, for example, states that 80% of those diagnosed with MCS are women (62). Biological factors, such as women's higher proportion of body fat, which retains many chemicals; the interactions between estrogen and chemicals; male-female immune system differences; and women's lower percentage of alcohol dehydrogenase, which breaks down toxins, may partly account for the sex difference (Gibson 476). Various gender-related practices, such as the use of cleaning products, perfumes, and cosmetics, may also contribute to the higher percentage of females who are chemically reactive.[5]

Apart from these rather debatable sex and gender disparities, it is also difficult to locate MCS within the usual socioeconomic and geographic maps of environmental justice. As discussed in chapter 3, in the United States, exposure to toxins correlates most directly with race, and then with class, as toxic waste sites, factories, and other sources are most often located near the neighborhoods of African Americans or other people of color. As the term *chemical injury* suggests, many people become ill through toxic workplaces, and those closest to the chemicals, such as factory workers and agricultural workers, face the most risk, suggesting that MCS is a class issue. Yet, some professionals, such as physicians, especially anesthesiologists, may also be at a higher risk for MCS. Thus, environmental justice models do not adequately capture the distribution of MCS. As Peter C. Van Wyck explains, drawing upon Ulrich Beck, "ecological threats construct a social cartography that is often, and largely, foreign to divisions such as class, property, and distribution and have a propensity to cut through social divisions, assembling new lines of affinity, new constituencies of those at risk" (91). Todd Haynes's film *Safe* dramatizes this new social cartography by focusing on Carol White, a wealthy Angla housewife who becomes severely ill. One scene portrays Carol at home with a domestic worker. As the fumes from the household toxins make the upper-class Carol increasingly ill, the Latina employee—who is in direct contact with the cleaning chemicals—remains unaffected, scrubbing away. Haynes, a smart and savvy filmmaker, marks the irony here.

And yet, it is not only the case that no one in industrialized culture is safe from MCS, but that affluence itself may multiply risks. Such things as *new* furniture, *new* carpeting, *new* clothing, fresh paint, dry-cleaning fumes, noxious fabric softeners, and all manner of cosmetic products are frequently the culprit. The more consumption and exposure, the more risk. To make things more complicated, race and class may factor differently for the symptoms of MCS versus the diagnosis of MCS. Stanley Caress and his colleagues conclude that MCS is evenly distributed across all categories of "race/ethnicity, age, household income, and educational level" ("Symptomology" 1). However, when these factors were cross-tabulated with people who had received an actual diagnosis of MCS from a physician, the results were striking: the vast majority of people who received a physician's diagnosis were white and the majority had some higher education (Caress, email).[6] It would make sense to conclude that, since "there are no agreed-upon criteria for defining EI as an official medical condition" and since physicians endure censure if they dare to make such a diagnosis (Kroll-Smith and Floyd 19), the route to the diagnosis category of MCS usually involves a fair amount of leisure time and other resources with which to conduct one's own research and search for a sympathetic physician. J. Dumit provocatively argues that MCS, and chronic fatigue syndrome, are "Illnesses You Have to Fight to Get," as he titles his 2006 article.

It takes resources not only to battle for a diagnosis, but to undergo treatment. Checking into one of the few EI treatment centers that exist, such as William Rea's Environmental Health Center in Dallas, Texas, costs thousands of dollars and would entail weeks of lost wages.[7] Moreover, although the primary treatment—avoidance—may sound inexpensive, the necessary air filters, water filters, organic clothes and bedding, organic food and personal care products are quite costly. Not to mention the costs of procuring a nontoxic home or making a home less toxic by replacing a gas stove with an electric one; replacing carpets, vinyl flooring, curtains, mattresses, and furniture; or, in more extreme cases, lining the walls with porcelain or aluminum. Most medical insurance covers costly cancer treatment, but it is not likely to pay for organic clothes or tile floors. When chemically reactive people cannot tolerate their workplaces or secure nontoxic housing, poverty, homelessness, and ravaged lives may result.[8] Thus, although EI departs from standard environmental justice models of the unequal distribution of risk, economic factors do affect access to information, diagnosis, treatment, employment, and housing. Most environmental justice struggles must demonstrate that particular places have exposed particular people to particular toxins. For those with MCS, however, nearly every human environment, even domestic space, is harmful.

Portraits of the Body-Space of Environmental Illness

The process of remaking one's domestic space blurs the commonsensical outlines of the human body, as one finds oneself vulnerable, or open, to ostensibly benign, utilitarian objects: a gas stove, a couch, a shower curtain. Suddenly, these things are no longer inert, but interact with one's body, causing particular symptoms.

Furniture made of particleboard, for example, may steadily release (or off-gas) formaldehyde, which may cause coughing, asthma attacks, skin rash, fatigue, severe allergic reactions, and cancer. (This may sound paranoid or comical, especially since it evokes the B-movie horror in which something benign becomes a killer: The Couch That Devoured Manhattan!) Even though it is standard medical practice to breach corporeal boundaries—with surgery, injections, transplants, dialysis, and other procedures—rarely does the medical model picture the human body as coextensive with the environment[9] or vulnerable to ostensibly inert objects, such as carpets or couches. And yet, those with EI vividly experience their contiguity with the material world and thus cannot be assured that anything is, or will remain, "external." Ironically, one psychiatric study in the *Journal of Nervous and Mental Disease* accounts for the phenomenon of MCS by labeling chemically reactive people as "externalizers" with "low private self-attentiveness." Constanze Hausteiner and his coauthors argue that these "'externalizers' could benefit from an intervention that teaches them to focus on their internal and emotional lives" (50). This treatment assumes that the healthy self is a rigidly enclosed, nonmaterial entity. Indeed, Hausteiner et al. partition corporeal experience from the self when they suggest that the "external attribution in EI might be reflected by a generally low self-attentiveness in contrast to the overestimation of physical sensations" (ibid.). Moreover, by fixing the blame on an individual's psyche, the treatment absolves government, industry, and indeed the entire material/political world from blame. By contrast, a forty-six-page report published in the *Journal of Nutritional and Environmental Medicine* concludes with a list of government recommendations (for the United Kingdom) for decreasing the population's exposure to xenobiotic chemicals (Eaton et al.). Rather than placing the onus upon individuals, this report points out that "individuals currently cannot choose to avoid chemical exposures, and even reducing them is both expensive and socially isolating" (27). People, in this report, are permeable beings enmeshed in a political/material world that they cannot avoid. Similarly, Janice Strubbe Wittenberg's provocatively titled book *The Rebellious Body: Reclaim Your Life from Environmental Illness or Chronic Fatigue Syndrome* asserts that "EI and CFS are symbols for what can happen when you take the world into your body" (274). (These "symbols" may be more accurately termed material metonyms, since EI results, literally, from taking the world into your body.) Seeing these illnesses as trans-corporeal catalyzes a self-help book in which political activism and personal healing are symbiotic. Strubbe Wittenberg advises people to undertake "activism," which includes healing oneself, educating oneself, engaging in green consumerism, voting for environmentally-oriented politicians, and writing letters to Congress.

Rhonda Zwillinger's book of photographs, *The Dispossessed: Living with Multiple Chemical Sensitivities,* captures the devastation wrought by extreme forms of MCS. Exhibiting disability is a risky enterprise because, as David Heavey argues in "The Enfreakment of Photography": "the photographic observation of disablement has increasingly become the art of categorization and surveillance" (36). While visual representations of disability risk becoming vehicles of surveillance, the lack of representations results in invisibility, especially for those with conditions that are not widely known or understood. Zwillinger's photos suggest the ongoing necessity for particular forms of identity politics (which, of course, can be a form of "categorization") for people who live with disputed illnesses.[10] Eriksen and Ursin, for example, dismiss MCS and other "complaints" on the grounds that "[t]here seem to be no sharp lines between what is a completely normal phenomenon, ignored by most people, and crippling conditions that require support, treatment, and can lead to disability" (3). (Oddly, for Eriksen and Ursin matters that exist on a continuum are excluded from mattering at all.) Zwillinger, who herself has MCS, portrays how severe forms of the illness profoundly alter people's lives. But her art also suggests the ontological shift that environmental illness entails; the photographs capture how EI dissolves something so basic to the sense of what it is to be human—a sense of being a discrete entity, separate from one's environs.

Since MCS is a hidden disability, nothing visually distinguishes the bodies of those who are chemically reactive. Most of the people gaze into the camera with solid, somewhat confrontational expressions, perhaps anticipating the viewer's skepticism or scorn. Each photograph is accompanied by a first-person narration, most of which begin with the catalyst for the illness. Most stories conclude by describing how and where each person lives; many must live outdoors, in tents, or in specially modified vans or porcelain-lined trailers. Thus, it is not the individual bodies and their symptoms that are of interest here, but rather the environment, broadly speaking. Unlike conventional portraits, the backgrounds are foregrounded and the subjects seem a bit marginal. Sometimes, an air mask obscures the subject's face. In the portrait of "Katherine D.," for example, the subject is hardly visible at all, as she sits within a dark sauna in the background. (See figure 5.1.) This photo suggests a sense of isolation and immobility, as its subject is contained within the frame of the sauna, while a child happily rides out of the frame on her bike. Even when the faces of the subjects are visible, their expressions reveal little about their interior lives. These photos are less about identity and more about the practices of habitation, replacing the question "who is this person?" with "how does this person manage to live?" The portrait of "Kelly S.," for example, reveals that she must live and sleep with a jumble of belongings in the narrow space of a carport because, as her interview explains, her rented house is not "chemically safe" for her. (See figure 5.2.) This photo depicts the gravity of her condition, as Kelly S. is not only hooked to an oxygen tank outdoors, but

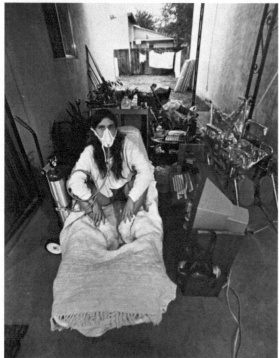

Figure 5.1. Above. "Katherine D." © 1998 Rhonda Zwillinger, from *The Dispossessed: Living with Multiple Chemical Sensitivities.*

Figure 5.2. Left. "Kelly S." © 1998 Rhonda Zwillinger, from *The Dispossessed: Living with Multiple Chemical Sensitivities.*

inhabits a hybrid indoor/outdoor space that is devoid of any aesthetic relief (no mountains or desert flora are in view). Furthermore, the personal belongings of Kelly S. hardly suggest the comforts of home, but instead they loom as the rather ominous detritus of late twentieth-century life. The photo suggests an inescapable irony as well, in that the ostensibly safe place that Kelly S. has cobbled together is nonetheless crowded with things that may well be hazardous.

As the portraits expand into landscapes, person and place converge. The viewer learns to read the inhabited landscapes as biographies of people who experience continual interchanges with their environments. It is difficult to locate "Janet M." in her portrait, for example, as she takes up very little space within a shot largely composed of the desert landscape, trailer homes, and the mountain. (See figure 5.3.) Tellingly, Janet M. poses on the threshold between the interior of her trailer, with its door open, and the wild desert plants in the foreground, suggesting that person, home, and environment are coextensive. Whereas portraits usually assume a clear demarcation of their subjects, Zwillinger brilliantly depicts human landscapes in which people blend into their living spaces, underscoring that, for people with environmental illness, places are never merely background. The photo "Arlene M., Larry M.," for example, shows a couple clad in white, sitting on white sheets, against white walls, nearly indistinguishable from their home. (See figure 5.4.) The photo references the famous Lennon-Ono "Bed In" for peace, importing a sense of hope and political activism into this seemingly empty environment.[11] One of the most striking characteristics of this collection as a whole is that the photos often confound distinctions between outside and inside, nature and domestic space, as they depict a mattress positioned out-of-doors, a backyard full of clothes and mail hanging to air out, a jumble of personal belongings huddled under a carport, and people posed next to or on the thresholds of the tents, automobiles, and trailers that serve as makeshift domestic spaces, floating within the expanse of southwestern deserts.

Zwillinger's compelling photographs of people inhabiting these "deviant" spaces conjure what cannot be seen: the pernicious spaces of "normal" human habitation that are riddled with toxins. These photographs function as an anti-spectacle, dispersing the surprise of the deviant to the normal, asking us to see, smell, or imagine the invisible toxins that permeate everyday life. Thus, Zwillinger's photos of the living spaces of those with MCS ultimately question the safety of normal, early twenty-first-century human habitats. The deviant spaces she represents have a political bite, as they insist upon the permeable boundaries of the individual.

Medical models of bounded human bodies make no sense for MCS, since the body is not separable from the environment, but disability models of accessibility, which focus on space and mobility, may provide a productive avenue of

Figure 5.3. "Janet M., MCS Community, Taos, New Mexico."
© 1998 Rhonda Zwillinger, from *The Dispossessed: Living with Multiple Chemical Sensitivities.*

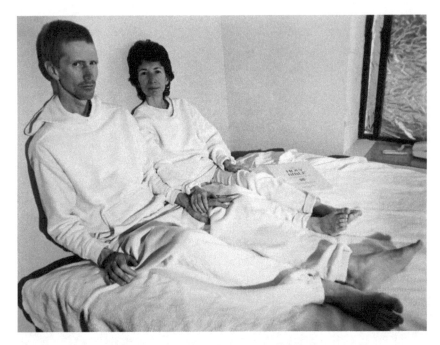

Figure 5.4. "Arlene M., Larry M." © 1998 Rhonda Zwillinger, from
The Dispossessed: Living with Multiple Chemical Sensitivities.

approach. Steve Kroll-Smith and H. Hugh Floyd claim that, because "the issue of
disabilities attends to functions and not cause," the chemically reactive are gain-
ing more recognition from the legal system than from the medical system (165).
Making public spaces accessible for chemically sensitive people would benefit
everyone.[12] Thus, the minoritizing, or disability model, which addresses the most
severe cases of MCS, can be complemented by broader, universalizing models in
which the ubiquitous xenobiotics of the twenty-first century threaten us all. Even
such universalizing arguments, however, are ultimately too humanist to account
for the traffic in toxins that ravage not only people but also animals, plants, and
entire ecosystems. Thus, MCS or, more appropriately in this context, *environmental illness,* needs to be allied not only with disability rights movements, but
with anti-toxin, environmental, and environmental justice movements in order
to forge an expansive, interwoven, material politics in which the political does
not become the merely personal. Rhonda Zwillinger's photos, as they intermesh
person, home, and wider environment, suggest how MCS requires that we rethink
the boundaries of our persons as well as our notions of safety and normalcy. The
chemically reactive manifest a corporeality that is always already trans-corpo-

real, as they help us to envision the invisible movement of xenobiotic substances across human bodies and more-than-human nature. Even as people with MCS engage in various boundary practices in order to create safe spaces, their constant vigilance demonstrates that ultimately no place is safe.[13] Such a realization recasts human health as a matter of environmental health, broadly conceived—as the human is substantially coextensive with the rest of the world.

Locating Materiality: Venom, Genes, and Cultural Theory

The scientific debates about the existence of MCS continue. Stephen Barrett, M.D., for example, includes MCS on his "Quackwatch" website. The National Institute of Environmental Health Sciences' website reports that, at an environmental health sciences meeting, "there was an old-fashioned debate on MCS and the proponents who believed that it was simply a psychiatric disorder won the debate!" The "simply" here not only discounts the testimony of people with MCS, but renders psychological conditions strangely immaterial. It is not surprising that various xenobiotic substances can produce psychological effects, since some of them affect neurological systems. Those who label MCS as a psychiatric condition, however, do so in order to contend that MCS is not a "real," physical illness. An article in the *Journal of Psychosomatic Research*, for example, argues that the "only limitation on the types of physical symptoms presented by the patient may be the patient's own imagination and knowledge about physical illnesses" (Eriksen and Ursin 5). Even though Eriksen and Ursin discuss the neurological mechanisms of sensitization and limbic kindling, which would seem to emphasize the materiality of MCS, they ultimately render MCS and similar conditions as strangely nonmaterial, concluding that there is no point in searching for a "nonexistent organic disease." They even begrudge these patients the term "symptoms," preferring to downgrade the phenomena to "complaints." Similarly, an article in *Toxicology Letters* by Hermann M. Bolt and Ernst Kiesswetter concludes that "MCS is not a conventional toxicological phenomenon," because it is not, poetically speaking, "the venom of the spider" that causes the effect but, quoting Shakespeare, "the 'infection of the knowledge'" (105). This metaphor not only dispels the materiality of this syndrome by making it a (mere) mental problem, but transforms myriad and diffuse environmental substances, which threaten, in part, because of the profound onto-epistemological problems that they pose, into the tangible, distinct figure of the venomous spider. (One can usually avoid, capture, compassionately relocate, or squash a spider—but how does an individual detect or avoid mercury in the air?) Dismissing MCS as a mere psychological problem is particularly odd in an age when the rapid increase in the use of psychopharmaceutical drugs jumbles mind/body, mental/material dichotomies. As Nicholas Ashford and Claudia Miller put it, patients with MCS whose symptoms have been "attributed to psychiatric causes" "wonder how psychiatrists, who routinely use minute doses of chemicals called *drugs* to effectuate behavior, fail to recognize that chemicals in the air or foods can impact the brain or cause marked behavioral changes" (114). The rather cavalier disregard for MCS as a material illness, with biological as well as psychological effects, may be tinged with misogyny, if the majority of those who are chemically reactive are, or are perceived to be, mere "complaining" women. In this instance, it is hardly progressive to discount the biology of MCS in favor of social constructionist or psychological models. Instead, it makes more sense to consider, along with Elizabeth Wilson, how "feminism can be deeply and happily complicit with biological explanation" (*Psychosomatic* 14).

Not surprisingly, chemical manufacturers fund some of this dismissive research. According to an article in *Rachel's Environment and Health Weekly,* "Corporate Manipulation of Scientific Evidence Linking Chemical Exposures to Human Disease": "The pesticide corporations have formed their own cigarette-science group called RISE (Responsible Industry for a Sound Environment). RISE is made up of executives from companies like Monsanto, Sandoz Agro, Dow-Elanco, DuPont Agricultural Products, The Scotts Company, and other pesticide manufacturers, formulators, and distributors." Most notoriously, Dr. Ronald Gots, who provides expert testimony on behalf of industry, contends that MCS is a psychological not a medical condition, calling it "a peculiar manifestation of our technophobic and chemophobic society" (quoted in "Corporate Manipulation").[14] Although Gots implies that irrational technophobic beliefs conjure up MCS, Caress's epidemiological study reports the contrary. He and his colleagues found that only 1.4% of their subjects "reported experiencing depression, anxiety, or other emotional problems prior to the onset of their hypersensitivity to chemicals." They suggest that the "emergence of emotional difficulties subsequent to hypersensitivity could be the result of physical symptoms so disruptive that they produce substantial emotional problems" or that they could result "from exposure to toxic agents that affect brain functions related to mood and emotions" ("Symptomology" 4–5). Similarly, Chris Winder, in a careful, comprehensive review of recent scientific research, explains why the many psychological explanations (of autosuggestion, conditioned response, malingering, and psychosomatic condition) are unlikely. He answers a key question in MCS research—why would some people be affected by such low doses of toxins?—by explaining that "[o]ne of the problems in dealing with toxic material is that if dose-response information is available, it usually refers to high level exposures at the upper end of the relationship, as effects are more likely to be evident" (86). The study of the "biological effects of low level exposures" may be an "important emerging area of toxicology" (ibid.), but chemical companies and other industries will probably not be so enthusiastic about this trend, since it focuses attention on the peskier side of the bell curve. Where science, law, and medicine make the cut—a demarcation that deems one side safe and the other harmful—has staggering political, economic, environmental, and ethical ramifications. The subtitle of Nicholas A. Ashford and Claudia S. Miller's book puts it succinctly: *Low Levels and High Stakes.*

Even though the mechanisms of EI are still highly debated, genetic studies of this syndrome are already under way. Gail McKeown-Eyssen and her colleagues undertook a study to determine "whether there are genetic differences in xenobiotic metabolism" (972), in other words, whether chemically reactive people have significant genetic differences that affect the metabolism of toxic chemicals. Focusing on the CYP2D6 enzyme, which is "known to activate and inactivate toxins and endogenous neurochemicals," they found that "individuals with higher CYP2D6 activity . . . are at increased risk for MCS compared with individuals with two non-functional alleles" (971, 975). They also found that this particular enzyme may interact with another (NAT2) "to substantially increase risk for MCS beyond the risk that is observed for each gene alone" (977). Genetic research is both promising and perilous. On the positive side, genetic research may help to uncover the mechanisms of MCS. In addition, the current cultural potency of "the gene" and its ability to signify what is scientifically deemed to be "real," may help MCS to gain wider cultural and medical legitimacy. Ironically, however, environmental illness, which could potentially breach the medical model of discrete, bounded bodies and encourage a trans-corporeal environmental ethic, may be constrained by the double helix of discrete, identifiable entities called "genes." Science studies scholars have criticized predominant conceptions of genes as isolated agents, disconnected from their environment.[15] Evelyn Fox Keller, for example, in *The Century of the Gene,* states, "The image of genes as clear and distinct causal agents, constituting the basis of all aspects of organismic life, has become so deeply embedded in both popular and scientific thought that it will take far more than good intentions, diligence, or conceptual critique to dislodge it" (136). The prevalent discourse of genetic agency may make the "environment" of environmental illness fade into immateriality. Labeling chemically reactive people as genetically defective places the onus on bad genes, instead of on injurious chemical, industrial, military, and governmental practices—a conclusion which has many economic, legal, and political implications. Giovanna Di Chiro explores a similar scenario in her disturbing essay "Producing 'Roundup Ready®' Communities? Human Genome Research and Environmental Justice Policy." Di Chiro explains that the Environmental Genome Project plans to catalog the genetic variances that "may render certain populations 'more susceptible to, or more resistant to, substances they may encounter at work, at home, or more generally, in the environment'" (142). As Di Chiro demonstrates, the discourse of this project "assumes we will live with environmental toxins—it naturalizes environmental toxicity and pathologizes some genomic subsets of the human population" (146).

Rather than engaging in a genetic reductionism that has pernicious environmental and social consequences, it is possible to undertake scientific studies that disclose gene-environment interactions. Sara Shostak explains that genetic epidemiology, molecular epidemiology, and toxicogenomics underscore the "importance of gene-environment interaction in the production of human health and illness" ("Locating Gene-Environment Interaction" 2338):

> [T]he promise of the study of gene-environment interaction is in its direction of scientific, biomedical, and public health attention simultaneously *inward*, towards the gene/genome and the interior of the body, and *outward*, towards particular practices, places and the exposures they contain and enable. Insofar as it places the reductionist paradigm of molecular genetics within the context of place, this dual focus helps to elucidate the inextricability of the biological and the social. (2328)

If the direction of genetic research is simultaneously inward and outward or, in my terms, trans-corporeal, scientists may be able to capture the ways in which the agencies of the body always interact with the substances and agencies of particular places. Research on gene-environment interaction may illuminate the phenomenon of MCS and, at the same time, expose the dangers of particular places, substances, products, industries, and labor practices.

The debate over whether MCS is a psychological or a medical condition is, of course, an argument about whether or not this illness is "real." Those who argue that MCS is psychosomatic not only conceive of the mind as strangely immaterial, but they sever the psyche, as well as the rest of the person, from the broader environment. Other scientists, such as toxicologists, neurologists, immunologists, and genetic researchers, search for the biological mechanisms that result in an intolerance to small doses of toxins. The fact that there is no medical treatment for MCS—certainly not drugs or surgery—means that it does not fit well within a medical model, and thus those practicing within standard medical paradigms may doubt its reality precisely because of that ill fit. Ironically, while those in science and medicine debate the material existence of EI, some cultural critics, immersed in models of social construction that tend to minimize the productive capacities of materiality, see it as breaking through those paradigms via corporeal agency. Environmental illness, in other words, provokes heretical departures from social construction by dramatizing material agency and corporeal ways of knowing.

Michelle Murphy's provocative article, "The 'Elsewhere within Here' and Environmental Illness; or, How to Build Yourself a Body in a Safe Space," admits that "[n]avigating the political tangles that ensnare writing about an abjected illness like MCS has been tricky, for the tools of social constructivism and cultural studies will not always perform in the interest of those with whom [her] political sympathies lie" (91). She explains, "historical and cultural accounts have tended to presuppose that an illness's historicity is inversely proportional to its reality"; thus, cultural construction performs a "delegitimizing or 'dematerializing' function" (ibid.). Murphy, however, puts forth a constructivist account that, "instead of chipping away, affirms the 'materiality'" of MCS (93). Murphy demonstrates, for example, the material agencies of bodies and built environments when she explains their "mutual constitution": "bodies reacting to the environment render it pathogenic, and the environment impinging on bodies renders them ill" (98). Murphy also imagines something akin to what I term trans-corporeality, when she expands the category of "ecology" to include "not simply moving from nature to a corporeal scale, but extending from the built environment through the skin" (110). Murphy's fine essay serves as a model for "relentlessly materialist" (119) science studies. Despite her use of the term *ecology*, however, Murphy contains most of her analysis within built environments, which risks diminishing the broader ecological ramifications of this disease.

Sociologists Steve Kroll-Smith and H. Hugh Floyd, in *Bodies in Protest: Environmental Illness and the Struggle over Medical Knowledge*, boldly emphasize the deviant corporeal agencies of those who are chemically reactive. They gathered their accounts of MCS via questionnaires, interviews, illness biographies, medical studies, and observation of a support group. One of the most compelling aspects of their argument is the extent to which they portray the agency of human bodies. Taking up Ulrich Beck's claim that "consciousness determines being," they argue that we should also acknowledge that "somatic states and conditions are shaping consciousness" (10). They posit, "the chemically reactive believe their bodies know things" (132). Moreover, MCS performs a mode of corporeal agency in that "bodies resist being the objects of biomedical theory" (97). Rather than censure this conception of corporeal agency by assuming that it requires a cognizance or intentionality that is incompatible with our notions of the body, we can read it as one particularly compelling instance of the possibilities for reconceiving materiality as itself agential. Karen Barad, in *Meeting the Universe Halfway*, develops a theory of "agential realism," in which "*matter is substance in its intra-active becoming—not a thing but a doing, a congealing of agency*" (151; emphasis in original). Agency does not require (or permit) a subject, rather "agency is a matter of intra-acting; it is an enactment, not something that someone or something has. It cannot be designated as an attribute of subjects or objects (as they do not preexist as such)" (ibid., 178). "Intra-action," unlike "interaction," denies the "prior existence of independent entities" (139). The bodies of chemically reactive people epitomize this sense of "intra-active becoming": "Humans are part of the world-body space in its dynamic structuration" (185).

Although Barad's theory, based on the philosophical physics of Niels Bohr, may seem worlds apart from an ordinary person's experience of MCS, it provides a potent onto-epistemology that helps us to make sense of the striking trans-corporeality of those who are chemically reactive. Furthermore, Barad's sense of material ethics seems to emanate from the peculiar predicament of those with MCS, since it urges us to take account "of the entangled materializations of which we are a part" (384). Chemically reactive people would likely appreciate a mode of ethics that does not preclude material entanglements—no matter how small or seemingly benign—from accountability.

Capturing Material Agency

As if responding to Lawrence Buell's contention that "toxic discourse" "is a dis-course of allegation or insinuation rather than proof" (*Writing* 48), the chemi-cally reactive submit the "proof" of their bodily reactions within a peculiar sort of (auto)biographical genre that seems more "scientific" than personal. The bare-bones listing of sequences of cause and effect may seek legitimacy through mimicking the scientific voice of "objective knowledge." This genre may also serve as a primer for life with MCS. Kroll-Smith and Floyd, provocatively, see MCS as a "practical epistemology—a strategy for knowing the world that works to reduce or make manageable a human trouble" (11). Kroll-Smith and Floyd's illuminating conception of MCS as a "practical epistemology" may be extended by way of Andrew Pickering's model of the "mangle" of (scientific) practice. Ac-counting for material agency, Pickering explains that much "of everyday life . . . has this character of coping with material agency, agency that comes at us from outside the human realm and that cannot be reduced to anything within that realm" (6). Against a representational model that opposes discourse and material reality, Pickering contends that scientific practice "captures" material agency. He explains how as "active, intentional beings, scientists tentatively construct some new machine. Then they adopt a passive role, monitoring the performance of the machine to see whatever capture of material agency it might effect" (21). The person with MCS may be understood as a sort of scientist, actively seek-ing knowledge about material agencies, and, simultaneously, as the instrument that registers those agencies. In MCS (auto)biographies, the body often appears as something akin to a scientific instrument, in that daily life becomes a sort of experiment: what happens when I go there, breathe that, touch this? In the foreword to Zwillinger's *The Dispossessed,* for example, Gunnar Heuser, M.D., writes that the "sensitivities" of people with MCS "in a way constitute very finely tuned instruments which can measure potentially toxic chemicals at very low levels" (4). Lynn Lawson, noting that the vast majority of industrial chemicals have never been tested for their long-term health effects, concludes: "Actually, of course, we are doing the testing. All of us, but especially those with environmental illness/multiple chemical sensitivities" (340). As Murphy puts it, for those with EI, "symptoms are not the signs of an underlying disease hidden within the body: symptoms provide MCSers with material information about the way various dimensions of their body ecologies are interacting. Symptoms are just as much indicators of what is going on in the environment, as they are indicators of health" (115). And, as Kroll-Smith and Floyd explain, "[P]eople with EI experience their bodies as sources of unmediated knowledge; importantly, they act toward that knowledge as if it were rational, that is, legitimate" (93). The "data" gathered from one's own corporeal intra-actions swirl together with information and frameworks taken from Western medicine, alternative medicine, law, science, environmentalism, green consumerism, and MCS subcultures.

The peculiar (auto)biographies of those with MCS have become a recognizable genre, featuring descriptions of toxins followed by descriptions of their effects. The sometimes eerie material/metonymic slide between toxic substance and self intimates an emerging ontology in which those with MCS are forced to see themselves as interconnected with their environs. Elizabeth Schuster, for example, describes walking into a room: "I had a panic-type reaction because it was one of those chemicals that I can feel moving into my brain and grabbing on, and it won't let go. One that affects me for three, four, five days" (quoted in McCormick 25). "Rand," a lawyer, reports that his "initial problems with perfume and diesel exhaust have exploded almost exponentially":

New books, new carpet, new paint, anything with phenol or formaldehyde, any pesticide or herbicide, everything from cassette tapes to car exhaust to the big bugaboo—cigarette smoke. Not just nuisance smells, these are agents that attack me with a sudden fury that can leave me totally disoriented, emotionally explosive, and utterly exhausted. (quoted in Johnson 201)

Each of Steen Hansen Hviid's paragraph-long "personal stories" of eighteen patients at the Environmental Health Center in Dallas details specific physical effects of numerous substances. Such accounts can only be written after one has concluded that one suffers from MCS, since without that epistemological frame, no one would ever imagine including such things as copy machines, perfume, or insecticides in one's autobiography or medical history. Lynn Lawson's "Notes from a Human Canary" employs a double-voiced discourse in which she recounts, with ironic hindsight, her own lack of awareness: "I remember playing, fascinated, with the mercury of a broken thermometer" (333). And even though she was an "ardent environmentalist" in the 1970s, writing papers about auto pollution and pesticides, she "failed to connect [her] headaches to those issues" (334). Jean MacKenzie writes with the dual perspective typical to the bildungsroman, of the knowing adult and the naïve youth:

> Early on, at about age fourteen, I had skin reactions to things like elastic and that sort of thing. I had worked a summer job as a silk presser in a dry cleaning establishment, and things began to bother me increasingly. Later I was doing window dressings and signs, and that involved a lot of solvents. I didn't realize what I was doing to myself. And I began to have a lot of trouble. Of course I never knew what it was. (quoted in McCormick 216)

The MCS bildungsroman is strangely material, with solvents and elastic as the antagonists—antagonists which, ultimately, permeate the self. Social relations fade in these eerie accounts, as the most influential forces in the authors' medical/environmental/life histories are objects and substances, commonplace matters that would escape notice were it not for a conception of MCS.

Receiving or claiming a diagnosis of MCS helps people to make sense of their baffling condition, offering them tangible things they can do to improve their health. But because there is no test for MCS and because its symptoms vary tremendously, procuring a diagnosis is no simple matter. Eric Hunting, on his harrowing website, which is both a compelling autobiography of an autodidact and an urgent plea for a safe place to live, contends that the "pattern of impoverishment through diagnosis chasing is one of the chief causes of homelessness among EI sufferers." "Diagnosis chasing" is a standard plot in longer MCS narratives, as many people seek help from a variety of physicians, psychologists, and psychiatrists, often to no avail. The turning point in the diagnosis plot usually comes when the person with EI happens to learn something from an unofficial source, such as a magazine, or a television story, or someone they happen to meet. While most people embrace a found framework, "Jeff," an industrial plant worker, created his own analogies "to help him understand [his] illness better, like fumeaholic [and] chemicalism." He rejected the need for authoritative discourse: "You don't have to open up a big two-foot book to try to explain why this stuff bothers me, you know. This is a tolerance thing, it's all about what you can tolerate" (quoted in Johnson 56). Denied workers' comp because doctors deemed him fine, denied legal recourse because of a corrupt lawyer, and denied even the names of the chemicals to which he was exposed while working in an eight-foot-deep pit (the company called them a "trade secret"), it is not surprising that he has become disenchanted with the power/knowledge systems symbolized by that big book.

The most captivating account of diagnosis chasing comes from Jacob B. Berkson, in his self-published book, *A Canary's Tale,* which documents nine years of life with MCS. Berkson, a former military man and lawyer, narrates his tale in crisp, no-nonsense, unadorned prose, with notes of irony, sarcasm, and dark humor. Like most descriptions of life with EI, *A Canary's Tale* begins by describing the initial cause of the illness: their home was sprayed with Dursban to kill termites. When Berkson and his wife have the drapes dry-cleaned to get rid of the lingering Dursban, readers hip to the anti-toxin subculture will notice the irony. Like other EI narratives, this tale details the frustrating and near-futile attempts to find a nontoxic place to live. He tries, at first, to live and work in a tent in his backyard, driving to the local YMCA every time he has to use the bathroom—but this is "not convenient" (30).

Dramatizing the assiduous struggle to make sense of his condition, Berkson includes medical, toxicological, and air-sampling test results as well as discussions with public health officials, allergists, toxicologists, a psychiatrist, and a wide range of physicians. The book's form, especially the extremely brief chapters, accentuates the confusing, piecemeal, episodic nature of his pursuit of knowledge. Berkson's minimalist, deadpan, darkly ironic style suggests, in a modernist fashion, the lack of moorings in this epistemological struggle. Moorings are swept away in the first few chapters, which question the wisdom of authorities. After documenting his initial suffering, Berkson includes a long excerpt from a Dow Chemical ad that touts Dursban as "the worry-free, peace of mind termiticide," assuring the consumer that "you can breathe easy." Berkson ends that chapter by commenting wryly, "If you can't believe Dow Chemical, one of the largest international petrochemical corporations in the world, who can you believe?" (14) only to begin the next chapter describing how the public health officer of the community (an M.D.) assures him that Dursban is safe. The absurdity rebounds when the same public health officer seems unable to recognize that the larger historical, political, and economic context unravels these declarations of safety. The official explains that Dursban is a replacement for Chlordane, which "[t]hey found out was a carcinogen" (16). Although the M.D. notes that Dursban has "only been on the market for a short time" (15), he seems unable to recognize that his guarantee of safety has fallen into an abyss of doubt. What, one wonders, will "they" find out about Dursban? Only time will tell.[16] When Berkson, who is still terribly ill, receives the air-sampling report on his house (which cost him more than a thousand dollars), he concludes this brief chapter, his dark irony intact: "The good news was that I now had a written report from scientific experts who had sampled the air and concluded that the house was safe" (45).

The voice of reason, in these first few chapters, comes not from an established authority, but from a contractor Berkson dubs "Dog," who gives him his first clue that something may be awry. He tells Berkson that he used to be an exterminator but quit because he "couldn't stand the stink of the chemicals!" (10):

"I got sick every day. I became confused, light-headed, nauseous, and then I had trouble with my vision and I started getting tremors. . . ."

"Dog, you mean to tell me those chemicals are dangerous to the people who work with them?"

"You bet your sweet ass! Those suckers are poison. They not only kill the bugs but they'll knock out your nervous system and make you sick as hell."

"I had no idea."

"I'm surprised a smart lawyer like you don't know that exposure to toxic chemicals can make you sick. . . . Boy, your house really stinks." (ibid.)

Dog makes the "smart lawyer" as well as the widespread, blasé use of pesticides look foolish. The conversation suggests that such ignorance—that denies common sense and experience—must be deliberately manufactured. The next chapter notes that neither the V.A. doctor nor the family physician suggested that Berkson leave his house, thereby underscoring the sense that his corporeal experience provides the most reliable evidence. Despite his razor-sharp critique of industry, science, and the medical establishment, Berkson continues to chase down a diagnosis, consulting, as he puts it, "an internist, gastroenterologist, psychiatrist, urologist, otolaryngologist, and a partridge in a pear tree" (87). He must contend not only with a variety of misdiagnoses, but with the absurd moments that can result when a layperson tries to decipher medical discourse. When, for example, he is diagnosed with "campylobacter pylori," he looks up the definition only to find that it is a venereal disease of cattle: "I knew damn well I had not been having sex with any goddamn sheep or cow" (88). He had read the wrong "campylobacter" definition.

Despite these difficulties, Berkson persists in tracking down more information about MCS. The quest for knowledge drives this narrative: what began as a personal story ends up being a compendium of information about pollution, environmentally induced disease, the legal status of MCS, sick building syndrome, Gulf War syndrome, and other environmental struggles. Volume 2 of *A Canary's Tale* is a 150-page bibliography not only on MCS, but on pollution and environmental public policy, culminating in a political "call to action." Although Berkson writes in a distinctive voice, one learns little about him, really, as his personal account extends into a vast network of knowledge, power, and activism, the "memoir" hijacked by long quotations from books, magazines, scientific essays, and his own medical records. One gets a vivid sense of the messy search for knowledge—knowledge that is crucial for survival. *A Canary's Tale* may well be the *Moby-Dick* of MCS, or even risk society more generally, in that it dramatizes a passionate, sometimes ironic, epistemological quest in an experimental form. Even as Berkson learns from his own corporeal reactions and the accounts of others, and even as he must contend with the ignorance or disbelief of many a medical professional, the point of his quest is not simply to critique science and medicine, but to get to the truth of the matter. Like Bruno Latour, he seeks to *add* "reality to matters of fact and not *subtract* reality" ("Why Has Critique Run Out of Steam? 232). Berkson needs scientific information to help him navigate his daily life. As Ulrich Beck explains, within a risk society, "the extent and the symptoms of people's endangerment are fundamentally *dependent on external knowledge*" (53; emphasis in original). Yet Beck's paradigm works only partially for those with MCS, since the need for external knowledge is inextricably intertwined with the ongoing experience of one's own body as it captures the agencies of the material world, a world that always intra-acts with one's emerging, corporeal self.

Berkson's quest for knowledge mushrooms, as domestic space, ordinary consumer practices, nonhuman natures, and human bodies intermingle. He realizes, for example, that it would be a mistake to consider his own health as a matter solely within the domain of the "human." Early on, after Dog tells him that pesticides not only kill bugs, but harm people, Berkson learns from a toxicologist that Dursban is a cholinesterase inhibitor and that "[c]holinesterase is some kind of enzyme that is essential for the nervous system to work properly" (36). "She seemed to be saying that termites and people are reliant upon the same—cholinesterase—for the health of the nervous system" (37). This may be no surprise to a biologist, but for an ordinary consumer who can't imagine life without pesticides, it is an astounding discovery. Realizing that one's own biological substance is not unlike that of a termite thrusts one into a trans-corporeal space. It is no surprise, then, that Berkson sees environmental illness as a phenomenon that demands not only more scientific and medical knowledge but more environmentally-oriented policies and practices.

Berkson's quest to figure out his own debilitating condition expands into a vast environmental health manifesto. *Detoxify or Die* by Sherry Rogers, M.D., moves in the opposite direction: she casts environmental illness as a nearly universal condition but ultimately shrinks the crisis down to the size of a pill. *Detoxify or Die* argues that "environmental toxins cause all human disease" (89). Rogers catalogs how various toxins cause specific problems, such as "[c]admium accumulation from seafood, dental work, or auto and incinerator exhausts can trigger osteoporosis, back pain, high blood pressure, hip pain, arthritis, kidney disease, BPH, chronic fatigue, [and] cancer" (90). A thoroughly environmental corporeality emerges from this account: bodies are not self-contained units; all are permeable, accumulating the various toxins that disseminate from innumerable sources. The devastating critique of the medical, pharmaceutical, and chemical industries proffered by this universalizing account of MCS is, unfortunately, tamed by Rogers's quasi-religious solutions. She advocates an expensive detoxification regimen in which one purchases a shelf full of antioxidants and phytonutrients that were, in her discourse, *specially created by God himself* to save us from industrialized society. It is an odd theology, indeed, in which the rather unpoetic antioxidant glutathione becomes the means of salvation! Even though Rogers cites the statistic that "27% of dead whales recovered from the St. Lawrence River . . . have cancer," which is the same percentage as that for humans, proving that "we are all a product of our polluted environment" (315), she does not consider that the "detoxify or die" solution is worthless for wild creatures, since they can purchase neither her book nor massive amounts of glutathione. Indeed, the individualistic and consumerist solution she offers is sublimated into a digital theology, as she concludes with her hope that the book has given "you a small appreciation for the magnificence of the natural, God-given healing capability that has been programmed into you" (ibid.). The "you" here is born of a digitized Genesis, not an ongoing evolutionary process in which species emerge from ongoing intra-actions with their environment.

Environmental illness provides a potent site from which to reconceptualize human corporeality as coextensive with the rest of the world. Emerging theories of material agency, especially those of Andrew Pickering and Karen Barad, offer compelling posthumanist models for reconceiving both corporeality and more-than-human nature. We all inhabit the "mangle of practice" in Pickering's terms, and we are all, according to Barad, "part of the world in its differential becoming" (*Meeting the Universe Halfway* 85). These accounts of emergent, intertwined, mangled, material agencies serve as antidotes to Sherry Rogers's vision in which detached, stable substances can save us from the world. Indeed, the agencies involved in environmental illness are as confounding as those of Barad's theory, in which there are, ultimately, no separate "things," and all matter acts and intra-acts in the ongoing "differential mattering" of the world. A material ethics may emerge from this trans-corporeal space, an ethics that is centered neither in individual humans nor in an external nature, but instead in the flows and interchanges between them.

No Place Is *Safe*

Jacob B. Berkson's *Canary's Tale* documents how an ostensibly private medical condition can provoke seemingly limitless forays into science, medicine, environmentalism, and political activism. Conversely, Todd Haynes's film *Safe* demonstrates how easily the vast environmental and political implications of MCS can become corralled into an echo chamber of psychological affirmations. Denying the trans-corporeality of MCS compresses it into a merely personal problem.

As mentioned above, *Safe* follows a suburban housewife, Carol White, who becomes violently ill when exposed to such things as automotive exhaust, a new couch, or dry-cleaning fumes. The black couch is introduced with sounds of horror that seem out of proportion for a piece of furniture.[17] Haynes, in his compelling liner notes for the DVD, explains, "Right away we are asking ourselves 'what is this really about?' . . . Immediately we are concerned with substances, the substance of Carol's life, the substances affecting her health, the substance of the film itself" (Haynes, *Safe*, DVD liner). Whether or not MCS is substantial, that is, whether it is a real material condition in which substances provoke corporeal effects, is debated by both the film's characters and its viewers.[18]

After being patronizingly dismissed by her physician, Carol, played by a wonderfully affect-less Julianne Moore, discovers an environmental illness subculture and seeks a cure in a supposedly "safe" place, a refuge in the desert named Wrenwood. This place turns out to be less safe, however—both materially and ideologically—than one would hope. Even though cars, with their noxious exhaust, are not allowed in Wrenwood, Carol discovers a road nearby when a car speeds around a corner and nearly hits her. Significantly, the film demonstrates that this near-collision with material reality is papered over by the positive-thinking discourse of Wrenwood, as this scene is sequestered within the voice-over of Carol writing an upbeat letter home. Carol, a compliant student, has absorbed the New Age psychobabble in which patients are led to blame themselves—not the toxins, not the lax government regulations, not the industries—for their illness. The moments of deviance from this unctuous orthodoxy provide a shard of hope. During a group therapy session, one woman answers the question "How did you feel when you got sick?" by responding, "I wanted to get a gun and blow the heads off" the people responsible for her illness. When Peter, the guru of Wrenwood, chides her that "the only person who can make you sick is you," she turns her head away with dignity, refusing to join in the self-blaming exercise. Surprisingly, even the compliant Carol glances away near the end of this scene. What she sees in this fleeting moment of rebellion is a haunting figure in the distance who can barely be discerned within the vast desert landscape. Carol glimpses this man several times, as he troubles the margins of Wrenwood. Despite the fact that nearly everyone within this community of people with MCS could be termed "disabled," this man with his strange walk serves as the disabled body that allows the others to become normalized, by contrast.[19]

In the next scene, as the rest of the community performs yet another psychological exercise, the strange-walking man—whose face we never see—is carted off by an ambulance.[20] Peter scolds the man, even after his death, "I tried to teach him this. To give up the rage." As Fiona Kumari Campbell puts it, "Disability and disabled bodies are effectively positioned in the nether regions of 'unthought.' For the ongoing stability of ableism, a diffuse network of thought, depends upon the capacity of that network to 'shut away,' to exteriorize, and unthink disability and its resemblance to the essential (ableist) human self" (109). The film *Safe*, then, warns of this sort of tendency to exteriorize physical disability and thus dematerialize MCS as an entirely psychological phenomenon. Here, "normalization" requires both the supposed transcendence of the physical body and a blissful ignorance of environmental, economic, and political forces. One wonders whether Peter is "treating" his patients according to Constanze Hausteiner's directions, which aim to make "externalizers" learn to "focus on their internal and emotional lives" (50), since the "normal" patients repeat affirmations of self-love. As Todd Haynes puts it, "[S]ince the potential for all illness and all wellness lies within the individual, society gets off scot free. This is how new age thought ultimately works in favor of the system while claiming to transcend it" (*Safe*, DVD liner). Furthermore, as this haunting figure awkwardly stalks the margins of the built community, the space he inhabits suggests the interface between human corporeality and more-than-human nature. This shadowy figure, then, paradoxically embodies the material reality of the illness and the disturbing, unpredictable agency of corporeality itself, in that his body will not simply be brought under control by the "talking cure." This figure suggests disability studies' "new realism of the body," which, according to Tobin Siebers, insists that "the body has its own forces. . . . It is not inert matter subject to easy manipulation by social representations" (749). The stylization of the figure encourages an appreciation of corporeal difference, a difference that will not be reined in nor talked away. According to Simi Linton, "Disabled people are expected to mask the behaviors that would disturb the public and certainly not to exaggerate or call attention to our odd forms or the way our forms function. Yet, in part, the art of our art is to exploit and expand on the quirkiness of our forms and to cultivate the interesting styles such bodies can produce" (521).

Deviant Agency

The person who stalks the margins of Wrenwood inhabits a materiality that cannot be transcended or ignored. This lived body departs from both the ableist norms of the dominant culture and the New Age spiritualism of the Wrenwood subculture. This haunting, quirky figure suggests a deviant material agency. Thinking through MCS as deviant agency works on several levels. First, the multitude of xenobiotic chemicals that humans have concocted are agents, chemical agents, which have effects—many of which are as yet unknown—on living, fleshy creatures. These xenobiotics can be said to deviate, often in destructive ways, from their intended uses and paths. Second, the chemically reactive body itself deviates from medical and scientific standards for the levels of toxic exposure that "normal" bodies should be able to withstand.[21]

Against the negative, deviant agencies of xenobiotic chemicals and chemically reactive bodies, it is striking to consider Ladelle McWhorter's queer, green redefinition of *deviance,* which casts it as the generative force of life itself. In her courageous autobiographical rumination on Foucault, McWhorter describes how she was institutionalized because of her "deviant" sexuality. Despite the suffering this categorization caused, she embraces the label of deviant, recasting it to link her sexuality with no less than the generative force of evolution. In the chapter entitled "Natural Bodies; or, Ain't Nobody Here but Us Deviants," she realizes that huge catalpa trees are first cousins to the lowly bean, the only difference being the development of bark:

> So when the woody stems first appeared, they were deviations merely, not improvements. They were abnormalities, freaks. In those days, though, there was no one around to propose therapeutic intervention. So they remained. . . . It was deviation in development that produced this grove, this landscape, this living planet. What is good is that the world remain ever open to deviation. (164)

As the "freaks" become more numerous, they are no longer anomalies, but a new and viable species of tree. Weaving in ironic references to her own psychiatric institutionalization for being queer, McWhorter proposes a thoroughly material sense of deviation as an ethical ideal of openness to unexpected change. McWhorter's compelling transvaluation of deviation as a positive, material force that traverses both human bodies and more-than-human natures creates new alliances among environmentalism, feminism, and queer theory. Thinking through deviation as both ideological and material, as both a form of critique and an ideal, may be less contradictory than it seems, if we consider deviation as a form of material/discursive agency of thoroughly embodied beings who are always inseparable from the environment. To do so would bring together the two seemingly unrelated definitions of *deviation:* "departure from an established ideology or party line" and "evolutionary differentiation." Environmental illness may provoke new ethical, epistemological, and political strategies and, above all, new material practices that deviate from the norms of the early twenty-first-century's chemical/industrial society. Chemically sensitive people and other transcorporeal subjects would caution, however, that not all deviations, in this world of toxicants and xenobiotic chemicals, should be embraced. To "remain ever open to deviation" would be revised, in this case, to take the onto-epistemological condition of chemically reactive people seriously by making the world more accessible for them. This would require a radical overhaul of industrial, consumer, and everyday practices, as well as a drastic departure from both philosophical and commonsensical conceptions of an enclosed, impervious human subject. Whereas both humanist subjects and contemporary consumers may, without hesitation, act upon an externalized world in innumerable ways that do not even begin to verge upon the traditional terrain of ethics, those with multiple chemical sensitivity and other trans-corporeal creatures require that the ethical terrain be expanded to include thorough assessments of a multitude of material entanglements, including (perhaps even especially) those of "normal," everyday life, such as the spraying of perfume or the use of fabric softener. These seemingly mundane matters become ethical concerns when the health, welfare, and mobility of chemically sensitive people are at stake.

The trans-corporeality of those with MCS urges us to foreground the *environment* of environmental illness—an environment that is fleshy, emergent, and ultimately inseparable from the stuff of the human. The next chapter will explore the possibilities for a posthuman environmental ethics—an ethics to be practiced by creatures who find themselves to be part of a maelstrom of material agencies, including the evolutionary force of deviation.

SIX

Genetics, Material Agency, and the Evolution of Posthuman Environmental Ethics in Science Fiction

Something pops out of our genes and makes monster babies . . . with a single huge ovary? . . . [W]hat in hell?

—Greg Bear, *Darwin's Radio*

[T]here is no time or place in which genetics ends and environment begins.

—Donna Haraway, *Companion Species Manifesto*

Wired magazine's cover story featured "Craig Venter's Epic Voyage to Redefine the Origin of Species": "He wanted to play God, so he cracked the human genome. Now he wants to play Darwin and collect the DNA of everything on the planet." Venter is portrayed as an intrepid explorer who having already "conquered the human genome" (Shreve 112) is now traveling the world to master the "bottom of the food chain," described as "a vast undiscovered world, the dark matter of life" (109). This comforting story of heroic individualism, scientific progress, and the mastery of nonhuman nature travels along familiar paths worn by sexism, racism, and colonialism. Unlike monster movies that reveal a terrifying truth—humans are made of the same genetic stuff as other creatures (as the mad scientist in the horror movie *Carnosaur* puts it, we're all "in the mix")—this account presents a reassuring gulf between the human and the "undiscovered ... dark matter of life."[1]

I would like to turn from this passive matter, which seemingly sits "out there" waiting to be "hunted," collected, and "smash[ed] ... to bits" (Shreve 112) by Venter and his high-tech arsenal that converts stuff to codes, toward a different sort of matter, portrayed by the science fiction of Greg Bear and the science studies of Karen Barad, Andrew Pickering, and others. I will argue for a posthuman environmental ethics in which the flows, interchanges, and interrelations between human corporeality and the more-than-human world resist the ideological forces of disconnection. I contend that a profound reconsideration of matter needs to be at the root of a posthumanist environmental ethics. Matter is not a passive resource for human manipulation and consumption, nor a deterministic force of biological reductionism, nor a library of codes, objects, and things to be collected and codified. As Barad puts it, "Matter, like meaning, is not an individually articulated or static entity. Matter is not little bits of nature, or a blank slate, surface, or site passively awaiting signification; nor is it an uncontested ground for scientific, feminist, or Marxist theories" (*Meeting the Universe Halfway* 150–151). Instead, as discussed earlier, she argues, "*matter is substance in its intra-active becoming—not a thing, but a doing, a congealing of agency*" (151; emphasis in original). This conception of matter as "intra-active becoming" may infuse a posthumanist environmentalist ethics that refuses to see the delineated shape of the human as distinct from the background of nature, and instead focuses on interfaces, interchanges, and transformative material/discursive practices.

Greg Bear's novels *Darwin's Radio* and *Darwin's Children* combine classic and more recent science fiction figures: the mad scientist, the monstrous mother, the horrific progeny, and the killer virus. The premise is that something—radiation from Chernobyl, stress, widespread environmental degradation, perhaps—has activated an endogenous retrovirus.[2] The particular retrovirus in this novel, named SHEVA, appropriately enough, runs the following course: women contract a flu-like illness, become pregnant (without insemination), miscarry that first pregnancy, and then bear a new species of child, one with flashing "squid cheeks" who can say "hello" after drawing her first breaths. Although fear of this new species of humans sparks widespread riots, mass executions, and the imprisonment of the new species in internment camps, a brave few accept their progeny, including the heroine of the tale, Kaye Lange, a biologist who eagerly sets about "becoming her own laboratory," giving birth to one of the first live members of the new species. These novels, like many monster movies, seem to fan the fear of nature, evolution, reproduction, and the female body. The premise of this series, however, in which something ancient within human DNA sparks another species that threatens to supersede the human, raises potent questions about the interface between nature and culture, the agency of nature, the constitution of the category of the human, and the nature of matter itself. Through a series of parallel "enfoldings," the novel reconfigures commonsensical landscapes of figure and ground, human agent and material resource, civilization and wilderness, presenting instead a kind of in-habitation, in which what is supposed to be outside the delineation of the human is always already inside. This stuff of matter generates, composes, transforms, and decomposes; it is both the stuff of (human) corporeality and the stuff that eviscerates the very notion of "human."

A Prelude: Material Agencies and the Emergent World

I will pause here to briefly consider the question of material agency. Attributing agency to the material world remains a rather questionable move, as agency is usually considered within the province of rational—and thus exclusively human—deliberation. A condensed version of this parceling of characteristics would attribute agency to humans, instinct to animals, and the deterministic forces of nature to everything else. Although this one-sentence summary of these scientific, philosophical, and cultural divisions is certainly oversimplified, the censure provoked by the mention of material agency suggests that those divisions, however simplistic, still hold sway. Thoroughgoing reconsiderations of materiality, especially those that are motivated by concern for nonhuman animals and the more-than-human world, must nonetheless grapple with the question of material agency, since the evacuation of agency from nature underwrites the transformation of the world into a passive repository of resources for human use. Alternative conceptions which accentuate the lively, active, emergent, agential aspects of nature foster ethical/epistemological stances that generate concern, care, wonder, respect, caution (or precaution), epistemological humility, kinship, difference, and deviance. The previous chapter, for example, included Ladelle McWhorter's redefinition of *deviance,* which provocatively combines the scientific meaning of the term as it pertains to evolutionary change and the more common meaning of deviance as the act of diverging from social norms (as in the case of "sexual deviants"). McWhorter's brilliant ruminations on the catalpa tree culminate in the ethical ideal that what is good "is that the world remain ever open to deviation" (164). An openness to material agencies, including those of evolutionary forces, entails an openness not only to the deviants that result but also to the wider sense that the world is ever-emergent.

Nancy Tuana's theory of "interactionalism" also insists upon emergent material agencies. She posits "a world of complex phenomena in dynamic relational-

ity": "Neither the materiality of the more-than-human world nor human materiality is an unchanging given. What exists is emergent, issuing from complex
interactions between our embodiment and the world" ("Material Locations" 239,
238). Charles E. Scott, in *The Lives of Things*, also stresses interconnections in
his account of what he calls "physicality" or "physical events." Although Scott
avoids the term "agency," the physicality that he outlines is one of actions, events,
happenings—intertwined occurrences that often do not fit within intellectual
schemes. Casting "lives" to mean "all physical events," he argues: "Lives in their
interconnections are so much *there* in their events, so rampant and fugitive in
their dispersions, so often ill suited to the orders we inflict upon them, so likely
to inflict their unregarding wildness on our orders" (77; emphasis in original).
Scott does not engage with environmental philosophy and its deliberations on
wildness, yet the idea that wildness disrupts human order nonetheless resonates
with that tradition. Wildness, in this sense, can be considered a form of material
agency, an agency without a (human) subject. Indeed, Scott is careful to reject the
term *nature* precisely because the word "nature" "signifies a kind of subjectivity"
(23). Scott also rejects the word "nature" because it draws "us to an abstracting process rather than to the lives of things in their nondiscursive, dynamic
interactions" (ibid.). His rejection of this abstracting process and his attempt to
characterize "physicality" suggest the ethos of his project: "an affirmation of what
we find in the world" (183). It may be useful to point out that, although the trans-
corporeal subjects discussed throughout *Bodily Natures* also recognize these
rampant and fugitive physical events, they are not at liberty to "affirm" what
they find in the world. Instead, they must struggle to understand these material
agencies and assess their risks. Trans-corporeality is a site not for affirmation, but
rather for epistemological reflection and precautionary principles.

Donna Haraway has long grappled with the epistemological, ethical, and political implications of nonhuman agency. In *Primate Visions*, Haraway explains
that it is nearly "impossible to avoid the trap of an appropriationist logic of domi-
nation built into the nature/culture binarism" (13). Such a logic casts the world
as "thing, not agent": "Nature is only the raw material of culture, appropriated,
preserved, enslaved, exalted, or otherwise made flexible for disposal by culture
in the logic of capitalist colonialism" (ibid.). Against this tradition, she asserts
that her story "must listen to the practices of interpretation of the primate order
in which primates themselves—monkeys, apes, and people—all have some sort
of 'authorship'" (8). Acknowledging nonhuman primates as "authors" acknowledges their "material-semiotic" agency. The lively figures populating Haraway's
work, in fact—cyborgs, primates, trickster coyotes, onco-mice, canines—embody material/semiotic agencies that reconfigure the nature/culture divide. The
trickster coyote of "Situated Knowledges: The Science Question in Feminism and
the Privilege of Partial Perspective," for example, encourages us to see "the world

as a witty agent" with an "independent sense of humor" (199). Haraway's more recent work, which develops a theory of "companion species," has far-reaching implications for our understanding of human and more-than-human agency. For one thing, the modest proposition that "there cannot be just one companion species" (*Haraway Reader* 300) means that the human, as such, emerges from an evolutionary history in which dogs, and perhaps other species, have been significant actors. Relations between humans and dogs are "co-constitutive relationships in which none of the partners pre-exist the relating" (ibid.). It would be strange, then, to imagine agency existing as an attribute within some ostensibly separate domain of the human, when the human itself emerges in relation to other species: "Historical specificity and contingent mutability rule all the way down" (ibid.). Companion species, then, provoke us to "think about liveliness and agency in different worlds" (308).

Dirt—typically scorned or overlooked—may well be one of the "different worlds." When Ladelle McWhorter attempts to grow her own tomatoes, she becomes entranced by the nature of dirt. Her sudden high regard for this substance may seem odd since most "people treat dirt as nothing more than the place where plants happen to be, like a kind of platform that plants stand on, or in. . . . Dirt is inactive. Inert. Nobody pays much attention to dirt" (165). McWhorter, however, grants dirt a great deal of philosophical attention, as she ruminates on its diffuse agency. After noting that dirt "has no integrity," she explains how it still acts:

> Dirt isn't a particular, identifiable thing. And yet it acts. It aggregates, and depending upon how it aggregates in a particular place, how it arranges itself around various sizes of empty space, it creates a complex water and air filtration system the rhythms of which both help to create more dirt from exposed stone and also to support the microscopic life necessary for turning dead organic matter back into dirt. Dirt perpetuates itself. (166)

Dirt demonstrates an agency without agents, a foundational, perpetual becoming that happens without will or intention or delineation. And yet, dirt, a rather nondiscrete substance, is necessary for the emergence of less diffuse life forms: "Whatever discreteness, integrity, and identity living things may have, it all comes from the activity of that undifferentiated, much maligned stuff we call dirt" (167).

Thinking through the agency of dirt in McWhorter's poetic narrative demands a reconceptualization of agency itself. Karen Barad's massive study *Meeting the Universe Halfway: Quantum Physics and the Entanglement of Matter and Meaning* radically rethinks materiality, agency, and realism, putting forth a coherent and comprehensive theory of science, knowledge, meaning, and mattering. Drawing upon the philosophy of Niels Bohr as well as feminist and queer theories of performativity, Barad constructs a theory of "agential realism," in which agency "is cut loose from its traditional humanist orbit": "Agency is not aligned with human intentionality or subjectivity. Nor does it merely entail re-signification or other specific kinds of moves within a social geometry of anti-humanism" (*Meeting the Universe Halfway* 177). Barad explains that "*agency is 'doing' or 'being' in its intra-activity*" (178; emphasis in original). Barad's account of Bohr's intra-activity, as opposed to inter-activity, rejects an ontology in which "things" precede their relations. Instead, "relata" (as opposed to discrete things) "do not preexist relations; rather, relata-within-phenomena emerge through spe-cific intra-actions" (140). Barad's agential realism, which rejects representational-ism in favor of a material/discursive form of performativity, insists that discourse and materiality are not external to each other, but instead "the material and the discursive are mutually implicated in the dynamics of intra-activity" (152).

Barad's compelling model of material agency will be taken up again at various points in the rest of this chapter. We should consider, however, that the question of material agency has run throughout most of this book. Trans-corporeality not only traces how various substances travel across and within the human body but how they *do* things—often unwelcome or unexpected things. The mercury that Greenpeace found in people's hair, the silica in the lungs of the Gauley Bridge miners, the anthrax threatening Robert Hawks and his Native American allies, the invisible substance that killed Fe, and the myriad toxicants taking up resi-dence in the substantial selves depicted by the material memoirs and the MCS au-tobiographies all dramatize that one of the central problematics of trans-corpo-reality is contending with dangerous, often imperceptible material agencies. The sense of being permeable to harmful substances may provoke denial, delusions of transcendence, or the desire for a magical fix, as in the case of Sherry Rogers's God-given glutathione, but it may also foster a posthuman environmentalism of co-constituted creatures, entangled knowledges, and precautionary practices.

Lorraine Code has observed how discourses of "[e]thical self mastery, politi-cal mastery over unruly and aberrent [*sic*] Others, and epistemic mastery over the external world . . . derive from and underwrite a reductive imaginary in which epistemic and moral agents are represented as isolated units on an indif-ferent landscape" (19). Trans-corporeality, as it insists that the human is never an isolated unit, has affinities with the "ecological thinking" advocated by Code. Furthermore, Code, drawing on Barad's theory, argues that ecological thinking "is capable of seeing nature and human nature as reciprocally engaged, intra-active" (32). The knowing "ecological subject" that Code describes is "materially situated" (91). The trans-corporeal subject, however, is not so much situated, which suggests stability and coherence, but rather caught up in and transformed by myriad, often unpredictable material agencies. Ulrich Beck, in a darkly funny moment, characterizes the agencies endemic to risk society: "Everywhere, pollut-ants and toxins laugh and play their tricks like devils in the Middle Ages. People are almost inescapably bound over to them" (73). The literature, films, photography, and websites included in this book depict the frustrations and confusions that result from contending with these devilish material agencies, especially as they are bound up with social, economic, and political forces.

Up to this point, *Bodily Natures* has examined trans-corporeality as it emerges from environmental health and environmental justice movements, which has meant that the predominant form of material agency so far has been that of toxicants. This chapter will take another direction entirely, becoming a bit more speculative, perhaps, as it explores evolution and other matters in Greg Bear's Darwin series. This chapter, however, is allied with the last three in that it puts forth potent instantiations of material and environmental agencies that contest the hegemony of genetics in the twenty-first century. Indeed, if trans-corporeality impacts our ethics, politics, and practices, it does so despite its prominent adversaries: Enlightenment conceptions of the human, capitalist consumerism that transforms matter into commodities, and a popular sense of the gene as an isolated, controlling, and controllable entity. As different as these three forces are, they all share an instrumental ethos, which is underwritten by a confidence in the solid boundaries of "things."

Genetic Engineering in Science Fiction and Science Studies

Theories of material agency are especially important, I would argue, as a corrective to current fixations on "the gene," which are consonant with the sense that mind (or code) should prevail over matter. Even though Greg Bear's Darwin series depicts the genetic transformation of human beings into something posthuman, these transformations are not engineered or masterminded but instead occur as a result of intricate, interwoven, and unpredictable material agencies. Written in a time when genetic engineering fills grocery store shelves, grabs media headlines, and sparks ethical and political debates, it is striking that Bear's series seems to ignore genetic engineering altogether. Thus, the Darwin series diverges from contemporary science fiction novels in which the posthuman species results from the conscious human manipulation of genes. Margaret Atwood's *Oryx and Crake,* for example, depicts a dystopia in which corporate prison houses—the ultimate gated communities—breed monstrous hybrid creatures for human consumption or organ replacement. The same culture that sentenced myriad creatures to extinction now reduces animals to malleable, unthinking material for genetic engineering. Students of "NeoAgriculture" (or "AgriCouture"), for example, design ghastly headless "chickens," whose bodies consist of consumable parts, some sprouting "drumsticks," others breasts, as ordered (202–203). This dystopia is superseded by a post-apocalyptic world in which nearly all humans have been destroyed and a new, kinder, gentler version of human has been engineered to take their place. *Oryx and Crake* presents a vivid denunciation of genetic engineering run amok. It does not, however, offer an alternative paradigm to counter or quell the march toward genetic "progress" that results in such things as a neurogeneration project in which "genuine human neocortex tissue" is grown in a "pigoon" (56).

More benign forms of genetic engineering appear in the work of Octavia Butler and Joan Slonczewski. In Butler's Xenogenesis series (now republished together as *Lilith's Brood*), the Oankali, motivated by their desire for difference, genetically engineer a human-Oankali hybrid, a post-apocalyptic creature that will, one hopes, lack the deadly hierarchical proclivities that led to global nuclear annihilation. Even though Butler's Oankali embody an environmental ethos in which the nature/culture divide is unthinkable,[3] their reproductive practices are akin to genetic engineering, in that the offspring are assembled via a conscious process of selection; there is little space for chance, random mutation, or the agency of material forces. Sex itself becomes a rather cerebral affair, as the various heterosexual pairs experience their pleasure not through touching each other, but through the mediation of the ooloi—the third sex that is also the genetic engineer. Although the genetic manipulation occurs within the ooloi's own body, in a special organ called the "yashi," and not in a separate laboratory, the Oankali sexual division of labor still suggests a divide between mind and matter, in that the ooloi engineers the offspring but cannot include its own genes in the mix.

In Joan Slonczewski's Elysium Cycle, the peaceful, parthenogenic, environmentally conscious, all-female culture of the Sharers lives on the aquatic planet of Shora. Like Butler's Oankali, the Sharers live in an entirely biotic environment; they "fulfill their needs entirely with organic 'lifestuff'" (*A Door into Ocean* 89). Crucial to the survival of the Sharers are the activities of the "lifeshapers," or genetic engineers, who store genetic information in living "clickflies" rather than in books or computers. The lifeshapers use genetic engineering not only to create such amenities as decorative wallpaper fungus but, more crucially, to shape "their own genes for aquatic life" (*The Children Star* 39).

Notwithstanding the fact that Butler and Slonczewski offer feminist, environmentally conscious versions of genetic engineering, the scenarios that they present still place mind over matter, since material substance is transformed through conscious control. By contrast, the posthuman species in Bear's *Darwin's Radio* is created through complex, interconnected, material processes. In fact, it is human "intelligence," as it is embodied through scientific and governmental institutions, that acts as the primary antagonist in the novel, threatening to prevent the new species from being born: "The human race had grown so cerebral, and had assumed so much control of its biology, that this unexpected and ancient form of reproduction, of creating variety in the species could be stopped in its tracks" (335). The plot and the narrative perspective persuade readers to identify with the material forces of evolutionary change—an unlikely and rather nonphotogenic protagonist, to be sure. Thus, *Darwin's Radio*, by seemingly ignoring the debates surrounding genetic engineering, may actually offer a compelling warning against the presumption of mastery that is manifested in the now widespread practice of genetic modification.

Even though various aspects of this intriguing novel can be read as embodying an environmental ethic, *Darwin's Radio* is not explicitly environmentalist fiction. Whether or not it is feminist fiction, others may decide. More problematic, from the standpoint of my particular argument, is that *Darwin's Radio* broadcasts mixed messages when it comes to genetics. Several characters, including, most strikingly, the brilliant heroine, proclaim surprisingly simplistic notions of genetics and material agency. Rather than alluding to a complex, interconnected sense of agency, some characters seem to attribute a "mind," a "self," or a teleological intent to evolution, "Mother Nature," or the SHEVA virus. Microbiologist Kaye Lange ruminates, for example, on the purpose behind the mysterious pregnancies, most of which are resulting in spontaneous abortions: "Not evolution, then. Perhaps Mother Nature had judged humans to be a malignant growth, a cancer" (212). This conclusion turns out to be wrong when the new species of children are born from this "cancer." (What it means to distinguish "Mother Nature" from evolution is another question.) Later, when Kaye is asked whether she is arguing that "the genome takes control of its own evolution, somehow sensing the right time to bring about change," she responds affirmatively, adding: "I believe our genome is much more clever than we are" (341). Although Bear is a fan of the work of Dorian Sagan and Lynn Margulis, it is difficult not to hear them insisting, "There is no life in a gene. There is no self. A gene never fits the minimal criterion of self, of a living system" (16).

Richard Lewontin and Richard Levins, Evelyn Fox Keller, Bonnie Spanier, Donna Haraway, and others have put forth comprehensive critiques of the scientific and popular discourses of genetics. Lewontin and Levins condemn the "evangelical enthusiasm of the modern Grail Knights" who have "so fetishized DNA." They expose the "ideological predispositions" that emphasize DNA as "blueprint, as plan, as master plan, as master molecule": "It is the transfer onto biology of the belief in the superiority of mental labor over the merely physical, of the planner and designer over the unskilled operative on the assembly line" (240). Evelyn Fox Keller explains that the "discourse of gene action," which attributes "agency, autonomy, and causal responsibility to genes," positions the gene as *the* basis of life" (*Refiguring Life* 11). Spanier argues, "The terms *gene, gene product,* and *gene expression*—because they are used within a conceptual framework of the current biology—increasingly become crystallized into 'things,' rather than fleshed out in complex processes" (93). Haraway critiques the "gene fetishism" that involves "'forgetting' that bodies are nodes in webs of integrations, forgetting the tropic quality of all knowledge claims" (*Modest_Witness* 142).

Although it is not possible to discuss the many scientific, philosophical, and ethical ramifications of "gene fetishism" within the scope of this chapter, it is crucial to consider the implications of the widespread fixation on the gene for environmental ethics. To put it simply, predominant conceptions of genetics are problematic for environmental ethics in at least three interrelated ways. First, understanding genes as mechanisms that can be turned on and off encourages humans to assume techno-scientific mastery of all life forms. This presumption of mastery breeds foolhardy policies and practices that dramatize the need for precautionary principles. Second, the presumption that humans can master the genetic code leads us to ignore multiple material agencies and the unpredictable transformations that these living forces will effect. Third, the overemphasis on genes places "the environment"—the entire material fabric of life, in other words—in the distant background where it plays little, if any, role. Take, for example, the popular and scientific obsession with finding genetic causes for diseases, which blinds us not only to environmental causes, such as the thousands of toxicants that reside in our bodies and interact with each other in often unpredictable ways, but to the manner in which even the "genetic" causes are inextricably interwoven with and sparked by environmental factors.

Even though many of the characters in *Darwin's Radio,* including the heroine, Kaye, put forth simplistic notions of the gene, the series can be read as a critique of popular and scientific genetic reductionism, which attributes a nearly God-like agency to discrete, delineated, isolated entities called "genes." Whereas in gene fetishism, as Haraway puts it, "[m]ere living flesh is derivative; the gene is the alpha and omega of the secular salvation drama of life itself" (*Modest_Witness* 133), in *Darwin's Radio* "living flesh"—in various forms, locations, and times—provides a generative matrix, a web of becomings, not a static originary point of departure. Whereas in popular thought, the science of genetics signals the progress of human knowledge and the hope that one day medicine will be able to simply "turn off" diseases such as cancer, genes in *Darwin's Radio* are not the sole determinants of anything, but instead are interwoven in a material and historical web of becomings.

Evolution and Material Agency

Although the bulk of posthumanist theories emphasize a techno-futurism that melds human and machine, often focusing on information systems,[4] another sort of posthumanism, more hospitable to an environmental ethics, may emerge from evolutionary paradigms that recognize the material interrelatedness of all beings, including the human. Charles Darwin, in *The Descent of Man*, which seeks to demonstrate that "man must be included with other organic beings in any general conclusion respecting his manner of appearance on this earth" (389), considers the evidence of "bodily structure":

> It is *notorious* that man is constructed on the same general type or model as other mammals. All the bones in his skeleton can be compared with corresponding bones in a monkey, bat, or seal. So it is with his muscles, nerves, blood-vessels and internal viscera. The brain, the most important of all the organs, follows the same law. (395–396; emphasis added)

The notoriety of the recognition that "man" is constructed like other mammals announces this striking resemblance as simultaneously accepted and unacceptable. Perhaps little has changed since Darwin's time, in that many humans remain repulsed by the idea of their own animality, as displayed by horror films such as *The Island of Dr. Moreau*. And yet, physical relatedness—such as the "similar framework of bones in the hand of a man, wing of a bat, fin of the porpoise, and leg of the horse" (Darwin, *Origin* 366)—may provoke a rich ethical sense of kinship between the human and other animals or, at the very least, deny us the mental or spiritual exceptionalism that underwrites the untrammeled use of the rest of the world. Darwin's term, "community of descent," in which all animals, including the human, are "members," is ethically resonant, especially when contrasted to the "prejudice" and "arrogance" that denies this community (411–412). Moreover, Darwin's vivid animal tales, in which wild and domestic animals act in intelligent, caring, or courageous ways, revoke the human's exclusive rights to our supposedly most defining attributes—"mental powers" and "moral sense." Demonstrating that the structure of the human body is comparable to that of animals and that animal behavior is comparable to that of the human, Darwin forges a scientific and philosophical "posthumanism" in which there are no solid demarcations between human and animal and in which the human is coextensive with the emergent natural/cultural world.

By alluding to the "father" of evolution, the titles—*Darwin's Radio* and *Darwin's Children*—broadcast Bear's novels as origin stories. Kaye Lange, the protagonist, explains the first title: "SHEVA's a messenger. . . . It's Darwin's radio" (275). The idea that the SHEVA virus acts as a medium for the "message" of evolution suggests a teleological trajectory, in which discrete genetic information, in this case a code for a new species of human, is transported from the past to the present. This sense of genetics is oddly akin to the consumerist and instrumentalist notion of genetics that currently predominates. As Sarah Franklin puts it, "[N]ature becomes biology becomes genetics, through which life itself becomes reprogrammable information" (190). The strange array of "mothers" who bring forth the new species, however, overwhelm the sense that DNA is disembodied information. Even though I've long been a critic of the Mother Earth figure, here, I think, the metonymic slide between the earth and various "mothers" may serve to reinstall a productive, as well as reproductive, sort of materiality that cannot be distilled into code. Nor can it be completely controlled by technoscience.[5] In fact, even though this series is riddled with genetics, the multiple origin stories in *Darwin's Radio* make it impossible to see "the gene" as a single determining point of origin.

The novel begins with two different origin stories, one from the male protagonist's point of view and the other from the female protagonist's perspective. The first six chapters bounce back and forth between these two perspectives. The larger narrative structure produces yet another origin story, since the protagonists, who are at this point strangers, will become the originators of the new species of human when they produce a "virus child," who will be born near the end of the novel. Thus, from the start, the structure of the novel undermines attempts to posit one discrete starting point for "Darwin's children," since each of the origin stories is already enveloped by the plot, which produces yet another origin story.

The first origin tale is told from the perspective of Mitch, a renegade anthropologist, who discovers the remains of a frozen, prehistoric, Neanderthal nuclear family in a cave. He immediately hails them as "everybody's ancestors," "Mama and Papa to the world" (*Darwin's Radio* 29). This particular family, however, includes a "human" child who was born to Neanderthal parents. That child marks a moment of rupture, of difference, not a homogeneous line of descent for the "human." (The novel supports punctuated equilibrium, rather than gradualism, in other words.) Mitch's anthropological origin story is followed by a biological one, in which Kaye Lange, after a day spent scouting bacteriophages in the Republic of Georgia, concludes an evening of revelry by toasting: "To bacteria, our worthy opponents, the little mothers of the world!" (49). The microbiological progenitors undermine the anthropological tale by insisting, as Darwin did, that human genealogy can be traced back to utterly nonhuman sorts of creatures. Unfortunately, Bear does not take advantage of the potential here to destabilize a gendered, heterosexist model of reproduction. Myra J. Hird, for example, includes bacteria in her queer biology, arguing, "Since bacteria recognize and avidly embrace diversity, they do not discriminate on the basis of 'sex' or 'gender' differences at all" (87). Yet, as we will see below, enfolded within the novel's seemingly straight reproductive paradigm is the slightly queer "matter" of the "interim daughter."

But first we should discuss the most conspicuous mother of the novel, Kaye Lange, hailed as "the next Eve" (*Darwin's Radio* 423). A biologist, she brazenly chooses to become her own laboratory, by fostering a SHEVA-virus pregnancy. Thus, she performs her mentor's satirical comment: "Remember, my dear, women are supposed to do science differently" (91). She undertakes this experiment, it should be noted, well before anyone had any idea what sort of creature would materialize from these pregnancies. Certainly, her bold scientific experiment, which could not be more personal and intimate, could never pretend to embody the scientific ideal of distanced (masculinist) objectivity.[6] Kaye tells her lover, the anthropologist Mitch, "I once worried that work and family wouldn't fit together. Now there's no conflict. I am my own laboratory" (357). Enfolding Pickering's "mangle of practice" within her own body, Kaye begins the "dance of agency." As Pickering puts it: "As active, intentional beings, scientists tentatively construct some new machine. Then they adopt a passive role, monitoring the performance of the machine to see whatever capture of material agency it might effect" (21). Interestingly, in this case, Kaye's "machine" is not an external entity but the pregnancy itself. As a mangle of practice, Kaye's pregnancy "captures" the material agency of the SHEVA virus and the creation of a new species. The novel also demonstrates how "the contours of material and social agency are mangled in practice" (Pickering 23), in the sense that even though Kaye is ready to accept the "unpredictable transformations" of enfolding the laboratory within her body, her economic status, her status as a scientist, her rights as a citizen, and her civil rights all become mangled. One could say that, after having gone through the wringer, Kaye becomes a different person. She is materially marked by the experience: her newly communicative "squid cheeks" make her status as a mother of a virus child quite apparent to anyone she encounters while they are in hiding. She exclaims: "We're *marked!*" (*Darwin's Radio* 517). "I felt like a leper. Worse, like a nigger" (516).

Within the space of Kaye's own personal laboratory, a particularly intriguing material agent performs. Perhaps the most fascinating "mother" in the series is not the cave woman, nor the bacteria, nor the protagonist, nor even the endogenous retrovirus, but "the fetus, or whatever they might call the bizarre growth" (119); they are later called the "interim daughters." These masses of matter have "a single huge ovary" that produces the "monster babies" (129). This mother—a monstrous bit of matter that exists solely to produce eggs—seems conjured by feminism's fear of biological reduction, a fear that is not unfounded, given centuries of misogynist definitions of women as passive and degraded nature. This monstrous matter exemplifies feminist theory's tendency to equate biology with a kind of "sinister materiality," as Elizabeth Wilson puts it ("Somatic Compliance" 2). As simultaneously fetus and mother, this creature seems to collapse developmental and historical time, epitomizing matter as inert substance. But yet, this monstrous creature, the discarded stuff of miscarriage, bears the unexpected evolution of the posthuman. An indispensable, though expelled, mass of biological tissue, it displaces the gene as sole determinant and the code as exalted and holy origin by doing nothing short of producing a new species. It may also recast how we understand matter itself. As Barad puts it:

> Matter's dynamism is generative not merely in the sense of bringing new things into the world but in the sense of bringing forth new worlds, of engaging in an ongoing reconfiguring of the world. Bodies do not simply take their places in the world. They are not simply situated in, or located in, particular environments. Rather, "environments" and "bodies" are intra-actively co-constituted. Bodies ("human," "environmental," or otherwise) are integral "parts" of or dynamic reconfigurings of, what is. (*Meeting the Universe Halfway* 170)

This undefinable, monstrous fetus/ovulator, daughter/mother, dramatizes the dynamism of matter in that it is "not a thing but a doing, a congealing of agency" (183–184). Moreover, its agency cannot be understood as emerging from a subject status, but rather emerges from its intra-actions in a web of relations in which bodies and environments are co-constituted. If, as Stephen Dougherty argues, the "killer virus novel" begins by "focusing so obscenely on the materiality of the flesh and the blood," only to transform the body into "a postorganic . . . entity whose being is merely a function of the fetishized code" (10), then *Darwin's Radio* takes the opposite path, discoursing on genetics, but ultimately immersing us within a fleshy matrix of generativity. Thus, the posthuman species materializes from intra-acting, nondiscrete agencies of bodies and environments, radically reconfiguring its world.

Despite this complex web of relations, in which all actions are better understood as intra-actions, in Barad's term, the title of a key scientific conference within the novel is "Controlling the En-Viron-Ment: New Techniques for the Conquest of Viral Illness" (*Darwin's Radio* 230). Even though the playful title— fit for the MLA—enfolds the outside "environment" into a microscopic virus, the "solution" here is simple conquest of the other. The other, in this case, is not indistinguishable from the self, however, since this endogenous retrovirus had been dwelling in human DNA for millennia. The ham-fisted terms "conquest" and "control" signal the need for an environmental ethics to emerge from this scenario, an ethics in which the environment can no longer figure as background, resource, or passive matter, discrete substances that remain below or behind the human. Instead, we can foster the sense of enfolding, in which the "outside" is always already within, inhabiting and transforming what may or may not be still "human" through continual intra-actions. In this dynamic scenario, matter— nature, if you will—is always an agent of change and always already within and without the permeable membrane of the human. This sense of trans-corporeality may best be understood as posthuman in that material agencies reconfigure the very boundaries of the human as such.

As Karen Barad puts it, "The iterative enfolding of phenomena and the shifting of boundaries entail an iterative reworking of the domains of interiority and exteriority thereby reconfiguring space itself, changing its topology" ("Re(con) figuring Space" 92). The most remarkable scene of enfolding occurs when Kaye, after investigating mass graves in the Republic of Georgia, transforms the nightmare outside into a beautiful dream:

> Biofilms, what most people thought of as slime: little industrious bacterial cities reducing these corpses, these once-living giant evolutionary offspring, back to their native materials. Lovely polysaccharide architectures being laid down within the interior channels, the gut and lungs, the heart and arteries and eyes and brain, the bacteria giving up their wild ways and becoming citified, recycling all; great garbage dump cities of bacteria, cheerfully ignorant of philosophy and history and the character of the dead hulks they now reclaimed. (41)

The human bodies become both "environment," the habitat for industrious bacteria who build cities within them, but also "matter," as the "gut and lungs, the heart and arteries" are "reduc[ed]" to "their native materials." In turn, abject matter—"what most people thought of as slime"—is transformed here into "[l]ovely polysaccharide architectures." But this is not just a reversal of nonhuman/human, nature/culture, but a kind of enfolding in which everything presumed to be outside of the properly human is always already within. Even the "wild" and, perhaps by extension, the wilderness are enacted within a human terrain, as the bacteria are said to have once reveled in their "wild ways," presumably traveling within and without the human habitat. This sort of wilderness or wildness— whether it be that of bacteria, virus, genetic material, or the monstrous ovulator—certainly can't be a mere resource for human mining; nor is it the product of genetic engineering, but instead matter is agency here, an agency that transforms the very stuff of the human.

Indeed, the "human" species, along with all of the other species, owes its very existence, according to Sagan and Margulis, to the "incorporation and integration of 'foreign' genomes, bacterial and other, [which] led to significant, useful, heritable variation" (205). Their emphasis on incorporation underscores a truism played out in the Darwin novels: humans are always already "other"; we *are* the aliens, the multitude of "foreign" creatures that inhabit and constitute our only seemingly distinct "selves."[7] Notwithstanding the fact that humans are 98% genetically identical to chimps, much of the discourse of *the* Human Genome Project resonates with the old-fashioned humanist sensibility of distinctiveness. For example, the Human Genome Project's website tells us, "In a material sense, then, all of the subtlety of our species, all of our art and science, is ultimately accounted for by a surprisingly small set of discrete genetic instructions." Moreover, the symbolic temporal trajectory of the science of genetics is toward a future in which we can finally control even ourselves. The premise of Greg Bear's *Darwin's Radio,* on the other hand, places genetic activity within a biological/historical realm of evolution, taking it, in a sense, from the laboratories of technoculture and situating it within the much more vast chronological context of natural history.[8] The premise stands as an important corrective to how dominant accounts not only isolate the gene as an agent, but separate genetics from evolution: the first being a comfortable resource for technological and medical advancement, the latter an incendiary story of origins.

Posthuman Environmental Ethics

In *Darwin's Radio,* strange matters, genetic jumbles, an evolutionary past as well as an evolutionary future result in a new species that is not exactly human.[9] The messy, multiple, material origins of this posthuman may suggest an environmental ethics that begins from the movement across—across time, across place, across species, across bodies, across scale—and reconfigures the human as a site of emergent material intra-actions inseparable from the very stuff of the rest of the world. *Darwin's Radio* enfolds various "natures" within the human: the wild bacteria, the virus that is already within the human gene, and the monstrous matter that enacts its agency without ever having been a subject.

We need not take an imaginative leap into science fiction in order to realize that we inhabit a corporeality that is never disconnected from our environment. As Bonnie Spanier puts it:

> [O]rganisms do not exist apart from their environs or from other organisms. Not only are organisms surrounded by and embedded in a dynamic interaction with their environs—and in that sense are contiguous with it—but we are contiguous with the environment from the inside as well, whether through our digestive and respiratory tracts, our skin pores, or the network of endoplasmic reticulum throughout the cytoplasm of many types of cells. A human body is many organisms, most of which are necessary for a healthy life: E. coli in the lower intestine, microorganisms on the skin. . . . A very different psychology of self and other would understand our beings as open to and connected with the environment around us through our external and internal surfaces, as well as what we project of ourselves (our exhalations, body head radiation, wastes, etc.). (90)

Humanism, capitalist individualism, transcendent religions, and utilitarian conceptions of nature have labored to deny the rather biophysical, yet also commonsensical realization that we are permeable, emergent beings, reliant upon the others within and outside our porous borders. The biological sense of trans-corporeality may be complemented by a philosophical recognition of the "trace" of the animal within the "human." Cary Wolfe argues that the "other-than-human resides at the very core of the human itself, not as the untouched, ethical antidote to reason but as part of reason itself" (17). Wolfe contends that a "truly postmodern ethical pluralism" "can take place . . . not by avoiding posthumanist theory but only by means of it": "theoretically and ethically speaking, the only way out is through, the only way to 'before' is 'to come,' and the only way to the 'there' in which the animals reside is to find them 'here,' in us and of us, as part of a plurality for which perhaps even 'the animals,' in the plural, is far too lame a word" (207).

A posthuman environmental ethics denies the human the sense of separation from the interconnected, mutually constitutive actions of material reality, thrusting us into an evolutionary narrative which, in Elizabeth Grosz's terms, "pushes toward a future with no real direction, no promise of any particular result, no guarantee of progress or improvement, but with every indication of proliferation and transformation" (*Time Travels* 26). Grosz's compelling philosophical reconsideration of Darwinian theory stresses its open dynamism:

> Darwin develops an ontology, an account of a real, that is profoundly different from that of his predecessors and contemporaries, in which life is now construed as an open and generative force of self-organization and growing material complexity, where life grows according to a materiality, a reality, that is itself dynamic, that has features of its own which, rather than exhibiting ongoing stability or given static qualities, rather than being seen as responsive or reactive, are as readily understood in terms of the active forces of interaction that generate and sustain change. (37)

Nature or the environment cannot serve as a mere resource within an ontology that sweeps us all up in interrelations of material dynamism. Grosz celebrates a rather extreme version of this openness by positing a "(non)moral" ontology of Darwinism, which "mourns no particular extinction, and which waits, with surprise, to see what takes the place of the extinct" (*Time Travels* 221n4). Whereas Grosz casts the recognition of the radical unpredictability of the future as a liberation from mourning and moralism, Barad insists that the human always exists within, not outside of, material intra-actions and thus must be accountable. Barad asserts, as part of her posthumanist ethics: "We are of the universe—there is no inside, no outside. There is only intra-acting from within and as part of the world in its becoming" (*Meeting the Universe Halfway* 396). An "ethics of mattering," she argues, "is not about right response to a radically exterior/ized other, but about responsibility and accountability for the lively relationalities of becoming of which we are a part" (393). In other words, "ethics is about accounting for our part of the tangled webs we weave" (384). Dwelling on the recognition that "'environments' and 'bodies' are intra-actively co-constituted" (170) can provoke a potent trans-corporeal ethics that attends to the material interrelations of bodies and places. Recognizing how the bodies of all living creatures intra-act with place—with the perpetual flows of water, nutrients, toxicants, and other substances—makes it imperative that we be accountable for our practices. Acknowl-edging the agency of all that is not human affirms the need for places in which creatures, ecological systems, and other nondiscrete life forms can flourish. Barad concludes *Meeting the Universe Halfway* with an enmeshed, intra-active, posthuman ethics: "Intra-acting responsibly as part of the world means taking account of the entangled phenomena that are intrinsic to the world's vitality and being responsive to the possibilities that might help us and it flourish" (396). This profound sense of entanglement, intra-activity, and perpetual emergence fosters an ethical stance that insists that the activities and knowledge practices of the human are always part of, and accountable to, the wider world.

Charles Darwin, exposing the human as a corporeal amalgamation of crea-tures both at hand and across vast temporal distances, may have given us our first glimpse of the always already "posthuman," a stance that insists upon our immersion within worldly material agencies, suggesting our accountability to our fellow creatures in this community of descent. In the midst of contemporary genetic fetishism that seeks human mastery over the stuff of life itself, Greg Bear's Darwin series casts the human within an evolutionary narrative in which we are not immune from the forces of messy, unpredictable materiality. *Darwin's Chil-dren*, set eleven years after *Darwin's Radio*, reports, "There was still controversy over exactly who and what they were—a diseased mutation, a subspecies, or a completely new species. Most simply called them virus children" (7). Born from an ancient endogenous retrovirus, an ovulating mass, and a microbiologist who became her own laboratory, there is a chance that these virus children may not disregard the world from which they materialized. And there is also the chance that the bodily natures of environmental health, environmental justice, multiple chemical sensitivity, science, science fiction, literature, material memoirs, pho-tography, film, activism, and theory will provoke an ethics that is not circum-scribed by the human but is instead accountable to a material world that is never merely an external place but always the very substance of our selves and others.

NOTES

1. Bodily Natures

1. I allude to the remarkable conference "Nature Matters," organized by Catriona Mortimer-Sandilands and Megan Salhus of York University, held in Toronto during October 2007. I regret that a broken ankle kept me from speaking at this important interdisciplinary event.

2. See Plumwood, *Feminism and the Mastery of Nature.*

3. Shannon Sullivan, in *Living across and through Skins: Transactional Bodies, Pragmatism, and Feminism,* also focuses on the relations between human bodies and their environments. She argues that, to think of bodies as "transactional" is to "conceive of bodies and their various environments as co-constituted in a nonviciously circular way" (1). She also argues for a "nonreductive recognition of the significance of bodily materiality to human lived existence" (2). Despite these striking parallels, I should note that *Living across and through Skins* focuses on pragmatism, bodily activities, and lived experiences, whereas *Bodily Natures* focuses on how the movement across bodies and environments necessitates engagements with scientific understandings of materiality. In a fascinating account of the reception of her book, Sullivan tells how she was surprised that the Library of Congress categorized her book under "ecology." But, she then reflects, "one of the main things the book does is present an ecological ontology, and as ecological, it is an ontology that intimately concerns social, political, and ethical issues. It is an ontology in which organisms and their various cultural, political, and physical environments co-constitute one another in dynamic, ongoing ways" (Sullivan, "Pragmatist Feminism" 202). Sullivan's work offers rich possibilities for environmental philosophy and material feminisms.

4. For more on queer ecologies, see Mortimer-Sandilands and Erickson, *Queer Ecologies.*

5. For a more extensive discussion of a wide range of material feminisms, see Alaimo and Hekman's introduction to the volume *Material Feminisms.* See also, of course, the other essays in that collection.

6. See, for example, the excellent collection of essays edited by Noel Castree and Bruce Braun, *Remaking Reality: Nature at the Millennium*, including their piece in that collection, "The Construction of Nature and the Nature of Construction."

7. See Alaimo, "Discomforting Creatures: Monstrous Natures in Recent Films" and "Endangered Humans? Wired Bodies and the Human Wilds."

8. This idea surfaced in conversation with Jeanne Hamming.

9. I discuss this in more depth in the essay "Insurgent Vulnerability: Masculinist Consumerism, Feminist Activism, and the Gendered Sciences of Global Climate Change."

10. Notwithstanding the allied aims of our projects and the feminist epistemologies that inform them both, *Bodily Natures* interrogates material interchanges and material agency as they emerge within risk society, environmental health, and environmental justice movements, whereas Code applies the concept of "ecological thinking" more broadly to epistemological situations that are unrelated to ecology or environment per se. I regret that I do not have the space here to undertake a more thorough analysis of Code's rich and provocative work, let alone to adequately chart the intriguing connections and divergences between her project and my own. It may be helpful to note one obvious difference, however: Code constructs a sustained philosophical elaboration of an epistemology, while my own work undertakes a more cultural studies analysis that explores the ethical and political ramifications of a jumble of theories, literature, cultural artifacts, activist sites, and scientific accounts.

11. See "Circulating Reference: Sampling the Soil in the Amazon Forest" in Latour, *Pandora's Hope: Essays on the Reality of Science Studies*. Against an ontology that assumes a "gap between words and the world," Latour argues that phenomena within scientific practice are "what *circulates* all along the reversible chain of transformations" (24, 71). Latour emphasizes the long chain of mediations from matter to form.

12. After reading Mark Lynas's *High Tide: The Truth about Our Climate Crisis,* the students in my spring 2009 Literature and Environment class had a keen sense of our collective complicity in climate change. The class periods subsequent to the discussion of that book were conducted without the benefit of electric lights.

13. Jeff Howard underscores the need for precautionary thinking by proposing the wonderful term "nasty surprise" to describe environmental catastrophe.

2. Eros and X-rays

1. For more on environmental justice, see Hofrichter, *Toxic Struggles: The Theory and Practice of Environmental Justice;* Bullard, *The Quest for Environmental Justice: Human Rights and the Politics of Pollution;* Pellow and Brulle, *Power, Justice, and the Environment: A Critical Appraisal of the Environmental Justice Movement;* Shrader-Frechette, *Environmental Justice: Creating Equality, Reclaiming Democracy;* and Stein, *New Perspectives on Environmental Justice: Gender, Sexuality, and Activism.*

2. See chapters 3 and 4 in Alaimo, *Undomesticated Ground.* For more on Hornaday, see ibid., 94–95.

3. See chapter 5 of this book for an analysis of a similar model of corporeal resistance, that of multiple chemical sensitivity or environmental illness.

4. See Alaimo, *Undomesticated Ground,* 102–105.

5. Indeed, in my earlier book *Undomesticated Ground: Recasting Nature as Feminist*

Space, which argues that nature has been a crucial site for feminist transformations, I ignored Le Sueur's writing. In that work, I argue that nature has been a site for many gender-minimizing, even nascent poststructuralist feminisms that recast nature in order to pry open the obdurate grip of gender, and Le Sueur's many fertile earth goddesses could not happily inhabit the same pages. Although I am still not uncritical of these particular figurations, as I will discuss below, I am rethinking the political aims and effects of Le Sueur's diverse representations of nature, especially in regard to social class.

6. See Alaimo, *Undomesticated Ground,* 87–93, for a more extensive analysis of how Emma Goldman employs Mother Earth for revolutionary, and nonreproductive, ends.

7. For a more extensive discussion, see Alaimo, *Undomesticated Ground,* 93–107.

8. Compare Lucia Trent's poem "Breed, Women, Breed," which includes such mordant lines as "Wrack your frail bodies with the pangs of birth / For the warlords who slaughter your sons." Although Le Sueur's own mother, Marian Wharton, fought for women's reproductive freedom, Le Sueur's untrammeled celebration of pregnancy vilifies reproductive control. "To Hell with You, Mr. Blue!" explicitly compares the protagonist's pregnancy with "love for this earth" (61) and concludes with her triumphantly proclaiming the eponymous line, asserting—against the deadly men—her desire not to have an abortion. Le Sueur's article "The Fetish of Being Outside" concludes: "The writer's action is full belief, from which follows a complete birth, not a fascistic abortion" (23). "The Girl," as Paula Rabinowitz ruefully notes, ends with a "separatist utopia of mothers" (*Labor & Desire* 136). Rabinowitz's generous, yet incisive, reading critiques the fact that Le Sueur does not question "the oppressiveness of motherhood." Yet, placing Le Sueur's work within the context of the Left, Rabinowitz also notes her feminist contribution, explaining that in "The Girl," Le Sueur "reminds us that women's labor brings children into the world, producing value and history just like men's labor" (ibid., 120). And, as Constance Coiner argues, Le Sueur, along with Tillie Olsen, "implicitly questioned Marxism's primacy-of-production theory, which defines production as the distinctively human activity. This theory encodes activities carried out in the home, to which women have historically been disproportionately consigned, as less valuable than men's activities outside of it" (163). Thus, Le Sueur's exaltation of pregnancy asserts the value of reproduction and motherhood against both capitalism and Marxism, which ignore or degrade them.

9. Le Sueur had to struggle to have this particular story printed, which demonstrates how difficult it was to have the subject matter taken seriously. Constance Coiner states that, when Le Sueur wrote "Annunciation," "pregnancy was considered unacceptable as a literary subject, as much by the *New Masses* as by the magazines that gave that reason for rejecting her manuscript (*Scribner's Magazine* and the *Atlantic Monthly*). Although the story has been frequently reprinted, it was originally published only in a small private edition" (152).

10. Even though Hartman does notice the relationship between "the worker's body and the land" in the Mearl Blankenship poem, her essay emphasizes modernization and the machine (213). Her rich analysis does account for the materiality of bodies, however, which is rare. I offer these comments in order to distinguish her reading from my own, not to critique her fine essay.

11. Tim Dayton notes that the term *mastery* is taken from the Egyptian Book of the Dead, where it means "not mastery of others, but mastery of their human destiny, mastery of the conditions in which people live" (76). He contends that it is crucial to

distinguish between a "sense of mastery" as "constructive human power" versus "coercive powers based on social structures" (77). Without this distinction, he argues, "the historical vision and the utopian resonance of *The Book of the Dead* are lost" (ibid.). I would contend that, as the poem struggles to trace various forces and substances that are simultaneously material and social, this sense of mastery is rendered an impossibility. See also Wolosky, "Medical-Industrial Discourses," which argues that Rukeyser forwards a discursive form of "affirmative individuality." It may also be useful to consider Rukeyser's use of the term *mastery* as an ironic echo of a newspaper article that glorified the Hawk's Nest tunnel, as I discuss at the end of the chapter.

12. Michael Thurston notes that "Mearl and the surrounding scene (river and rock) are intertwined," but he then argues that the "scene is Mearl himself writ large" (181), a reading which, I would contend, inflates the person at the expense of the place.

13. In support of this reading, Kadlec contrasts Rukeyser's lines with the original testimony of the African American George Robison. Rukeyser wrote: "As dark as I am, when I came out at morning after the tunnel at night, / with a white man, nobody could have told which man was white. / The dust had covered us both and the dust was white." Robison's original testimony, as cited in Kadlec, reads: "Nobody could have told which was the white man. The white man was just as black as the colored man" (24).

14. Beverly Hendrix Wright and Robert D. Bullard, writing in 2002, state, "[T]he lower life expectancy and higher incidence of cancer and death rates incurred by nonwhite (especially African American) workers [are] often attributed to either bad habits or genetics." One example they give is that the steel industry justifies assigning African Americans to the coke ovens because they "absorb heat better" (157). See Cherniak, *The Hawk's Nest Incident,* for more on the racist labor practices at the Hawk's Nest site, which included assigning African Americans to the most difficult and dangerous jobs and physically abusing them.

15. Despite Rukeyser's vision and its consonance with the transition from industrial hygiene to environmental health science, silicosis itself was, as David Rosner and Gerald Markowitz point out, "specifically a worker's disease" that was "never perceived as an environmental threat or a threat to the broader population" (231). Rukeyser's poetic vision, however, is significant, because it raises larger questions about how hazardous substances circulate across ostensible borders.

16. The workplace, according to Charles Noble, remains "the most dangerous environment." Noble states, for example, that due to Republican administrations' hostility toward workplace regulation in the United States, "OSHA rules today cover only a small percentage of the toxic substances that threaten workers" (177). Shrader-Frechette notes that, "in terms of permissible levels of chemicals in the work environment, U.S. regulations are less strict than those of countries such as Germany, Sweden, and Czechoslovakia" (138). Claudia Clark notes that "little progress has been made in ensuring workplace health after over a century of research and reform involving industrial diseases." She states that the "best estimate is that occupational diseases kill about 100,000 Americans each year and cause 400,000 new illnesses" (11). Sheldon Rampton and John Stauber lament that today's workers "are not much different from the worker[s] at Hawk's Nest." Since the federal government "makes no attempt to track silicosis," no one knows "how many men are dying from exposure to the deadly dust, and perhaps no one ever will" (82).

3. Invisible Matters

1. Michael Hames-Garcia critiques scholarship on race, offering a provocative alternative in his essay "How Real Is Race?" He contends that race cannot be easily dismissed as "only cultural" or "just ideological." Drawing upon Karen Barad's theory, he argues that race "emerges from the intra-action of history, culture, economics, and material human bodies" (331). See also Troy Duster's "heretical" contention that whether "race is a legitimate concept for scientific inquiry depends on the criteria for defining race, and will in turn be related to the analytic purposes for which the concept is deployed" (259).

2. I am grateful to Ursula Heise for introducing me to risk theory through her ASLE/SLSA papers, her published work, and conversations. Heise not only presents an extensive analysis of Beck's work and its relevance for ecocriticism, but also contributes to risk theory more generally by "foregrounding how new risk perceptions are shaped by already existing cultural tropes and narrative templates" (*Sense of Place and Sense of Planet* 13).

3. Although I am working through the commonalities between environmental justice and risk society, Heise points out the "deep seated difference of social vision between the two":

> Environmental justice advocates tend to see the current global ecological crisis in its manifold manifestations as a logical consequence and exacerbation of a socioeconomic organization based on capitalism, and of an approach to knowledge shaped by the rationalism of the Enlightenment. . . . Beck, by contrast, sees in the same ecological crisis a sign of the disintegration of the capitalist class society and of modernist approaches to knowledge. (*Sense of Place and Sense of Planet* 149)

4. Ursula Heise argues that Beck underestimates the impact of cultural differences: "he seems to infer that shared risk automatically implies enough cultural commonality to serve as the basis for new kinds of communities" (*Sense of Place and Sense of Planet* 158). As Heise points out, however, "environmental justice advocates who have actually tried to force such alliances . . . tell a more complex story" in which not only cultural differences but more pernicious legacies of oppression and inequality impede alliances (ibid.).

5. For example, Hawks becomes unwittingly bound up in the Plata Indians' struggle before he has any idea what is going on. Because of his own family history with racist police, he just couldn't tell the truth to the FBI. His "lie" is ironically juxtaposed with a description of the medical dissection of a tongue, which seems to reference the clichéd saying that whites "speak with forked tongues" in their systemic lies, as documented by the many Indian treaties sprinkled through the text. Thus, his scientific practice, which documents the illegal anthrax dump, emerges from a vast historical fabric of African American and Native American histories.

6. By contrast, see Jason Coburn's analysis of the "street science" practiced by another group of activists who took lead samples and monitored the lead levels in children's blood. In "Science as a Double-Edged Sword," Azibuike Akaba, a community technical assistance coordinator, urges environmental justice activists "to strategically use science as a tool" (10).

7. Kamala Platt argues that Fe is "held accountable to her lifestyle and her 'faith' in a system of structural oppression":

> After all, Fe's labor does not produce seemingly innocent products like grapes or even computer chips, which to varying degrees serve useful purposes meeting basic needs, despite the harm caused to workers, sometimes consumers, and the environment when the industries are unregulated and those in charge are unconscionable. Rather, Fe is involved in the production of the deadliest of weapons—one of which may even have killed her sister Esperanza during the Gulf War. (87)

8. Notwithstanding the sheer horror of Fe's tale, Acme International, which echoes the fictional "Acme Corporation" that appears in many cartoons, including *The Road-runner,* brings to mind the absurdly apparent, but somehow survivable, assaults that the Roadrunner endures—as when boulders smash him flat. The cartoon clarifies Beck's concept of ubiquitous, invisible risks—by stark contrast.

9. Marta Caminero-Santangelo presents a fascinating reading of this novel, in which she contrasts its magical realist elements with its more political episodes, including Fe's death. She argues that the political episodes "strikingly lack magical realism," while the magical realist moments embody "threats" to "any sort of active resistance" (82). I am intrigued by her reading, but I still suggest that Fe's plot dramatizes an onto-epistemological rupture emblematic of risk culture.

10. Dorothy Ann Purley (Keres) testified that the Jackpile mine left the area a "vast wasteland." In the 1970s, the health effects of the mining became evident: "We started hearing about people being affected by upper respiratory ailments like emphysema. Our younger generations were afflicted by leukemia and tumors. Babies were born with birth defects. We wondered what was going on and did not realize that our people were being affected from the exposure to radiation" (Navajo Uranium Miner Oral History and Photography Project 16).

11. Kenneth M. Roemer argues, "Ortiz is a master of tactile imagery, and he uses this mastery to transform topics as remote and small as a dry root in a wash and as hidden and apocalyptic as the Jackpile uranium mine into living parts of us" (69). Although Roemer's point is that Ortiz's mastery of tactile imagery allows him to bridge the distances of place and time that would separate the reader from the poetry, one could also see (or feel) the tactile imagery as insistent upon particular landscapes and material substances.

12. Vegetarians, including myself, will balk at that assessment.

13. For what else you could do with chickens, see Margaret Atwood's dystopian, near-futuristic novel *Oryx and Crake,* which will be discussed in the last chapter of this book.

14. Joni Adamson interprets work, in this poem, as offering a common ground: "Because all the elements of human survival are extracted from the natural world, and because most of us must work to live, work is the link that binds humans to other humans and to nature" (85).

15. *Sovereignty* is an overdetermined term in this context, as it is a key term for Native American political, legal, and, more recently, intellectual movements (e.g., the work of Craig Womack and Robert Allen Warrior) as well as one of Ulrich Beck's terms for what the individual loses in risk society. Interestingly, Allan Kanner, Ryan Casey, and Barrett Ristroph explain that "environmentalism" and "environmental racism" are "new concerns" for "advocates of Native American sovereignty." "They viewed the positions

advocated by environmentalists as a manifestation of their lack of sovereignty problem, and not as a solution to an impending health crisis" (157–158). Noriko Ishiyama critiques the predominant model of distributive justice within environmental justice scholarship, arguing that, for Native Americans, the key to environmental justice is sovereignty: "In the context of Indian country, environmental justice depends on tribes' sovereign capacity to pursue politically, economically, and ecologically sound options for sustainable development. Accordingly, reinforcement of both political and economic sovereignty of tribes will lead to the long-term accomplishment of environmental justice" (135–136).

16. See also Arun Agrawal's essay "Dismantling the Divide between Indigenous and Scientific Knowledge," which concludes:

> It is only when we move away from the sterile dichotomy between indigenous and western; when we begin to recognize intra-group differentiation; and when we seek out bridges across the constructed chasm between the traditional and the scientific, that we will initiate a productive dialogue to safeguard the interests of those who are disadvantaged. (433)

17. Bauer provides this definition of biomonitoring: "the assessment of human exposure to an environmental chemical via the measurement of that chemical, its metabolite(s), or reaction product(s) in human blood, urine, milk, saliva, adipose or other tissue in individuals taken separately but generally taken together to constitute a population" (3).

4. Material Memoirs

1. Information on environmental causes of cancer is not readily available on the website of the American Cancer Society. A search for "environment" and "prevention" brings up an article that labels radiation, chemicals, and toxic waste as "unproven risks." The site even lauds the use of pesticides: "pesticides play a valuable role in maintaining the food supply" ("The Environment and Cancer Risks"). By stark contrast, Breast Cancer Action, the "bad girls of breast cancer," emphasizes "prevention first" and "public health before private profit." In its "Think before You Pink" campaign, the organization exposes the fact that cosmetics companies that market their products with pink ribbons for breast cancer awareness actually include many carcinogenic chemicals within the products. See also Proctor, *Cancer Wars*.

2. The material memoir also marks an extreme departure from the "tradition of autobiography itself," which, Shirley Neumann argues, "has established access to public discourse about the self as synonymous with spiritual quest and has consequently repressed representations of bodies within the genre" (294). K. Wesley Berry has identified "ecospiritual autobiographies," which map "an author's interaction with the 'holy' in a particular physical environment," such as the writings of Annie Dillard, Wendell Berry, and Gretel Erhlich (149). The material memoir departs from this model in its relentless attention to corporeal substance rather than spirituality. What I'm terming the *material memoir* is most akin to what Cecilia Konchar Farr terms "American ecobiographies," which are "nonfiction autobiographical narratives centered on place" (94), such as the work of Edward Abbey and Terry Tempest Williams. Konchar Farr's analysis of ecobiographies has some affinities with my emphasis on trans-corporeality, as she argues

that "in ecobiographies nature becomes us" (ibid., 95). My analysis, however, focuses on emerging models of materiality in the memoir, as well as the epistemological and ethical issues arising from the need for scientific understandings of the trans-corporeal self. Mark Allister discusses books that mix the genres of nature writing and autobiography in his study *Refiguring the Map of Sorrow,* focusing on how "the literary act of self-creation can bring an end to grieving" (5). An analysis of the many contemporary memoirs and autobiographies that emphasize geographic, physical places would require much more space than I have here. For a start, see Ray, *Ecology of a Cracker Childhood;* Swander, *Out of This World: A Journey of Healing;* Grover, *North Enough: AIDS and Other Clearcuts;* Harris, *Mississippi Solo: A River Quest;* Masumuto, *Harvest Son.* Terry Tempest Williams's *Refuge* is probably the best known place-based autobiography; it has generated many critical essays, including "Nature Writing as Refuge" by Brooke Libby, who notes that *Refuge* "crystallizes what is the general though perhaps unstated aim of most nature writing: to write about the natural world and about oneself simultaneously, to look mutually outward and inward" (252). See also the fine collection edited by Chandler and Goldthwaite, *Surveying the Literary Landscape of Terry Tempest Williams: New Critical Essays.* Chip Ward's *Canaries on the Rim: Living Downwind in the West* is especially notable for its extensive discussions of environmental health, scientific evidence, and the politics of information. Many of its arguments are akin to those of Steingraber and Antonetta. The memoirs of people with multiple chemical sensitivity (discussed in the next chapter) epitomize—maybe even exaggerate—the material memoir as formulated in this chapter.

3. Joni Seager argues that it "has taken relentless pressure from environmental justice and women's health advocates to shift paradigms—to put human health issues on the mainstream environmental movement agenda and to put environmental issues on the health map" (957). For analyses of industry backlash, see Stauber and Rampton, *Toxic Sludge Is Good for You: Lies, Damn Lies, and the Public Relations Industry;* and Rampton and Stauber, *Trust Us, We're Experts! How Industry Manipulates Science and Gambles on Your Future.* The latter exposes industry's twisted public relations campaign against the precautionary principle, which claims that this principle is itself hazardous.

4. These quotes come from the websites of the World Health Organization, the Centers for Disease Control, and the European Union Portal: http://www.who.int/topics/environmental_health/en; http://www.cdc.gov/node.do?id=0900f3ec8000e044; http://ec.europa.eu/health-eu/my_environment/environmental_health/index_en.htm.

5. Phil Brown and Judith Kirwan Kelley note that physicians lack training in environmental health:

> Many environmental health effects often go unrecognized, and thus untreated, in nonspecialist physicians' practices primarily because of a lack of knowledge of environmental health effects on the part of physicians. Despite the increasing public interest in environmental health issues, a number of studies have documented a critical shortage in the number of physicians who have been trained to recognize and treat environmental health effects. (47)

See also Ausubel, *Ecological Medicine: Healing the Earth, Healing Ourselves;* and Hofrichter, *Reclaiming the Environmental Debate: The Politics of Health in a Toxic Culture.*

6. Ursula K. Heise makes a similar critique of Richard Powers's novel *Gain:* "the self-assurance of the narrator's command of the global and his transparent (though complex) language remain in tension with the scenario of individual powerlessness vis-à-vis the global power networks that the novel portrays. In this respect, the novel's formal accomplishment lags behind its conceptual sophistication" ("Toxins" 773).

7. See Alaimo, *Undomesticated Ground,* for how women in various historical moments have transformed associations between woman and nature.

8. See the collection edited by Mortimer-Sandilands and Erickson, *Queer Ecologies: Sex, Nature, Biopolitics and Desire.* Michael Warner defines *reprosexuality* as "the interweaving of heterosexuality, biological reproduction, cultural reproduction, and personal identity" (9).

9. Daniel Martineau et al. have studied the higher-than-average cancer rates of both people and beluga whales who live near or in the St. Lawrence estuary in Quebec, concluding that "a human population and a population of long-lived, highly evolved mammals may be affected by specific types of cancer because they share the same habitat and are exposed to the same environmental contaminants" (290). In a 2009 article in *Nature Reviews: Cancer,* "Wildlife Cancer: A Conservation Perspective," Denise McAloose and Alisa L. Newton observe that cancer in wildlife is more prevalent than scientists have thought. They conclude by noting that they see a great potential for research on epizootics to "drive timely environmental mitigation and influence environmental policy" (524).

5. Deviant Agents

1. I use the term *environmental illness* (EI) to underscore how this illness articulates human health with environmental health, emphasizing that human bodies are coextensive with the natural, unnatural, and hybridized material world. I will use the term *multiple chemical sensitivity* (MCS) to emphasize that the thousands of xenobiotic chemicals in our shared world are a likely cause for this illness. *Chemical injury* is an important term for those who have been damaged by particular events, such as industrial accidents. I hesitate to use that term as a general name for this condition, however, because it does not include the many people who become ill from ordinary, seemingly benign exposures. Moreover, the term *chemical injury,* which implies isolated accidents rather than pervasive industrial and consumer practices, suggests that better safety measures at particular sites—rather than a massive overhaul of our entire chemical/industrial society—would prevent this illness.

2. William Rea defines "Total Toxic (Body) Load (Burden)" as "the sum of all pollutants in the body at one time." In his theory, toxic load is important because when "this accumulation overloads the system, chemical sensitivity can occur" (12).

3. A 2004 epidemiological study by Stanley Caress and his co-investigators finds that 12.6% of their sample reported hypersensitivity to chemicals ("Prevalence of Multiple Chemical Sensitivities"). Martin Pall contends that EI has a prevalence "roughly similar to that of diabetes and glucose intolerance," but EI receives "less than a thousandth" of the funding given for diabetes research (11).

4. Neither Gail McCormick, *Living with Multiple Chemical Sensitivity,* nor Rhonda Zwillinger, *The Dispossessed,* include a preponderance of women with MCS in their

books. Alison Johnson's *Casualties of Progress: Personal Histories from the Chemically Sensitive* not only includes roughly the same number of men and women with MCS, but alternates, for the most part, between male and female accounts, which highlights gender parity. Her table of contents also identifies each person by profession, implicitly arguing that MCS can affect any "type" of person. It is not clear, however, whether the gender parity that McCormick, Zwillinger, and Johnson portray is representative or strategic. In their epidemiological study, Caress et al. reported that 71.7% of the respondents with hypersensitivity were female (and 28.3% male), but stated that this difference was exaggerated by the preponderance of females in the sample itself ("Prevalence of Multiple Chemical Sensitivities"). Clearly, more research needs to be done to determine the extent to which MCS is more prevalent among women and, more important, to investigate the environmental and biological factors (and their interactions) that might make MCS more prevalent among women.

5. Gibson argues that women are more likely to experience the trivialization of their illness by family members, friends, employers, co-workers, and physicians. She cites several studies showing that, even when men and women suffer from identical conditions, physicians are more likely to dismiss women's symptoms as hysteria or stress (478).

6. Stanley Caress generously calculated the cross tabulation at my request but asked that I not cite the actual figures since they were rounded and there were some missing cases.

7. Readers may be curious about what the treatment entails. The Environmental Health Center of Dallas offers diagnostic tests, many of which determine the levels and types of chemicals within one's body, along with treatments such as immunotherapy, nutrient therapy, oxygen therapy, massage, and sauna sessions.

8. Alison Johnson reports that "[m]any people with MCS have committed suicide because they were unable to find housing that did not make them terribly sick" (251).

9. A notable exception here, of course, would be the medical fields of clinical ecology and human ecology. As early as 1962, Theron G. Randolph, in *Human Ecology and Susceptibility to the Chemical Environment,* argued that medicine needs a "wider frame of reference": "It is the relationship between man and his environment, including his diet—so called human ecology—that is of prime importance. Strangely, the basic biologic laws of human ecology have not been adequately stated. Neither has the full range of environmental incitants capable of eliciting clinical responses been fully described" (v). Almost fifty years later, the predominant medical paradigms still fail to encompass this wider frame of reference.

10. Mary Swander, for example, struggled with the invisibility of her environmental illness: "I wanted the able-bodied to grasp I was different, very different, and couldn't 'function normally,' couldn't eat, sleep, dress, work, or socialize the same way they did" (102). Although her friends suggested she "go underground" with her condition, especially with prospective employers, she insisted that, even if she "had wanted to pass as able-bodied, [she] couldn't" (ibid.).

11. Rhonda Zwillinger informed me that this was her intent in a conversation, July 2009. Many of the black-and-white photos of the Lennon-Ono "Bed In" for peace depict a contrast between the white sheets and light pajamas of the activists in their bed and the dark suits of the reporters and photographers.

12. Air fresheners, for example, "work either by using a nerve-deadening agent which

interferes with the ability to smell, or by covering up one smell with another." "Freshening" chemicals, such as xylene, have serious health effects: "xylene may cause liver and kidney damage, as well as damage to a developing fetus" ("Fresh or Foul?"). No one, it would seem, should be breathing xylene.

13. See, for example, Fiona Coyle's study of how eighteen Canadian women address the "corporeal chaos" of MCS by practicing a "spatial and bodily regime that entails the reconstruction of everyday environments into safe spaces" (72).

14. See also Eric Nelson, "The MCS Debate: A Medical Streetfight," about a toxicologist who was paid a large sum by Boeing and who concluded that the symptoms the workers were experiencing could be explained by "psychological morbidity."

15. See work by Lewontin, Haraway, Oyama, and Keller. See also chapter 6 in this book.

16. Time, of course, can be bought and sold, as the article "Corporate Manipulation of Scientific Evidence Linking Chemical Exposures to Human Disease" attests:

> As the scientific evidence piles up, linking chemical exposures to serious human diseases, many chemical-dependent industries, such as pesticide purveyors, are searching for a strategy to buy themselves some time, to put off the inevitable. They needn't look far. The tobacco industry has demonstrated that 40 years of scientific bad news can be deflected and neutralized with relative ease.

Dursban was finally banned on June 8, 2000, by the U.S. Environmental Protection Agency for "virtually all home and garden uses" and is supposed to be phased out of other products (Browner).

17. For more about the black couch, see Alaimo, "Discomforting Creatures"; and Reid, "UnSafe at Any Distance: Todd Haynes' Visual Culture of Health and Risk."

18. Lawrence Buell asks:

> Does her final retreat to a hermetic igloo-like "safehouse" at an exclusive holistic health ranch in the hills above Albuquerque result from undiagnosed physiological vulnerabilities or from psychic dysfunctionality? The film insinuates the former possibility by making it the ostensible catalyst, but equivocates by suggesting the alternative possibility throughout. (*Writing for an Endangered World* 49)

When I taught *Safe* in an undergraduate course on Nature in Film and Literature, about a third of the class thought Carol White was simply crazy. This was especially surprising given that one of the students in the class bravely spoke about her daughter who nearly died from exposure to new carpeting.

19. The process parallels that described by Robert McRuer in his incisive critique of *Queer Eye for the Straight Guy*, in which he argues that "the seemingly marginal flashes of disability in the show . . . attest to" the "normalizing processes" that discipline and contain both disability and queerness (176).

20. Rhonda Zwillinger says that this character in Haynes's film was based on one of her portraits in *The Dispossessed*, which Haynes had seen (Zwillinger, telephone conversation).

21. Pamela Reed Gibson notes that chemically reactive people are defined as "deviant": "we have conventional medical practitioners (untrained in toxicology) and chemical companies (with a vested financial and legal interest) drawing the boundaries between patients and chemical context with the result that women who re-experience the

salience of the chemical context are defined as deviant and unbalanced" (484). More generally, the chronically ill body may be marked as deviant, as Pamela Moss explains, because it is "neither good at being ill nor good at being healthy." As Moss struggled to receive partial long-term disability coverage, the administrators at her university denied her "experience of illness" and instead inscribed her body "discursively and materially as *deviant*" (161). The apparently clear-cut category of "disabled," which often assumes rather static corporeal conditions, does not serve those with chronic, fluctuating, or undiagnosed conditions. Such categories need to be challenged by alternative models that emphasize the full range of disabling conditions, including those, such as autoimmune diseases, in which relative ability and disability fluctuate in often unpredictable ways. Insisting upon the material agency of the body, as well as its ever-emergent intra-actions, is one way to challenge rigid, bounded conceptions of corporeality.

6. Genetics, Material Agency, and the Evolution of Posthuman Environmental Ethics in Science Fiction

1. For a reading of the *Carnosaur* films, see Alaimo, "Endangered Humans?"

2. Bear defines an *endogenous retrovirus* as a "virus that inserts its genetic material into the DNA of a host" (*Darwin's Children* 378). According to Matt Ridley, endogenous retroviruses account for a surprisingly large percentage of the human genome: 1.3%, compared to "proper" genes, which account for 3%. As he puts it, "If you think being descended from apes is bad for your self-esteem, then get used to the idea that you are also descended from viruses" (125).

3. See Alaimo, *Undomesticated Ground,* 144–147, for an analysis of the environmentalist/feminist ethics of Octavia Butler's Xenogenesis series.

4. Notable exceptions to prevalent models of techno- or cyber-posthumanism would be the work of Donna Haraway, especially in her attention to coevolution and companion species, *The Companion Species Manifesto;* and Cary Wolfe, in his critique of the discourse of species and his attention to the animal, *Animal Rites.* Katherine Hayles, in *How We Became Posthuman: Virtual Bodies in Cybernetics, Literature, and Informatics,* a central text of posthuman theory, critiques the disembodiment of the posthuman in ways hospitable to environmentalist concerns: "As we rush to explore the new vistas that cyberspace has made available for colonization, let us remember the fragility of a material world that cannot be replaced" (49). Manuela Rossini argues for a "critical posthumanism" in which "the experience of embodiment in all its richness and variety marks post/humanity and in which the lived body remains the ground not only of individual subjectivity but also of the interaction and connection with the world and with others" (33). Drawing upon Haraway, Vicki Kirby, and Hayles, Sherryl Vint argues for an "embodied posthumanism," asserting that it is "only by remaining faithful to the material context in which we and other subjects are embedded that we can begin to negotiate a collective bodily ethics" (188).

5. Interestingly, both *Darwin's Radio* and *Darwin's Children* echo Lynn Margulis's remark that "Gaia is a tough bitch" (Margulis 140). In *Darwin's Children,* Kaye thinks "Nature is a bitch goddess" (336), and in *Darwin's Radio,* Mitch says, "Mother Nature has always been something of a bitch" (380). From the standpoints of feminism and of environmental ethics, nature as bitch—a potent, unruly, indomitable, and unpredict-

able force—is preferable to the image of the long-suffering, always forgiving, endlessly bountiful maternal figure.

6. There are many compelling feminist critiques of scientific epistemology, including Carolyn Merchant, *The Death of Nature;* Sandra Harding, *Whose Science? Whose Knowledge? Thinking from Women's Lives;* and Haraway, "Situated Knowledges."

7. Eric White's wonderful term for "the evolutionist perspective on the human body as an assemblage of nonhuman parts" is "the menagerie within" (244).

8. Lisa Lynch reads *Darwin's Radio* quite differently, arguing that, despite its critique of medical institutions, it fails to envision social reform but instead "sounds a rallying cry for the arrival of the posthuman, [as] the 'reform' Bear champions comes from within the genome" (72). Whereas she critiques the sociobiology and the gene fetishism of the novel, I argue that multiple material agencies, including those of evolution, disrupt contemporary genetic reductionism.

9. A bit of scientific context may be of interest here. Although evolutionary biologists would answer the question "are humans still evolving?" in the affirmative, a retrovirus is not considered to be the most likely cause of future human evolution. Instead, as Floyd A. Reed from the Max Planck Institute for Evolutionary Biology explains, environmental/ social conditions, such as "changes in newly emerging diseases, wars, availability of cheap energy and food resources, climate change and nuclear and chemical pollution . . . are likely to expose our genomes to intense Darwinian selection and/or increased genetic drift," making it "inevitable" that "we will continue to undergo some form of evolutionary change" (4).

WORKS CITED

Abram, David. *The Spell of the Sensuous: Perception and Language in a More-than-Human World*. New York: Vintage, 1997.

Adamson, Joni. *American Indian Literature, Environmental Justice, and Ecocriticism: The Middle Place*. Tucson: University of Arizona Press, 2001.

Agrawal, Arun. "Dismantling the Divide between Indigenous and Scientific Knowledge." *Development and Change* 26.3 (1995): 413–439.

Akaba, Azibuike. "Science as a Double-Edged Sword." *Race, Poverty, and the Environment: A Journal for Social and Environmental Justice* 11.2 (Winter 2004–2005): 9–11.

Alaimo, Stacy. "Discomforting Creatures: Monstrous Natures in Recent Films." In *Beyond Nature Writing*, ed. Karla Armbruster and Kathleen Wallace. Charlottesville: University of Virginia Press, 2001: 279–296.

———. "Endangered Humans? Wired Bodies and the Human Wilds." *Camera Obscura* 40–41 (May 1997): 227–244.

———. "Insurgent Vulnerability: Masculinist Consumerism, Feminist Activism, and the Gendered Sciences of Global Climate Change." *Women, Gender & Research* (*Kvinder, Kon og Forskning*, Denmark) (Fall 2009): 22–35.

———. *Undomesticated Ground: Recasting Nature as Feminist Space*. Ithaca, N.Y.: Cornell University Press, 2000.

Alaimo, Stacy, and Susan J. Hekman. "Introduction." In *Material Feminisms*, ed. Stacy Alaimo and Susan J. Hekman. Bloomington: Indiana University Press, 2007: 1–19.

Alaimo, Stacy, and Susan J. Hekman, eds. *Material Feminisms*. Bloomington: Indiana University Press, 2007.

Alexie, Sherman. "Introduction." In Percival Everett, *Watershed*. Boston: Beacon, 1996.

Allister, Mark. *Refiguring the Map of Sorrow: Nature Writing and Autobiography*. Charlottesville: University of Virginia Press, 2001.

American Cancer Society. "The Environment and Cancer Risks." *American Cancer Society.* http://www.cancer.org/docroot/NWS/content/NWS_2_1x_The_Environment_and_Cancer_Risk.asp, Jan. 14, 2000 (accessed Dec. 21, 2007).

Antonetta, Susanne. *Body Toxic.* Washington, D.C.: Counterpoint, 2001.

Ashford, Nicholas A., and Claudia S. Miller. *Chemical Exposures: Low Levels and High Stakes.* New York: Van Nostrand Reinhold, 1991.

Atwood, Margaret. *Oryx and Crake.* New York: Anchor, 2003.

Ausubel, Kenny. *Ecological Medicine: Healing the Earth, Healing Ourselves.* San Francisco: Sierra Club Books, 2004.

Barad, Karen. *Meeting the Universe Halfway: Quantum Physics and the Entanglement of Matter and Meaning.* Durham, N.C.: Duke University Press, 2007.

———. "Posthumanist Performativity: Toward an Understanding of How Matter Comes to Matter." *Signs* 28.3 (Spring 2003): 801–831.

———. "Re(con)figuring Space, Time, and Matter." In *Feminist Locations: Global and Local, Theory and Practice,* ed. Marianne DeKoven. New Brunswick, N.J.: Rutgers University Press, 2001: 75–109.

Barrett, Stephen. *Quackwatch: Your Guide to Quackery, Health Fraud, and Intelligent Decisions.* www.quackwatch.org/00AboutQuackwatch/mission.html (accessed July 2008).

Bauer, Susanne. "Societal and Ethical Issues in Human Biomonitoring: A View from Science Studies." *Environmental Health* 7, suppl. 1 (2008): 1–10.

Bear, Greg. *Darwin's Children.* New York: Ballantine, 2003.

———. *Darwin's Radio.* New York: Ballantine, 1999.

Beck, Ulrich. *Risk Society: Towards a New Modernity.* Trans. Mark Ritter. London: Sage, 1992.

Benford, Robert. "The Half-Life of the Environmental Justice Frame: Innovation, Diffusion, Stagnation." In *Power, Justice, and the Environment: A Critical Appraisal of the Environmental Justice Movement,* ed. David Naguib Pellow and Robert J. Brulle. Cambridge, Mass.: MIT Press, 2005: 37–54.

Berkson, Jacob B. *A Canary's Tale: The Final Battle: Politics, Poisons, and Pollution vs. the Environment and the Public Health,* vols. 1 and 2. Hagerstown, Md.: Berkson, 1996.

Berry, K. Wesley. "Bioregional Pedagogy, Ecospiritual Autobiography, and the Horn Island Logs of Walter Inglis Anderson." *Southern Quarterly: A Journal of the Arts in the South* 38.1 (Fall 1999): 147–158.

Birke, Lynda. "Bodies and Biology." In *Feminist Theory and the Body: A Reader,* ed. Janet Price and Margrit Shildrick. New York: Routledge, 1999: 42–49.

BlueVoice. http://www.bluevoice.org/sections/ocean/ocean-pollution.shtml (accessed Aug. 1, 2009).

Bolt, Hermann M., and Ernst Kiesswetter. "Is Multiple Chemical Sensitivity a Clinically Defined Entity?" *Toxicology Letters* 128 (Mar. 2002): 99–106.

Bolton Valencius, Conevery. *The Health of the Country: How American Settlers Understood Themselves and Their Land.* New York: Basic, 2002.

Breast Cancer Action. http://www.bcaction.org (accessed Dec. 21, 2007).

———. *Think before You Pink.* http://thinkbeforeyoupink.org/Pages/FocusOnPinkwashers.html (accessed Nov. 7, 2007).

Brown, Phil. "When the Public Knows Better: Popular Epidemiology." *Environment* 35.8 (Oct. 1993): 17–41.

Brown, Phil, and Judith Kirwan Kelley. "Physicians' Knowledge, Attitudes, and Practice Regarding Environmental Health Hazards." In *Illness and the Environment: A Reader in Contested Medicine,* ed. Steve Kroll-Smith, Phil Brown, and Valerie J. Gunter. New York: NYU Press, 2000: 46–71.

Brown, Phil, Steve Kroll-Smith, and Valerie J. Gunter. "Knowledge, Citizens, and Organizations: An Overview of Environments, Diseases, and Social Conflict." In *Illness and the Environment: A Reader in Contested Medicine,* ed. Steve Kroll-Smith, Phil Brown, and Valerie J. Gunter. New York: NYU Press, 2000: 9–25.

Browner, Carol. "Dursban Announcement." *U.S. Environmental Protection Agency.* http://www.epa.gov/history/topics/legal/03.htm (accessed Aug. 3, 2009).

Bryson, Michael A. "It's Worth the Risk: Science and Autobiography in Sandra Steingraber's *Living Downstream.*" *Women's Studies Quarterly* 1–2 (2001): 170–182.

Buell, Lawrence. *The Environmental Imagination: Thoreau, Nature Writing, and the Formation of American Culture.* Cambridge, Mass.: Harvard University Press, 1995.

———. *Writing for an Endangered World: Literature, Culture, and Environment in the U.S. and Beyond.* Cambridge, Mass.: Harvard University Press, 2001.

Bullard, Robert. *The Quest for Environmental Justice: Human Rights and the Politics of Pollution.* San Francisco: Sierra Club Books, 2005.

Burke, Fielding. *Call Home the Heart.* Old Westbury, N.Y.: Feminist Press, 1983.

Butler, Judith. *Giving an Account of Oneself.* New York: Fordham University Press, 2005.

Butler, Octavia E. *Lilith's Brood.* New York: Warner, 2000.

Caminero-Santangelo, Marta. "'The Pleas of the Desperate': Collective Agency versus Magical Realism in Ana Castillo's *So Far from God.*" *Tulsa Studies in Women's Literature* 24.1 (Spring 2005): 81–103.

Campbell, Fiona Kumari. "Legislating Disability: Negative Ontologies and the Government of Legal Identities." In *Foucault and the Government of Disability,* ed. S. Tremain. Ann Arbor: University of Michigan Press, 2005: 108–130.

Caress, Stanley. Personal email. Oct. 2005.

Caress, Stanley, et al. "Prevalence of Multiple Chemical Sensitivities: A Population-Based Study in the Southeastern United States." *American Journal of Public Health* 94.5 (May 1, 2004): 746–747.

———. "Symptomology and Etiology of Multiple Chemical Sensitivities in the Southeastern United States." *Archives of Environmental Health* 57.5 (Sept. 1, 2002): 429–436.

Carson, Rachel. *Silent Spring.* New York: Houghton Mifflin, 1962.

Casey, Edward. *Getting Back into Place: Toward a Renewed Understanding of the Place-World.* Bloomington: Indiana University Press, 1993.

Castillo, Ana. *So Far from God.* New York: Norton, 1993.

Castree, Noel, and Bruce Braun. "The Construction of Nature and the Nature of Construction: Analytical and Political Tools for Building Survivable Futures." In *Remaking Reality: Nature at the Millennium,* ed. Bruce Braun and Noel Castree. London: Routledge, 1998.

Chandler, Katherine R., and Melissa A. Goldthwaite. *Surveying the Literary Landscape of Terry Tempest Williams: New Critical Essays.* Salt Lake City: University of Utah Press, 2003.

Cheah, Pheng. "Mattering." *Diacritics* 26.1 (Spring 1996): 109–139.

"Chemical Trespass 2004." *Pesticide Action Network North America.* http://www.panna.org/docsTrespass/chemicalTrespass2004.dv.html (accessed Jan. 24, 2010).

Cherniak, Martin. *The Hawk's Nest Incident: America's Worst Industrial Disaster.* New Haven, Conn.: Yale University Press, 1986.

Clark, Claudia. *Radium Girls: Women and Industrial Health Reform, 1910–1935.* Chapel Hill: University of North Carolina Press, 1997.

Coburn, Jason. *Street Science: Community Knowledge and Environmental Health Science.* Cambridge, Mass.: MIT Press, 2005.

Code, Lorraine. *Ecological Thinking: The Politics of Epistemic Location.* Oxford: Oxford University Press, 2006.

Coiner, Constance. "Literature of Resistance: The Intersection of Feminism and the Communist Left in Meridel Le Sueur and Tillie Olsen." In *Radical Revisions: Rereading 1930s Culture,* ed. Bill Mullen and Sherry Linkon. Urbana: University of Illinois Press, 1996: 144–166.

Cornell, Drucilla. *Beyond Accommodation: Ethical Feminism, Deconstruction, and the Law.* New York: Routledge, 1991.

"Corporate Manipulation of Scientific Evidence Linking Chemical Exposures to Human Disease: A Case in Point—Cigarette Science at Johns Hopkins." *Rachel's Environment and Health Weekly* 464 (Oct. 18, 1995). http://www.rachel.org/en/node/3977 (accessed Aug. 2009, title changed to "Cigarette Science at Johns Hopkins").

Couch, Stephen R., and Steve Kroll-Smith. "Environmental Movements and Expert Knowledge." In *Illness and the Environment: A Reader in Contested Medicine,* ed. Steve Kroll-Smith, Phil Brown, and Valerie J. Gunter. New York: NYU Press, 2000.

Coyle, Fiona. "Safe Space as Counter Space: Women, Environmental Illness and 'Corporeal Chaos.'" *Canadian Geographer* 48.1 (2004): 62–75.

Darwin, Charles. *The Origin of Species by Means of Natural Selection and the Descent of Man and Selection in Relation to Sex.* New York: Modern Library, n.d.

Davidson, Michael. *Ghostlier Demarcations: Modern Poetry and the Material World.* Berkeley: University of California Press, 1997.

Dawahare, Anthony. "Modernity and 'Village Communism' in Depression-Era America: The Utopian Literature of Meridel Le Sueur." *Criticism* 39.3 (Summer 1997): 409–431.

Dayton, Tim. *Muriel Rukeyser's "The Book of the Dead."* Columbia: University of Missouri Press, 2003.

"Death in Small Doses." *Environmental Justice Foundation.* http://www.ejfoundation.org/modules.php?set_albumName=album14&op=modload&name=gallery&file=index&include=view_album.php&page=1 (accessed Feb. 7, 2009).

De Lauretis, Teresa. "Statement Due." *Critical Inquiry* 30.2 (2004): 365–368.

Deleuze, Gilles, and Felix Guattari. *A Thousand Plateaus: Capitalism and Schizophrenia.* Trans. Brian Massumi. Minneapolis: University of Minnesota Press, 1987.

Di Chiro, Giovanna. "Indigenous Peoples and Biocolonialism: Defining the 'Science of Environmental Justice' in the Century of the Gene." In *Environmental Justice and Environmentalism: The Social Justice Challenge to the Environmental Movement,* ed. Ronald Sandler and Phaedra C. Pezzulo. Cambridge, Mass.: MIT Press, 2007: 251–283.

——. "'Living Is for Everyone': Border Crossings for Community, Environment, and Health." *Osiris* 19 (2004): 112–130.

——. "Local Actions, Global Visions: Remaking Environmental Expertise." *Frontiers* 18.2 (1997): 203–231.

——. "Producing 'Roundup Ready®' Communities? Human Genome Research and Environmental Justice Policy." In *New Perspectives on Environmental Justice: Gender, Sexuality, and Activism,* ed. Rachel Stein. New Brunswick, N.J.: Rutgers University Press, 2004: 139–160.

Dougherty, Stephen. "The Biopolitics of the Killer Virus Novel." *Cultural Critique* 48 (Spring 2001): 1–29.

Dumit, J. "Illnesses You Have to Fight to Get: Facts as Forces in Uncertain, Emergent Illnesses." *Social Science and Medicine* 62.3 (2006): 577–590.

Dunaway, Finis. *Natural Visions: The Power of Images in American Environmental Reform.* Chicago: University of Chicago Press, 2005.

Duncan, David Ewing. "The Chemicals within Us." *National Geographic* 210.4 (Oct. 2006): 116–137.

——. "A World of Hurt." *National Geographic* 210.4 (Oct. 2006): 139–143.

Duster, Troy. "Buried Alive: The Concept of Race in Science." In *Genetic Nature/Culture: Anthropology and Science beyond the Two Culture Divide,* ed. Alan H. Goodman, Deborah Heath, and M. Susan Lindee. Berkeley: University of California Press, 2003.

Eaton, K., et al. "Multiple Chemical Sensitivity: Recognition and Management. A Document on the Health Effects of Everyday Chemical Exposures and Their Limitations." *Journal of Nutritional and Environmental Medicine* 10.1 (Mar. 1, 2000): 39–84.

Eichstadt, Peter. *If You Poison Us: Uranium and Native Americans.* Santa Fe, N.M.: Red Crane, 2008.

Eisenstein, Zillah. *Manmade Breast Cancers.* Ithaca, N.Y.: Cornell University Press, 2001.

Environmental Health Center of Dallas. www.ehcd.com/services/patientsservices (accessed Oct. 18, 2004).

Environmental Justice Foundation. http://www.ejfoundation.org/page124.html (accessed Sept. 15, 2008).

Environmental Working Group. *Human Toxome Project.* http://www.ewg.org/sites/humantoxome/participants/index.php?country=USA&state=TX (accessed Dec. 18, 2007).

"EPA Warns Human Beings No Longer Biodegradable." *Onion* 43.30 (July 26, 2007). http://www.theonion.com/content/news_briefs/epa_warns_human_beings_no (accessed June 20, 2009).

Eriksen, H. R., and H. Ursin. "Subjective Health Complaints, Sensitization, and Sustained Cognitive Activation (Stress)." *Journal of Psychosomatic Research* 56.4 (Apr. 1994): 445–448.

Everett, Percival. *Watershed.* Boston: Beacon, 1996.

FitzSimmons, Margaret, and David Goodman. "Incorporating Nature: Environmental Narratives and the Reproduction of Food." In *Remaking Reality: Nature at the Millennium,* ed. Bruce Braun and Noel Castree. London: Routledge, 1998: 194–220.

Frank, Arthur W. *The Wounded Storyteller: Body, Illness, and Ethics.* Chicago: University of Chicago Press, 1995.

Franklin, Sarah. "Life Itself: Global Nature and the Genetic Imaginary." In *Global Nature, Global Culture,* ed. Sarah Franklin, Celia Lury, and Jackie Stacie. London: Sage, 2000.

"Fresh or Foul? Air Fresheners in Public Spaces." *Environmental Health Association Nova Scotia.* www.environmentalhealth.ca/fall02foul.html (accessed May 27, 2005).

Frickel, Scott. "Just Science? Organizing Scientific Activism in the U.S. Environmental Justice Movement." *Science as Culture* 13.4 (Dec. 2004): 449–469.

Fromm, Harold. "The 'Environment' Is Us." *Electronic Book Review,* Jan. 1, 1997. http://www.altx.com/ebr/reviews/rev8/r8fromm.html (accessed Sept. 9, 2005).

Garland-Thomson, Rosemarie. "Disability and Representation." *PMLA* 120.2 (Mar. 2005): 522–527.

Gatens, Moira. *Imaginary Bodies: Ethics, Power and Corporeality.* New York: Routledge, 1996.

Gibson, Pamela Reed. "Multiple Chemical Sensitivity, Culture, and Delegitimization: A Feminist Analysis." *Feminism and Psychology* 7.4 (1997): 475–493.

Goldman, Emma, and Max Baginski. "Mother Earth." *Mother Earth* 1.1 (Mar. 1906): 1–4.

Gompers, Samuel. "Wages and Health." *American Federationist* 21 (Aug. 1914): 642–646.

Grosz, Elizabeth. *The Nick of Time: Politics, Evolution and the Untimely.* Durham, N.C.: Duke University Press, 2004.

———. *Time Travels: Feminism, Nature, Power.* Durham, N.C.: Duke University Press, 2005.

———. *Volatile Bodies: Toward a Corporeal Feminism.* Bloomington: Indiana University Press, 1994.

Grover, Jan Zita. *North Enough: AIDS and Other Clearcuts.* Minneapolis, Minn.: Graywolf, 1997.

Hames-Garcia, Michael. "How Real Is Race?" In *Material Feminisms,* ed. Stacy Alaimo and Susan Hekman. Bloomington: Indiana University Press, 2007: 308–339.

Hansen Hviid, Steen. "Personal Stories from Environmentally Ill Patients around the Environmental Health Center in Dallas." http://www.ehcd.com/websteen/ehcd_patient_stories.htm (accessed May 29, 2005).

Haraway, Donna J. "A Cyborg Manifesto: Science, Technology, and Socialist Feminism in the Late 20th Century." Reprinted in her *Simians, Cyborgs, and Women.* New York: Routledge, 1991.

———. *The Companion Species Manifesto: Dogs, People, and Significant Otherness.* Chicago: Prickly Paradigm, 2003.

———. *The Haraway Reader.* New York: Routledge, 2004.

———. *Modest_Witness@Second_Millennium: FemaleMan©_Meets_OncoMouse™.* New York: Routledge, 1997.

———. *Primate Visions: Gender, Race, and Nature in the World of Modern Science.* New York: Routledge, 1989.

———. "Situated Knowledges: The Science Question in Feminism and the Privilege of Partial Perspective." Reprinted in her *Simians, Cyborgs, and Women: The Reinvention of Nature.* New York: Routledge, 1991.

Harding, Sandra. *Science and Social Inequality: Feminist and Postcolonial Issues.* Urbana: University of Illinois Press, 2006.

———. *Whose Science? Whose Knowledge? Thinking from Women's Lives.* Ithaca, N.Y.: Cornell University Press, 1991.

Harris, Eddy L. *Mississippi Solo: A River Quest.* New York: Holt, 1998.

Hartman, Stephanie. "All Systems Go: Muriel Rukeyser's *The Book of the Dead* and the Reinvention of Modernist Poetics." In *How Shall We Tell Each Other of the Poet? The Life and Writing of Muriel Rukeyser,* ed. Anne F. Herzog and Janet E. Kaufman. New York: Macmillan, 1999: 209–223.

Hausman, Bernice. "Virtual Sex, Real Gender: Body and Identity in Transgender Discourse." In *Virtual Gender: Fantasies of Subjectivity and Embodiment,* ed. Mary Ann O'Farrell and Lynne Vallone. Ann Arbor: University of Michigan Press, 2006: 190–216.

Hausteiner, Constanze, et al. "Psychiatric Morbidity and Low Self-Attentiveness in Patients with Environmental Illness." *Journal of Nervous and Mental Disease* 191.1 (Jan. 2003): 50–55.

Hayles, N. Katherine. "Constrained Constructivism: Locating Scientific Inquiry in the Theater of Representation." In *Realism and Representation: Essays on the Problem of Realism in Relation to Science, Literature, and Culture,* ed. George Levine. Madison: University of Wisconsin Press, 1993: 27–43.

———. *How We Became Posthuman: Virtual Bodies in Cybernetics, Literature, and Informatics.* Chicago: University of Chicago Press, 1999.

Haynes, Todd, dir. *Safe.* DVD liner. Chemical Films Limited Partnership, 1995.

Heavey, David. "The Enfreakment of Photography." In *Disability Studies Reader,* ed. Lennard J. Davis. New York: Routledge, 1997: 332–347.

Heise, Ursula K. *Sense of Place and Sense of Planet: The Environmental Imagination of the Global.* New York: Oxford University Press, 2008.

———."Toxins, Drugs, and Global Systems: Risk and Narrative in the Contemporary Novel." *American Literature* 74.4 (Dec. 2002): 747–748.

Heuser, Gunnar. "Foreword." In Rhonda Zwillinger, *The Dispossessed: Living with Multiple Chemical Sensitivities.* Paulden, Ariz.: Dispossessed Project, 1998.

Hileman, Bette. "Chemical Intolerance: Researchers Explore Relationships between This Environmentally Induced Illness and Addiction." *Chemical and Engineering News* 83.41 (Oct. 10, 2005): 24–29.

Hird, Myra J. "Naturally Queer." *Feminist Theory* 5.1 (2004): 85–89.

Hochman, Jhan. *Green Cultural Studies: Nature in Film, Novel, and Theory.* Moscow: University of Idaho Press, 1998.

Hofrichter, Richard, ed. *Reclaiming the Environmental Debate: The Politics of Health in a Toxic Culture.* Cambridge, Mass.: MIT Press, 2000

———. *Toxic Struggles: The Theory and Practice of Environmental Justice.* Salt Lake City: University of Utah Press, 2002.

Howard, J. "Environmental 'Nasty Surprise' as a Window on Precautionary Thinking." *Technology and Society Magazine* (IEEE) 21.4 (2003): 19–22.

Human Genome Project. http://www.ornl.gov/sci/techresources/Human_Genome/publicat/tko/03_introducing.html (accessed July 2008).

Hunting, Eric. "Shelter: Documenting a Personal Quest for Nontoxic Housing." http://radio.weblogs.com/0119080/stories/2003/01/31/introduction.html (accessed May 26, 2005).

Irigaray, Luce. *This Sex Which Is Not One.* Trans. Catherine Porter. Ithaca, N.Y.: Cornell University Press, 1985.

Ishiyama, Noriko. "Environmental Justice and American Indian Tribal Sovereignty: Case Study of a Land-Use Conflict in Skull Valley, Utah." *Antipode* 35.1 (2003): 119–139.

Johnson, Alison, ed. *Casualties of Progress: Personal Histories from the Chemically Sensitive.* Brunswick, Maine: MCS Information Exchange, 2000.

Kadlec, David. "X-Ray Testimonials in Muriel Rukeyser." *Modernism/Modernity* 5.1 (1998): 23–47.

Kalaidjian, Walter. *American Culture between the Wars: Revisionary Modernism and Postmodern Critique.* New York: Columbia University Press, 1993.

Kanner, Allan, Ryan Casey, and Barrett Ristroph. "New Opportunities for Native American Tribes to Pursue Environmental and Natural Resource Claims." *Duke Environmental Law and Policy Forum* 14.1 (2003): 155–183.

Keller, Evelyn Fox. *The Century of the Gene.* Cambridge, Mass.: Harvard University Press, 2002.

———. *Refiguring Life: Metaphors of Twentieth-Century Biology.* New York: Columbia University Press, 1995.

Kidner, David W. "Fabricating Nature: A Critique of the Social Construction of Nature." *Environmental Ethics* 22.4 (Winter 2000): 339–357.

Kingston, Maxine Hong. *The Woman Warrior: Memoirs of a Girlhood among Ghosts.* New York: Vintage, 1989.

Kirby, Vicki. *Telling Flesh: The Substance of the Corporeal.* New York: Routledge, 1997.

Knopf-Newman, Marcy Jane. *Beyond Slash, Burn, and Poison: Transforming Breast Cancer Stories into Action.* New Brunswick, N.J.: Rutgers University Press, 2004.

Konchar Farr, Cecilia. "American Ecobiography." In *Literature of Nature: An International Sourcebook,* ed. Patrick D. Murphy. Chicago: Fitzroy Dearborn, 1998: 94–97.

Kroll-Smith, Steve, Phil Brown, and Valerie J. Gunter. "Knowledge, Citizens, and Organizations: An Overview of Environments, Diseases, and Social Conflict." In *Illness and the Environment: A Reader in Contested Medicine,* ed. Steve Kroll-Smith, Phil Brown, and Valerie J. Gunter. New York: NYU Press, 2000: 9–25.

Kroll-Smith, Steve, and H. Hugh Floyd. *Bodies in Protest: Environmental Illness and the Struggle over Medical Knowledge.* New York: NYU Press, 1997.

Latour, Bruno. *Pandora's Hope: Essays on the Reality of Science Studies.* Cambridge, Mass.: Harvard University Press, 1999.

———. *Politics of Nature: How to Bring the Sciences into Democracy.* Trans. Catherine Porter. Cambridge, Mass.: Harvard University Press, 2004.

———. *We Have Never Been Modern.* Trans. Catherine Porter. Cambridge, Mass.: Harvard University Press, 1993.

———. "Why Has Critique Run Out of Steam? From Matters of Fact to Matters of Concern." *Critical Inquiry* 30 (Winter 2004): 225–248.

Lawrence, Candida. *Fear Itself: A Memoir.* Denver, Colo.: Unbridled, 2004.

Lawson, Lynn. "Notes from a Human Canary." In *Illness and the Environment: A Reader in Contested Medicine,* ed. Steve Kroll-Smith, Phil Brown, and Valerie J. Gunter. New York: NYU Press, 2000: 333–341.

Le Sueur, Meridel. "American Bus." In *Harvest and Song for My Time.*

———. "Annunciation." In *Salute to Spring.*

———. "Autumnal Village." In *Harvest and Song for My Time.*

———. "Corn Village." In *Salute to Spring.*

——. *Crusaders: The Radical Legacy of Marian and Arthur Le Sueur.* St. Paul: Minnesota Historical Society Press, 1984.

——. "The Dark of the Time." In *Harvest and Song for My Time.*

——. "Eroded Woman." In *Harvest and Song for My Time.*

——. "Evening in a Lumber Town." *New Masses* (July 1926): 22–23.

——. "The Fetish of Being Outside." *New Masses* (Feb. 26, 1935): 22–23.

——. "The Girl." In *Salute to Spring.*

——. "Harvest." In *Harvest and Song for My Time.*

——. *Harvest and Song for My Time.* Minneapolis: West End, and MEP, 1977.

——. *I Hear Men Talking: Stories of the Early Decades,* ed. Linda Ray Pratt. Minneapolis, Minn.: West End, 1984.

——. "Iron Country." *Masses and Mainstream* 2.3 (Mar. 1949): 53–60.

——. "Memorial." In *Ripening.*

——. "Nests." *Poetry* 24.2 (May 1924): 80–81.

——. "No Wine in His Cart." In *Salute to Spring.*

——. "The Origins of Corn." Excerpted in *New America* 2.3 (1976): 20–23.

——. *Ripening: Selected Work, 1927–1980,* ed. Elaine Hedges. Old Westbury, N.Y.: Feminist Press, 1982.

——. *Salute to Spring.* New York: International, 1940.

——. "Spring Story." *Scribner's Magazine* 89 (May 1931): 553–562.

——. "To Hell with You, Mr. Blue!" In *Harvest and Song for My Time.*

——. "We'll Make Your Bed." In *Harvest and Song for My Time.*

——. "Women Know a Lot of Things." In *Ripening.*

Lewontin, Richard, and Richard Levins. *Biology under the Influence: Dialectical Essays on Ecology, Agriculture, and Health.* New York: Monthly Review Press, 2007.

Libby, Brooke. "Nature Writing as Refuge: Autobiography in the Natural World." In *Reading under the Sign of Nature: New Essays in Ecocriticism,* ed. John Tallmadge and Henry Harrington. Salt Lake City: University of Utah Press, 2000.

Light, Andrew, and Holmes Rolston III. "Introduction: Ethics and Environmental Ethics." In *Environmental Ethics: An Anthology,* ed. Andrew Light and Holmes Rolston III. Malden, Mass.: Blackwell, 2003: 1–11.

Linton, Simi. "What Is Disability Studies?" *PMLA* 120.2 (Mar. 2005): 518–522.

Lorde, Audre. *The Cancer Journals.* San Francisco: Aunt Lute, 1980.

Lowney, John. *History, Memory, and the American Left: Modern American Poetry, 1935–1968.* Iowa City: University of Iowa Press, 2006.

Luke, Timothy W. "Rethinking Technoscience in Risk Society: Toxicity as Textuality." In *Reclaiming the Environmental Debate: The Politics of Health in a Toxic Culture,* ed. Richard Hofrichter. Cambridge, Mass.: MIT Press, 2000: 239–254.

Lynas, Mark. *High Tide: The Truth about Our Climate Crisis.* New York: Picador, 2004.

Lynch, Lisa. "Not a Virus, but an Upgrade: The Ethics of Epidemic Evolution in Greg Bear's *Darwin's Radio.*" *Literature and Medicine* 20.1 (Spring 2001): 71–93.

Margulis, Lynn. "Gaia Is a Tough Bitch." In *The Third Culture: Beyond the Scientific Revolution,* ed. John Brockman. New York: Touchstone, 1995: 129–151.

Martineau, Daniel, et al. "Cancer in Wildlife, a Case Study: Beluga from the St. Lawrence Estuary, Québec, Canada." *Environmental Health Perspectives* 110.3 (Mar. 2002): 285–292.

Massumi, Brian. *Parables for the Virtual: Movement, Affect, Sensation.* Durham, N.C.: Duke University Press, 2002.

Masumoto, David. *Harvest Son.* New York: Norton, 1999.

McAloose, Denise, and Alisa L. Newton. "Wildlife Cancer: A Conservation Perspective." *Nature Reviews: Cancer* 9.7 (July 2009): 517–526.

McCormick, Gail. *Living with Multiple Chemical Sensitivity: Narratives of Coping.* Jefferson, N.C.: McFarland, 2001.

McKeown-Eyssen, Gail, et al. "Case-Control Study of Genotypes in Multiple Chemical Sensitivity: CYP2D6, NAT1, NAT2, PON1, PON2 and MTHFR." *International Journal of Epidemiology* 33 (2004): 971–978.

McKone, Thomas. *Berkeley Center for Environmental Public Health Tracking.* http://ehtracking.berkeley.edu/projects/assess.htm (accessed Sept. 1, 2008).

McRuer, Robert. *Crip Theory: Cultural Signs of Queerness and Disability.* New York: NYU Press, 2006.

McWhorter, Ladelle. *Bodies and Pleasures: Foucault and the Politics of Sexual Normalization.* Bloomington: Indiana University Press, 1999.

Merchant, Carolyn. *The Death of Nature: Women, Ecology and the Scientific Revolution.* New York: Harper and Row, 1980.

Mortimer-Sandilands, Catriona, and Bruce Erickson, eds. *Queer Ecologies: Sex, Nature, Biopolitics and Desire.* Bloomington: Indiana University Press, 2010.

Moss, Pamela. "Autobiographical Notes on Chronic Illness." In *Mind and Body Spaces: Geographies of Illness, Impairment, and Disability,* ed. Ruth Butler and Hester Parr. London: Routledge, 1999: 155–166.

Moss, Pamela, and Isabel van Dyck. "Inquiry into Environment and Body: Women, Work, and Chronic Illness." *Environment and Planning: Society and Space* 14 (1996): 737–753.

Murphy, Michelle. "The 'Elsewhere within Here' and Environmental Illness; or, How to Build Yourself a Body in a Safe Space." *Configurations* 8 (2000): 87–120.

Nash, Linda. *Inescapable Ecologies: A History of Environment, Disease, and Knowledge.* Berkeley: University of California Press, 2006.

National Association for the Advancement of Colored People. http://www.naacp.org/legal/expertise (accessed Sept. 6, 2008).

National Institute of Environmental Health Sciences. http://www.niehs.nih.gov/external/faq/mcss.html (accessed Sept. 2005).

Navajo Uranium Miner Oral History and Photography Project. *Memories Come to Us in the Rain and the Wind: Oral Histories and Photographs of Navajo Uranium Miners and Their Families.* Jamaica Plain, Mass.: Red Sun, 1997.

Nelson, Cary. *Repression and Recovery: Modern American Poetry and the Politics of Cultural Memory, 1910–1945.* Madison: University of Wisconsin Press, 1989.

———. *Revolutionary Memory: Recovering the Poetry of the American Left.* New York: Routledge, 2003.

Nelson, Eric. "The MCS Debate: A Medical Streetfight." *Free Press* 8 (Feb.–Mar. 1994). http://www.washingtonfreepress.org/08/Boeing4.html (accessed May 2005).

Neumann, Shirley. "'An Appearance Walking in a Forest the Sexes Burn': Autobiography and the Construction of the Feminine Body." In *Autobiography and Postmodernism,* ed. Kathleen Ashley, Leigh Gilmore, and Gerald Peters. Amherst: University of Massachusetts Press, 1994: 293–315.

Noble, Charles. "Work: The Most Dangerous Environment." In *Toxic Struggles: The Theory and Practice of Environmental Justice*, ed. Richard Hofrichter. Salt Lake City: University of Utah Press, 2002.

Olsen, Tillie. *Yonnondio: From the Thirties*. New York: Dell, 1974.

Ortiz, Simon J. *Woven Stone*. Tucson: University of Arizona Press, 1992.

Oyama, Susan. *The Ontogeny of Information: Developmental Systems and Evolution*. Durham, N.C.: Duke University Press, 2000.

Pall, Martin L. "NMDA Sensitization and Stimulation by Peroxynitrite, Nitric Oxide, and Organic Solvents as the Mechanism of Chemical Sensitivity in Multiple Chemical Sensitivity." *FASEB Journal* 16 (2002): 1407–1417.

Pellow, David Naguib, and Robert J. Brulle, eds. *Power, Justice, and the Environment: A Critical Appraisal of the Environmental Justice Movement*. Cambridge, Mass.: MIT Press, 2005.

Pickering, Andrew. *The Mangle of Practice: Time, Agency, and Science*. Chicago: University of Chicago Press, 1995.

Platt, Kamala. "Ecocritical Chicana Literature: Ana Castillo's 'Virtual Realism'." *ISLE: Interdisciplinary Studies in Literature and Environment* 3.1 (Summer 1996): 67–96.

Plumwood, Val. *Feminism and the Mastery of Nature*. New York: Routledge, 1993.

Pratt, Linda Ray. "Afterword." In Meridel Le Sueur, *I Hear Men Talking and Other Stories*. Minneapolis, Minn.: West End, 1984.

Proctor, Robert N. *Cancer Wars: How Politics Shapes What We Know and Don't Know about Cancer*. New York: Basic, 1995.

Rabinowitz, Paula. *Labor & Desire: Women's Revolutionary Fiction in Depression America*. Chapel Hill: University of North Carolina Press, 1991.

———. *They Must Be Represented: The Politics of Documentary*. London: Verso, 1994.

Radetsky, Peter. *Allergic to the Twentieth Century: The Explosion in Environmental Allergies—From Sick Buildings to Multiple Chemical Sensitivity*. Boston: Little, Brown, 1997.

Raglon, Rebecca, and Marian Scholtmeijer. "Heading Off the Trail: Language, Literature, and Nature's Resistance to Narrative." In *Beyond Nature Writing: Expanding the Boundaries of Ecocriticism*, ed. Karla Armbruster and Kathleen Wallace. Charlottesville: University of Virginia Press, 2001.

Rampton, Sheldon, and John Stauber. *Trust Us, We're Experts! How Industry Manipulates Science and Gambles with Your Future*. New York: Tarcher, 2001.

Randolph, Theron G. *Human Ecology and Susceptibility to the Chemical Environment*. Springfield, Ill.: Thomas, 1962.

Ray, Janisse. *Ecology of a Cracker Childhood*. Minneapolis, Minn.: Milkweed, 2000.

Rea, William. *Chemical Sensitivity*, vol. 1. Boca Raton, Fla.: Lewis, 1992.

Reed, Floyd A. "Are Humans Still Evolving?" In *Encyclopedia of Life Sciences*. Hoboken, N.J.: Wiley, 2008: 1–6.

Reid, Roddey. "UnSafe at Any Distance: Todd Haynes' Visual Culture of Health and Risk." *Film Quarterly* 51.3 (1998): 32–44.

"Resolution of the Navajo Nation Council." *20th Navajo Nation Council*, 2005 www.sric.org/uranium/DNRPA.pdf (accessed Dec. 1, 2008).

Ridley, Matt. *Genome: The Autobiography of a Species in 23 Chapters*. New York: Perennial, 1999.

Roemer, Kenneth M. "A 'Touching Man' Brings Aacqu Close." *Studies in American Indian Literatures* 16.4 (Winter 2004): 69–78.

Rogers, Sherry. *Detoxify or Die.* Sarasota, Fla.: Sand Key, 2002.

Rolfe, John. "Asbestos." 1928. In *Anthology of Modern American Poetry,* ed. Cary Nelson. Oxford: Oxford University Press, 2000.

Rose, Nikolas. *The Politics of Life Itself: Biomedicine, Power, and Subjectivity in the Twenty-First Century.* Princeton, N.J.: Princeton University Press, 2007.

Rosner, David, and Gerald Markowitz. *Deadly Dust: Silicosis and the On-Going Struggle to Protect Workers' Health.* Ann Arbor: University of Michigan Press, 2006.

Rossini, Manuela. "Figurations of Post/Humanity in Contemporary Science/Fiction: All Too Human(ist)?" *Revista Canaria de Estudios Ingleses* 50 (2005): 21–35.

Rukeyser, Muriel. *The Book of the Dead.* In *The Collected Poems of Muriel Rukeyser,* ed. Janet E. Kaufman and Anne F. Herzog, with Jan Heller Levi. Pittsburgh, Pa.: University of Pittsburgh Press, 2005.

———. *The Life of Poetry.* Ashfield, Mass.: Paris Press, 1996.

———. Radio interview with Sam Sillen. In Tim Dayton, *Muriel Rukeyser's "The Book of the Dead."* Columbia: University of Missouri Press, 2003.

Sagan, Dorian, and Lynn Margulis. *Acquiring Genomes: A Theory of the Origin of Species.* New York: Basic Books, 2002.

Sandilands, Catriona. *The Good-Natured Feminist: Ecofeminism and the Quest for Democracy.* Minneapolis: University of Minnesota Press, 1999.

Science and Environmental Health Network. http://www.sehn.org/ecomedicine.html (accessed Aug. 8, 2007).

Scigaj, Leonard. "Ecology, Egyptology, and Dialectics in Muriel Rukeyser's *The Book of the Dead.*" *Mosaic* 38.3 (Sept. 2005): n.p.

Scorecard: The Pollution Information Site. http://www.scorecard.org (accessed July 2008).

Scott, Charles E. *The Lives of Things.* Bloomington: Indiana University Press, 2002.

Scott, Joan. "Experience." In *Feminists Theorize the Political,* ed. Judith Butler and Joan W. Scott. New York: Routledge, 1992: 22–40.

Seager, Joni. "Rachel Carson Died of Breast Cancer: The Coming Age of Feminist Environmentalism." *Signs* 28.3 (2003): 945–972.

Sellers, Christopher. "Factory as Environment: Industrial Hygiene, Professional Collaboration and the Modern Sciences of Pollution." *Environmental History Review* 18.1 (Spring 1994): 55–83.

———. *Hazards of the Job: From Industrial Disease to Environmental Health Science.* Chapel Hill: University of North Carolina Press, 1997.

———. "Thoreau's Body: Toward an Embodied Environmental History." *Environmental History* 4.1 (Jan. 1999): 486–514.

Shiva, Vandana. *Biopiracy: The Plunder of Nature and Knowledge.* Cambridge, Mass.: South End, 1997.

———. *Monocultures of the Mind: Perspectives on Biodiversity and Biotechnology.* London: Zed, 1993.

Shostak, Sara. "Environmental Justice and Genomics: Acting on the Futures of Environmental Health." *Science as Culture* 13.4 (Dec. 2004): 540–562.

———. "Locating Gene-Environment Interaction: At the Intersection of Genetics and

Public Health." *Social Science and Medicine* 56 (2003): 2327–2342.

Shrader-Frechette, Kristin. *Environmental Justice: Creating Equality, Reclaiming Democracy.* Oxford: Oxford University Press, 2002.

Shreve, James. "Craig Venter's Epic Voyage to Redefine the Origin of Species." *Wired* (Aug. 2004): 106–113, 146.

Siebers, Tobin. "Disability in Theory: From Social Constructionism to the New Realism of the Body." *American Literary History* 13.4 (Winter 2001): 737–754.

Slicer, Deborah. "Toward an Ecofeminist Standpoint Theory." In *Ecofeminist Literary Criticism: Theory, Interpretation, Pedagogy,* ed. Greta Gaard and Patrick D. Murphy. Urbana: University of Illinois Press, 1998.

Slonczewski, Joan. *The Children Star.* New York: Doherty Associates, 1998.

———. *A Door into Ocean.* New York: Doherty Associates, 1986.

Smedley, Agnes. *Daughter of Earth.* Old Westbury, N.Y.: Feminist Press, 1987.

Sontag, Susan. *Illness as Metaphor and AIDS and Its Metaphors.* 1977. Rpt., Garden City, N.Y.: Doubleday, 1988.

———. *Regarding the Pain of Others.* New York: Farrar, Straus and Giroux, 2003.

Sorg, Barbara A. "Multiple Chemical Sensitivity: Potential Role for Neural Sensitization." *Critical Reviews in Neurobiology* 13.3 (1999): 283–316.

Spanier, Bonnie B. *Impartial Science: Gender Ideology in Molecular Biology.* Bloomington: Indiana University Press, 1995.

Squier, Susan Merrill. *Liminal Lives: Imagining the Human at the Frontiers of Biomedicine.* Durham, N.C.: Duke University Press, 2004.

Stauber, John C., and Sheldon Rampton. *Toxic Sludge Is Good for You: Lies, Damn Lies, and the Public Relations Industry.* Monroe: Common Courage Press, 1995. New York: Putnam, 2001.

Stein, Rachel, ed. *New Perspectives on Environmental Justice: Gender, Sexuality, and Activism.* New Brunswick, N.J.: Rutgers University Press, 2004.

Steinberg, Ted. "Down to Earth: Nature, Agency, and Power in History." *American Historical Review* 107.3 (June 2002). http://continuuum.uta.edu;2190/journals/ahr/107.3/aho302000798.

———. *Down to Earth: Nature's Role in American History.* New York: Oxford University Press, 2002.

Steingraber, Sandra. *Having Faith: An Ecologist's Journey to Motherhood.* New York: Berkeley Trade, 2001.

———. *Living Downstream: A Scientist's Personal Investigation of Cancer and the Environment.* New York: Vintage, 1998.

Strubbe Wittenberg, Janice. *The Rebellious Body: Reclaim Your Life from Environmental Illness or Chronic Fatigue Syndrome.* New York: Insight, 1996.

Sullivan, Shannon. *Living across and through Skins: Transactional Bodies, Pragmatism, and Feminism.* Bloomington: Indiana University Press, 2001.

———. "Pragmatist Feminism as Ecological Ontology: Reflections on Living across and through Skins." *Hypatia* 17.4 (Fall 2002): 201–217.

Supersize Me, dir. Morgan Spurlock. Samuel Goldwyn Films, Roadside Attractions, 2004.

Susan G. Komen for the Cure. ww5.komen.org (accessed June 18, 2009).

Swander, Mary. *Out of This World: A Journey of Healing.* Iowa City: University of Iowa Press, 2008.

Thurston, Michael. *Making Something Happen: American Political Poetry between the World Wars.* Chapel Hill: University of North Carolina Press, 2001.

"Toxics and Health." *Physicians for Social Responsibility.* http://www.psr.org/site/PageServer?pagename=Toxics_main (accessed Sept. 1, 2008).

"Trade Secrets." *Candide Media Works for Washington Media Associates and Public Affairs Television.* http://www.pbs.org/tradesecrets (accessed 2008).

Trent, Lucia. "Breed, Women, Breed." 1929. In *Anthology of Modern American Poetry,* ed. Cary Nelson. Oxford: Oxford University Press, 2000.

Tuana, Nancy. "Fleshing Gender, Sexing the Body: Refiguring the Sex/Gender Distinction." *Southern Journal of Philosophy* 35, suppl. (1996): 53–71.

———. "Material Locations: An Interactionist Alternative to Realism/Social Constructivism." In *Engendering Rationalities,* ed. Nancy Tuana and Sandra Morgen. Albany: State University of New York Press, 2001: 221–243.

———. "Viscous Porosity." In *Material Feminisms,* ed. Stacy Alaimo and Susan J. Hekman. Bloomington: Indiana University Press, 2007: 188–213.

Van Dijck, José. *The Transparent Body: A Cultural Analysis of Medical Imaging.* Seattle: University of Washington Press, 2005.

Van Wyck, Peter C. *Signs of Danger: Waste, Trauma, and Nuclear Threat.* Minneapolis: University of Minnesota Press, 2004.

Vint, Sherryl. *Bodies of Tomorrow: Technology, Subjectivity, Science Fiction.* Toronto: University of Toronto Press, 2007.

Wadley, Jared. "Detroit Mothers Reveal Environmental Abuses through Photography." *University Record Online* (University of Michigan). http://www.ur.umich.edu/0607/Jun25_07/13.shtml (accessed Sept. 15, 2008).

Ward, Chip. *Canaries on the Rim: Living Downwind in the West.* New York: Verso, 1999.

Warner, Michael. "Introduction: Fear of a Queer Planet." *Social Text* 9.4 (1991): 3–17.

WebMD. http://my.webmd.com/hw/allergies/zp3200.asp (accessed July 8, 2004).

Wechsler, Shoshana. "A Ma(t)ter of Fact and Vision: The Objectivity Question in Muriel Rukeyser's *The Book of the Dead.*" *Twentieth Century Literature* 45.2 (Summer 1999): 121–137.

White, Eric. "'Once They Were Men, Now They're Land Crabs': Monstrous Becomings in Evolutionist Cinema." In *Posthuman Bodies,* ed. Judith Halberstam and Ira Livingston. Bloomington: Indiana University Press, 1995: 244–266.

Williams, Joy. *Ill Nature.* New York: Vintage, 2002.

Wilson, Elizabeth. *Neural Geographies: Feminism and the Microstructure of Cognition.* New York: Routledge, 1998.

———. *Psychosomatic: Feminism and the Neurological Body.* Durham, N.C.: Duke University Press, 2004.

———. "Somatic Compliance—Feminism, Biology, and Science." *Australian Feminist Studies* 14.29 (Apr. 1999): 7–19.

Winder, Chris. "Mechanisms of Multiple Chemical Sensitivity." *Toxicology Letters* 128.1–3 (Mar. 10, 2002): 85–97.

Wing, Steve. "Environmental Justice, Science, and Public Health." *Environmental Health Perspectives,* 2005. http://www.ehponline.org/docs/2005/7900/7900.html (accessed Dec. 1, 2008).

———. "Objectivity and Ethics in Environmental Health Science." *Environmental Health Perspectives* 111.4 (Nov. 2003): 1809–1818.

Wolfe, Cary. *Animal Rites: American Culture, the Discourse of Species, and Posthumanist Theory.* Chicago: University of Chicago Press, 2003.

Wolosky, Shira. "Medical-Industrial Discourses: Muriel Rukeyser's *The Book of the Dead.*" *Literature and Medicine* 25.1 (Spring 2006): 156–171.

World Health Organization. "Environmental Health." http://www.who.int/topics/environmental_health/en (accessed Jan. 23, 2010).

Wright, Beverly Hendrix, and Robert D. Bullard. "The Effects of Occupational Injury, Illness, and Disease on the Health Status of Black Americans: A Review." In *Toxic Struggles: The Theory and Practice of Environmental Justice,* ed. Richard Hofrichter. Salt Lake City: University of Utah Press, 2002.

Zwillinger, Rhonda. *The Dispossessed: Living with Multiple Chemical Sensitivities.* Paulden, Ariz.: Dispossessed Project, 1998.

———. Telephone conversation. July 2009.

INDEX

activism, environmental, 18–20, 61–66, 71–74, 81–83, 92, 94–95, 98, 106–107, 109–112

agency, material, 2–3, 21–25, 31, 33, 87, 107, 115–116, 128–131, 135–136, 138–140, 142–158; as deviance, 116, 138–140, 143, 169n21

Alaimo, Stacy, 4–5, 29, 31–32

Alexie, Sherman, 65

animals, 59, 69–70, 77, 104, 110–112, 134, 136, 143–145, 147, 151, 156–158, 167n9

Antonetta, Susanne, 23, 98–100, 102–103, 105–108

Ashford, Nicholas and Claudia Miller, 126–127

Atwood, Margaret, 147–148

autobiography. *See* memoir, material

Barad, Karen, 1–2, 21, 40, 111, 115, 129–130, 136, 142, 145–146, 154–155

Bear, Greg, 24–25, 142–143, 148–158

Beck, Ulrich, 19, 21, 55, 62, 64–65, 68, 72, 93, 135, 146–147

Berkson, Jacob B., 132–135

biomonitoring, 62–63, 81–83, 88, 97, 107–112; defined, 165n17

Birke, Lynda, 5

BlueVoice, 111–112

bodies: biological, 3, 5–6, 27–28, 151, 156; coextensive with environment, 2–4, 52–53, 55, 70, 89, 101–104, 113–140; in feminist theory, 4–7; as scientific instrument, 130–131, 153; toxic, 17–22, 105–112, 113–140; of working-class people, 27–59. *See also* animals; biomonitoring; disability, disability studies; environmental health; environmental history; environmental illness, multiple chemical sensitivity; environmental justice; evolution; gender; genes, genetics; materiality, matter; medicine; memoir, material; race, racism; trans-corporeality

Body Toxic (Susanne Antonetta), 98–100, 100–102, 105–108

Bolton Valencius, Conevery, 89–90

The Book of the Dead (Muriel Rukeyser), 32, 44–59
Breast Cancer Action, 18–19, 165n1
Brown, Phil, 94
Brown, Phil, Steve Kroll-Smith, and Valerie J. Gunter, 94
Bryson, Michael A., 95
Buell, Lawrence, 8, 88–89, 130, 169n17
Butler, Judith, 89
Butler, Octavia, 148

A Canary's Tale (Jacob B. Berkson), 132–135
cancer, 18–21, 85–87, 91, 96–98, 112, 165n1, 167n9
The Cancer Journals (Audre Lorde), 85–88
Caress, Stanley, 118, 126
Carson, Rachel, 95
Casey, Edward S., 8, 11
Castillo, Ana, 23, 72–76
Cheah, Pheng, 4
Cherniak, Martin, 45–46, 54
Clark, Claudia, 30–31
class, 27–40, 44, 54, 82–83, 117–118
Code, Lorraine, 17, 146, 160n10
Couch, Stephen R., and Steve Kroll-Smith, 62–63, 94
Coyle, Fiona, 117
cultural studies, 4, 39
cyborg, 6–7

Darwin, Charles, 10–11, 141, 151, 157–158. *See also* evolution
Darwin's Children (Greg Bear) 142, 151, 158
Darwin's Radio (Greg Bear), 142, 148–158
Dawahare, Anthony, 38–40
de Lauretis, Teresa, 6
Detoxify or Die (Sherry Rogers), 135–136
Di Chiro, Giovanna, 80, 92–94, 106, 127
Diné Natural Resources Protection Act, 79
disability, disability studies, 7, 12, 120, 122, 124, 137–138, 169n21. *See also* environmental illness, multiple chemical sensitivity

The Dispossessed: Living with Multiple Chemical Sensitivities (Rhonda Zwillinger), 119–125, *121, 123, 124*
Dougherty, Stephen, 154
Dumit, J., 118
Dunaway, Finis, 48
Duncan, David Ewing, 107–109

Eichstadt, Peter, 81
Eisenstein, Zillah, 23, 96–97
environmental health, 3, 81–83, 85–112, 113–140
environmental history, 8, 11–12, 29, 55–56, 89–91
environmental humanities, 7–8
environmental illness, multiple chemical sensitivity, 113–140; as a term, 167n1
environmental justice, 3, 28–29, 32, 54, 58, 61–83, 116–118, 124, 160n1
Environmental Justice Foundation, 71–74, *73, 74*
Environmental Working Group (EWG), 110
environmentalism, 15–22, 29, 32, 58–59, 106–112, 139–140, 157–158
epistemology, 3, 17, 19–24, 27–28, 41–43, 52–53, 63–65, 67–68, 71–72, 76–81, 88–89, 93–100, 104–105, 111, 114–115, 125–135, 144–145
ethics, 2–3, 16–25, 70, 83, 98, 104–105, 111–112, 130, 136, 139–140, 150–151, 154, 156–158
Everett, Percival, 23, 65–70
evolution, 139, 142–143, 147, 149–153, 156–158. *See also* Darwin, Charles
expertise. *See* epistemology

Fear Itself: A Memoir (Candida Lawrence), 87–88
feminism, 85–87, 95, 104, 148, 160n5, 161n8. *See also* feminist theory; gender
feminist theory, 4–7, 14, 96, 153. *See also* feminism; gender
FitzSimmons, Margaret, and David Goodman, 13
Fox Keller, Evelyn, 127, 149
Frank, Arthur W., 100

Franklin, Sarah, 151–152
Frickel, Scott, 64
Fromm, Harold, 11

Garland-Thomson, Rosemarie, 12
Gatens, Moira, 13
gender, 36–38, 95, 104, 108–109, 116–117, 126, 167n4, 168n5. *See also* feminism; feminist theory
genes, genetics, 3, 105–107, 127–128, 141–142, 147–152, 154–156, 158
genetic engineering, 147–148, 155
Gibson, Pamela, 117
Goldman, Emma, 34–35
Gompers, Samuel, 30–31
Greenpeace, 19–20
Grosz, Elizabeth, 10–11, 40, 157

Hames-Garcia, Michael, 7
Haraway, Donna J., 6–7, 106, 144–145, 150
Harding, Sandra, 64, 79
Hartman, Stephanie, 46
Hausman, Bernice, 7
Hausteiner, Constanze, et al., 119
Having Faith: An Ecologist's Journey into Motherhood (Sandra Steingraber), 103–106
Hayles, Katherine N., 42
Haynes, Todd, 24, 117, 136–138
Heise, Ursula, 15–16, 93, 163nn2,3,4
Hird, Myra J., 5–6, 152
Hochman, Jhan, 15

industrial hygiene. *See* occupational hazards, occupational illness
invisible risks, 47, 53, 61–83, 88, 118–125, 146
Irigaray, Luce, 36

Kadlec, David, 53–54
Kalaidjian, Walter, 51
Kidner, David W., 8
Kirby, Vicki, 14, 41
Knopf-Newman, Marcy Jane, 86
knowledge. *See* epistemology
Kroll-Smith, Steve, and H. Hugh Floyd, 115, 124, 129–131

Kumari Campbell, Fiona, 137

Latour, Bruno, 8–9, 28, 50, 100–101, 135
Lawrence, Candida, 23, 87–88
Lawson, Lynn, 131–132
Le Sueur, Meridel, 22, 32–45, 161–162nn5,8,9
Lewontin, Richard, and Richard Levins, 27–28, 149
Lilith's Brood (Octavia Butler), 148
Linton, Simi, 138
Living Downstream: An Ecologist's Personal Investigation of Cancer and the Environment (Sandra Steingraber), 97–98, 112
Lorde, Audre, 23, 85–87
Luke, Timothy W., 92, 101–102

Manmade Breast Cancers (Zillah Eisenstein), 96–97
materiality, matter, 1–4, 6–11, 33, 38–41, 43–44, 52–53, 62–63, 69–71, 76–77, 86–89, 102–103, 105, 111, 115–116, 118–136, 138–140, 141–158. *See also* agency, material; bodies; memoir, material; and subjectivity
McKeown-Eyssen, Gail, et al., 127
McKone, Thomas, 81
McWhorter, Ladelle, 12–13, 95, 139, 142, 145
medicine, 28, 30, 32–33, 50–51, 53, 82, 90–92, 103–107, 113–114, 118–119, 126–129, 131–136, 166n5, 168n9
memoir, material, 85–112, 131–135; as compared to other genres, 165–166n2; more examples, 165–166n2
Memories Come to us in the Rain and the Wind: Oral Histories and Photographs of Navajo Uranium Miners and their Families (Navajo Uranium Miner Oral History Photography Project), 78–80
Moss, Pamela, and Isabel van Dyck, 10
Moyers, Bill, 109–110
multiple chemical sensitivity. *See* environmental illness, multiple chemical sensitivity
Murphy, Michelle, 128–129, 131

Nash, Linda, 11–12, 32–33, 90–91
National Geographic, 107–109
Nelson, Cary, 30

occupational hazards, occupational illness, 28, 30–32, 45–59, 75–77, 117, 162n16
Ortiz, Simon J., 76–78
Oryx and Crake (Margaret Atwood), 147–148
"Our Homeland: A National Sacrifice Area" (Simon J. Ortiz), 78

Pesticide Action Network North America (PANNA), 83
Photo Voice Project, 71
photography, 48, 67–74, *73, 74,* 81, 107–109, 119–125, *121, 123, 124*
Physicians for Social Responsibility, 82–83
Pickering, Andrew, 44, 115, 130, 136, 153
Plumwood, Val, 2
posthumanism, 14, 44, 110–112, 136, 142, 146, 150–151, 153–158, 170n4
Proctor, Robert N., 20, 91

queer biology, queer ecology, queer natures, 5–6, 105, 139, 152

Rabinowitz, Paula, 47
race, racism, 7, 28–29, 33, 45, 54, 61–63, 65–66, 70, 81–83, 117–118, 162n14, 163n1
Radetsky, Peter, 114–115
Raglon, Rebecca, and Marian Scholtmeijer, 42
risk society, 19–21, 55, 62–83, 89, 93, 101, 114, 117, 135, 146–147, 163nn2,3,4
Rogers, Sherry, 135–136
Rolfe, John, 30
Rose, Nikolas, 62–63
Rukeyser, Muriel, 22, 32, 44–59

Safe, 24, 117, 136–138
Sandilands, Catriona, 42–43
science, 17–22, 53–54, 61–83, 87–89, 93–112, 113–116, 125–128, 130, 134–136, 141–142, 147–158. See also biomonitoring; epistemology; risk society; science studies
science fiction, 142–143, 147–158
science studies, 8–9, 144–146, 149–150, 153–154
Scigaj, Leonard, 46–47, 51
Scorecard: The Pollution Information Site, 109
Scott, Charles E., 8, 144
Seager, Joni, 95–96
Sellers, Christopher, 11, 29–31, 56
Shiva, Vandana, 44
Shostak, Sara, 82, 107, 128
Siebers, 7, 138
Slicer, Deborah, 33
Slonczewski, Joan, 148
So Far from God (Ana Castillo), 72–76
Sorg, Barbara A., 117
Spanier, Bonnie, 149–150, 156
Squier, Susan, 9, 87, 95
Steinberg, Ted, 8
Steingraber, Sandra, 21, 23, 97–98, 103–106, 108, 112
Strubbe Wittenberg, Janice, 119
"Stuff: Chickens and Bombs" (Simon J. Ortiz), 76–77
subjectivity, 20, 23–24, 51, 85–89, 94–105, 118–125, 139–140, 144
Sullivan, Shannon, 159n3

Thurston, Michael, 52
Trade Secrets, 109–110
transcendence, 51–53, 57, 138, 146
trans-corporeality, 2–4, 11–25, 28, 31, 48, 62–63, 68–69, 83, 86–89, 95–96, 102–105, 111–112, 114–116, 118–140, 144, 146, 154–158
Tuana, Nancy, 5, 14–15, 70, 143–144

Van Wyck, Peter C., 117

Ward, Chip, 98
Watershed (Percival Everett), 65–70
"We Have Been Told Many Things but We Know this to be True" (Simon J. Ortiz), 77–78
Weschler, Shoshana, 47

Williams, Joy, 1–2
Wilson, Elizabeth, 3, 126, 153
Winder, Chris, 126
Wing, Steve, 64
Wolfe, Cary, 156–157

Wolosky, Shira, 47
Woven Stone (Simon J. Ortiz), 76–78

Zwillinger, Rhonda, 24, 119–125, *121, 123, 124*

STACY ALAIMO is Professor of English at the University of Texas at Arlington, where she also serves as co-chair of the President's Sustainability Committee. She publishes widely on North American literatures, environmental humanities, green cultural studies, science studies, and feminist theory. Her publications include *Undomesticated Ground: Recasting Nature as Feminist Space* (2000) and a collection edited with Susan J. Hekman, *Material Feminisms* (Indiana University Press, 2008). Alaimo has written essays on literature and the environment, environmental art and architecture, performance art, feminist theory and nature, environmental pedagogy, gender and climate change, and the science and culture of queer animals.